D0870278

The Essentials of Living Aboard a Boat

The Definitive Guide for Liveaboards

Mark Nicholas

Copyright © 2019 by Mark Nicholas

Fourth edition enlarged, revised, and updated.
First edition copyright © 2004 Mark Nicholas, published by Aventine Press
Second edition (2005), third edition (2008), updated and revised edition
(2013), and fourth edition (2019), published by Paradise Cay

All rights reserved. No part of this book may be used or reproduced in any
manner whatsoever without written permission, except in the case of brief
quotations embodied in critical articles and reviews. For information, contact
the publisher.

Cover design by Robert Tripp

Contact the author:
mark@livingaboard.net
www.livingaboard.net

Photo credits:
  Interior photos by Mark Nicholas
  Photo of Rafthouse by Bob and Connie Hull at C&B, Inc.

Printed in the United States of America

ISBN 978-1951116026

Published by:
Paradise Cay Publications, Inc.
P. O. Box 29
Arcata, CA 95518-0029
800-736-4509
707-822-9163 Fax
orders@paracay.com
www.paracay.com

To Max the Cat

1993 - 2006

Rest well, my liveaboard friend

Contents

Mark Nicholas
Aboard *Morning Fog*
In Coastal Waters in New England

1

Introduction

So you want to be a liveaboard. Or maybe you are just examining the lifestyle—or maybe you have already taken the plunge. In any event, let me welcome you to what I believe is a truly terrific lifestyle.

There are countless joys to life aboard. The good parts of life aboard include the gentle movement of the boat, smell of the air and breeze, ability to leave civilization at any time, freedom of movement, sunsets, unity with nature, and wonderful neighbors. Other benefits might include the sounds of the water, view of a skyline, special times with friends and family, or just the open water. We can go on and on. This is oceanside or waterside living at its best, sometimes at a fraction of the price.

Despite all of these benefits, living aboard is typically outside of the average human comfort zone. While some decide on this lifestyle for more practical reasons (such as economics, commute proximity, etc.), many of the reasons are not as practical—falling for the romance and allure of the water and waves. The romance is presented to us in movies, television, and magazines. We see the pictures and dream. We fall in love with our boats just as we do with a significant other, although we more rarely divorce our boats. The lifestyle, however, has its share of challenges and surprises.

We can learn a great deal from those liveaboards who have preceded us. The art and practice of boating by its nature demands experience, not for the summer days when the water is calm and the breeze fresh and light, but for those moments when things aren't going as smoothly. If you are cruising, the difference between a beautiful experience and a life-threatening one may be separated by he smallest of factors. An unexpected gale or a broken piece of equipment or a drunk or clumsy person on board can turn a great day into hell in a fraction of a second. Anticipating that the weather may turn and that equipment might fail requires experience as well as a calm mind. While many problems can be fixed, or at least improved with common-sense solutions, there are true complexities that only the words of our ancestors and years of experience can teach us.

When I first decided to live aboard, I wasn't aware of either the common-sense issues *or* the issues that come with experience. All I knew was how to sail, and though I studied books on sailing and seamanship, none provided me with any true insight into the practical subtleties of boating or living aboard. For me, this lifestyle was a true trial by fire—and in the beginning I was burned more often than I wasn't. It was easy for me to think that I was alone, the only one learning the harsh lessons this way, but in talking to other liveaboards it became clear to me that we all learn this way, and it is a true shame that the most prominent issues were not encapsulated in a meaningful, educational, and commonsensical way. And that is how this book was born.

The bottom line is that there are essentials to living aboard, although even many of the most experienced liveaboards don't often realize how *many* essentials there really are. We are all very similar and experience many of the same challenges as our neighbors.

A prominent boat broker told me that most decisions that must be made when choosing a boat are simple common sense—and yet it is amazing to him how many smart and logical boat buyers must be reminded again and again what common sense really dictates. Our objectives are often clouded by our dreams, desires, and emotions, or the novelty of it all, as we fall in love with our boats and become absorbed by our aspirations. Then we forget our practical needs, ignore our budget requirements, and forget what our fundamental goal was in the first place: to have a safe place to live.

As liveaboards, we face a most fundamental question of how best to survive and enjoy our day-to-day lives. In the liveaboard endeavor, there are few resources that speak about achieving the status quo. Issues such as safety and sanitation and methods of enhancing comfort are generally not able to be effectively learned from movies, articles or videos, but rather are taught through experience, marina rules, and from social visits to our boating neighbors. There are so many of us, we do deserve better.

While I want this book to be an *all-inclusive* resource on the essentials of living aboard, that would be an insurmountable standard to set. All you have to do is visit the Internet and you will see how many different opinions exist as to the right solution for our most simple day-to-day problems. On an e-mail discussion list, the type of toilet recommended for use might generate days or weeks of online conversations that will probably result in hurt feelings caused by peoples' strong beliefs (note: I vote for manual toilets—less potential for breakdown, less maintenance, and little energy requirement). While I am only one person with an opinion, there are many others with equally valid opinions—some are better for your needs, and some are worse. Find a salesperson at your marine store who likes to talk, and then take the time to ask questions and listen. Talk to your boating neighbors. Walk the docks at local marinas. Use the Internet.

Luckily, boaters (especially liveaboards) love to talk. Unfortunately, boaters (particularly inexperienced ones) sometimes forget to listen.

Boaters, particularly liveaboards, have far more in common with each other than landlubbers do with their landlubbing neighbors. While homeowners might make choices that show very little correlation to each other, almost no boat or boating system is unique. Though we, as liveaboards, may be unique in terms of our desires, needs, and goals—and most dramatically, our lifestyles—our boats are all very similar. Many of the same conversations occur with our boating neighbors day in and day out, regardless of whether our boats and those of our neighbors are powerboats or sailboats, wood or fiberglass, luxury or practical, cruising or dockbound, big or small, bluewater or coastal. While not every system is the identical, many systems are, and the ones that are different often work on exactly the same principles.

For example, there are typically* only two kinds of marine heads (a.k.a. toilets), manual and electric (yes, we're back to the all-important topic of the head). All boats have holding tanks and the same concerns with the storage of waste, including how to ultimately get rid of the waste and how to avoid the smell which is sure to invade our living quarters, which are often just a few feet away from our waste holding tank. NOTE: Liveaboards seem to enjoy talking about our septic systems because this issue is paramount to the enjoyment of our lifestyle.

Who is the author?

(See also, "About the Author")

* Typically does not mean without exception. One can always find exceptions.

Nobody, really, just a guy who decided to live aboard a boat—and who then bought the wrong boat, hired the wrong boat inspector (surveyor), and wasn't prepared for the problems that would soon be experienced.

For instance, I had shore power and two batteries, but had no idea that plugging my particular boat into the dock did not automatically charge my batteries (some boats do, others don't, all should). Only running the engine and using the alternator would charge my batteries. A liveaboard (or any boater for that matter) might well need a separate battery charger to charge the batteries for periods at the dock or during other times when the engine isn't running. And here in the Northeast, once the engine is winterized, the engine cannot be operated. As my batteries died, there was no way for me to use my 12-volt systems, which included all of my lights. Funny, but as the lights got dimmer and dimmer, I didn't understand why, even though my boat was plugged in. Then there was no more light. That battery charger cost $120 that I hadn't bargained on - and that just was on day 1.

Unfortunately, that wasn't the first expense, nor the last expense, nor the biggest expense related to the things that I had not expected. I lived in the Northeast as a young liveaboard (now I live in Southern California), took ownership of the boat in the winter, and wasn't prepared for the temperature or the systems necessary to heat the boat. For goodness sake, I didn't even know exactly what "shrinkwrapping" meant to a cold-weather winter liveaboard!

The stories I can tell are egregious examples of what can happen to the unprepared liveaboard. I'll tell some of the stories within this book, but I find them all entertaining in retrospect. The advantage to my experiences is that I survived and learned my boat, *The Morning Fog,* and all of its systems and quirks at a dramatic pace. After only a few months, I had already rebuilt and reinstalled all of the electric lines and systems of the *Fog*. If I had done this myself, I would have done this wrong, thinking that wires were connected in a similar fashion to those of a house. They aren't. I paid an expert $50 per hour for his time to help me do this. While the cost of my boat was going up exponentially, the work was being done right and I was getting one hell of an education.

Speaking of expenses, I hadn't bargained on all of the new tools I would need, such as a heat gun (used for electrical work) and stuffing box wrenches, and it was a shock to watch my good tools rust away in the salt air.

Before that winter had ended, we (my hired marine technician and I) had rebuilt the entire plumbing system, except for the holding tank, which I replaced myself in one of the most disgusting, horrendous activities that I have ever undertaken. (Visualizing a casual swim in a septic tank, my neighbors all decided to spend that day elsewhere.) We added a diesel heating system, resealed and bedded key sections of the deck, worked on the rigging, updated the engine, installed a new alternator, replaced many of the lines, and on and on and on. Under the tutelage of my trusty and well-paid technician, I made tough decisions, and survived those things that we just couldn't work on or economically fix, such as fixing a delaminated deck.

Perhaps you are thinking that I did not get the boat properly surveyed prior to purchase. Not so. I paid top dollar for a survey. My surveyor told me that replacing five gate valves with seacocks would cost $750; they ended up costing upwards of $2,000. He also missed about twenty rather significant problems with the boat, a few of which did end up putting at risk not only the lives of those on board, but also the well-being of the boat herself. The most crucial error was failing to notice that the rudder stops were bolted to wood that had completely disintegrated. On the very first 'delivery' cruise, the vessel lost steering in 20 degree weather and we had to be rescued by the Coast Guard just as we floated dead stick toward the shoals (another $750). I was paying dearly for my education.

My sailing experience had been rather substantial as well. I grew up on the Jersey shore and sailed quite often through my childhood. My problems arose not through an unfamiliarity with boats, but rather from the transition to cruising-capable liveaboard-worthy, budget-conscious boat ownership, with complex countless systems, excessive wear, and other complicating factors.

As a new boat owner of three weeks, I had a major flood aboard when it turned out that the wires to the bilge pump had rusted away and I had a stuffing box that had been overtightened (causing a moderate leak). The surveyor never noticed that the wires were falling off and rusted (they were under heat shrink so not obvious to the casual eye). [This is just an example of my early problems. The letter to the surveyor included a list of items four pages long as well as a recap of the events that put us in a highly precarious position at sea for things that were missed or surveyed incorrectly.]

After the flood (which damaged the floor and other key components of my new floating home), I replaced the bilge pump in subfreezing weather, rewired the pump, and installed a manual pump to the cockpit deck. Again, what made this process particularly painful was that I'd thought I had purchased a turn-key boat with every system in good shape on the day that I took ownership of the *Fog*. What an unfortunate surprise.

This book came about because I decided that if there was anything I could do to help ensure that future boaters and liveaboards might benefit from many of the preventable mistakes that I made, then it was my obligation to write this.

So am I an expert? Yes. I'm an expert at what can go wrong.

Is living aboard a good thing?

An emphatic yes! Maybe. It depends.

This is a romantic life, different than the norm and often more economical than life ashore. The lifestyle offers all of the benefits mentioned above. These are truly amazing benefits.

So what does the quality of liveaboard life depend on? Well . . . are you doing this by yourself or with your mate? If you are doing this with someone else, then it depends upon whether your mate wants to do this as much as you do. In the course of my discussions with liveaboards, close-quarter-compatibility seems to be one of the most significant reasons why some couples that commit to this lifestyle cease living aboard after just a month or two.

And success depends on whether the reality of living aboard is acceptable once you realize that the lifestyle is not all romance. The deck still needs to be maintained, wood varnished, systems maintained, and so forth. Unless you have a boat that you don't want or need to maintain, which many liveaboards do, this lifestyle is not entirely about sitting on deck off of a beautiful tropical island with a drink in your hand.

And it depends upon whether you can handle the motion of the boat, particularly in storms. And if you live in a setting with other boats going past, it depends upon whether you can stand the wakes that are thrown off by those boats. I have a friend who, for instance, gets thrown into the air every morning at 0800 when the police boats speed past heading out for their patrols (in an otherwise coastal no-wake zone).

After a couple of years living aboard in a marina that was well protected from the rough waters of Boston Harbor, I moved to a marina in Salem, Massachusetts that was exposed to the elements.

I thought that I could handle any motion, but had to leave after four days of bouncing more than three feet up and down under what I would have considered steady but not overwhelming 12-knot winds. To make matters worse, my cat (Max The Cat) was getting seasick. It was horrible—and the only time I have ever gone to a motel room for refuge.

And it depends on whether you can take boating problems in stride, and find some enjoyment in the repairs and routine maintenance without letting the little things drive you crazy.

Another challenge of being a liveaboard with a faulty boat (and all boats are—or will be—faulty) is that there is no place to go when you need to perform repairs or upgrades. Many liveaboards allow nonessential problems to persist, since it is so difficult to perform repairs and concurrently live in such a small space. If you need to drill a hole, for instance, to run some wires or plumbing or install equipment, it is likely that your possessions will spread onto every flat space and you will smelling, as well as inhaling, fiberglass fibers and dust for days. That's not a good thing, let me tell you. It's even worse if your mate spends those days complaining about the clutter and smell.

Do you think those are your only challenges? They aren't. My lockers (closets) were forward, toward the bow (the pointy tip at the front of the boat), where the hull sloped both forward and down. Boats can be damp because of both humidity and condensation. The suits I wore to work every day were thoroughly wrinkled on the right side, while the left side was pretty nice. I then started keeping every suit jacket in my office and had my shirts put into boxes so that the wrinkles were more predictable (there was no room aboard the *Fog* for an iron). At least I was symmetrical. Funny, isn't it?

Not as funny, though, as when the mold started setting in. Because of the condensation in the closet, the clothes that weren't worn as often started to get a bit funky. Mold provides for a lovely aroma that presents its own set of challenges. I then turned my aft (toward the stern, or the back) berth (bed) into a locker (closet) to avoid the wrinkles and mold, because I could heat the cabin much more evenly. That meant that I lost a main storage area and second berth—but at least my home and I didn't smell. Now, however, the boat always looked cluttered, something I hated. I soon employed solutions to the mold problem in the locker, although I never did overcome the problem of the left half of every outfit being wrinkled.

That leads me to one of the biggest challenges of all: storage. On a boat there is no attic, no basement, and no walk-in closet. I owned nine guitars—and could take only one aboard. I had a great sofa—once. That went into storage and was later sold, along with a multimedia collection, paintings, desktop computer, printer, dining room furniture, and TV. Treasured memories recorded in a photo album also do not take kindly to water. After I loaded all of my photos onto a photo website, my albums went into storage as well,

And no discussion of life aboard is complete without a discussion of the toilet (head). It is uncomfortable and cramped. If you don't remember (having been sheltered on land for too long), sewage smells—worse as the temperature gets warmer. Unlike a homeowner's, a liveaboard's septic tank is stored very close to his living room and sleeping quarters. We can hide from the world, but not from this.

In return for these and other challenges, you receive genuinely wonderful benefits. You're outside every day. You get to watch the rain bounce off the water. You get rocked (hopefully gently) to sleep. You get interesting and quirky neighbors (whether they are liveaboards or not). You get to be a part of the sunsets, and you are in a perfect position to take sunset cruises because you are, after all, already on your boat. As a matter of fact, you can go cruising any time you want! You get to experience the sounds and smell of the water. And you get the freedom to move your home wherever you want.

The philosophy of this book:

The first questions I faced when deciding to write this book were determining what we should *not* spend time discussing.

When discussing the essentials to living aboard, it is certainly necessary to consider the process of choosing a boat, choosing a location for that boat, lifestyle issues, amenities, sanitation, and so forth. These are truly all essential to your undertaking.

It doesn't, however, make any sense to spend much of our time discussing the benefits to living aboard. I think the fact that you are reading this book means that you are already prepared (or preparing) for this undertaking; consequently, I suppose that you already know the benefits to living aboard. You probably already know how wonderful sunsets can be. And of course you are looking forward to the gentle motion. You might even be so focused on the benefits that you are about to undertake this endeavor without knowing or preparing for the challenges that might be forthcoming. Therefore, we will spend the majority of our time talking about problems, costs, concerns, and issues.

One important point is that you need to learn how to be a boater on your own. We won't discuss that either. The Coast Guard, for instance, has safety rules that apply to all boaters. If you plan on taking your boat out for a cruise, then it is incumbent upon you to be a competent captain and to take the Coast Guard's safety course. You need to know the navigation rules and rights of way and how to captain and master your own vessel, if not for your own safety, then for the safety of your passengers and neighbors. You need to know how to handle engine maintenance and emergencies that may arise. This applies to all boaters, and there are many courses and books and videos already out there that will teach you this. We're here to focus on issues that affect liveaboards. And while sometimes there might be some overlap, this resource is not a source for maintenance techniques, safety requirements or legal requirements for boating or boaters.

While there are many kinds of liveaboards, there are three in particular for our purposes. The first is the dreamer and planner. This book can be a great resource in that regard. The second liveaboard category is the liveaboard who lives in a marina, and who may or may not dream of blue water cruising. This book was intended for that category as well. The third category of liveaboards are the cruisers. It is important to recognize that cruising is a very different beast altogether, although we'll offer some thoughts a bit farther into the book. Cruisers should have as a starting point a tremendous amount of experience on the water, and there are some terrific resources out there written by cruisers who seem to rarely if ever touch land. For our topic we have more than enough to discuss and I'll leave the bulk of the cruising commentary to my brethren who have set out to discuss those very topics. Our perspective is life aboard in the most common condition of all, gently touching land with departures as often as possible while maintaining a home base. In our case, the boat is largely a replacement for a house, or a second home, a fort/hideaway, hobby, escape, or whatever.

It is important to remember that while our focus on the challenges and solutions of life aboard could be interpreted to suggest that I am trying to scare you away from this lifestyle, that couldn't be more wrong. This book is about preparation: trying to educate and prepare the future liveaboard for the challenges that this lifestyle will present.

The bottom line is that I love the lifestyle and everything about it—almost. I have had many brilliant days. I have also faced some significant challenges and unexpected costs. But don't confuse our spending time on the challenges of living aboard with thinking that I believe this lifestyle to be less than ideal. I do not. I just don't want you to think that it is easy.

Now that I've told you what we *won't* cover . . .

My Friends Tom and Lynne Cox
Lounging Aboard *Rosinante*
Constitution Marina, Boston, Massachusetts

2

Let's Get Started

Well, we have quite a bit to do. There seems to be a paralyzing amount of variables among boats and lifestyles—but by being methodical, the endeavor of living aboard becomes simpler. An uninformed novice can easily fall into an emotional pattern: He or she first decides to live aboard, then picks a boat by falling in love with aspects of it, ignoring mundane details such as general condition, comfort and storage. So with the best of intentions, the infatuated liveaboard starts with inadequate preparation and a less-than-ideal liveaboard boat. Moreover, attempts to cut initial costs, or to buy a boat because it has certain amenities, can be followed by extreme and unexpected expenditures, totally undercutting one of the primary reasons the new liveaboard became interested in this undertaking in the first place.

What Is Your Motivation?

Freedom? Cost cutting? Luxury living? A dream to cross oceans? Social aspects? To be closer to work? To be different than the norm? To escape a marriage or difficult relationship? To escape from the law?

There are as many variations of liveaboards as there are liveaboards, and it is important to know who you want to be and what you want to achieve. Without this understanding, it is difficult or impossible for you to choose the best boat, the perfect marina, and the "right" amenities and equipment. Know thyself.

What Kind Of Liveaboard Are You?

There are many kinds of liveaboards, each with his or her own personality as well as specific needs, wants, desires, and aspirations, probably no two alike. You need to have an idea of which kind of liveaboard you want to be, and your goals, as well as your needs and wants, should be decided carefully. The cost of a boat for a cruising "bluewater" liveaboard is substantially more than that of a boat purchased for non-cruising purposes, and the cost of a coastal/day cruiser can be substantially more than that of a non-cruising floating home. Unfortunately, many liveaboards often spend a substantial amount of time, energy, and money buying their expensive boat (or money pit fixer-upper) and installing complex systems for a voyage that is never taken. It's hard to preach practicality for an endeavor which, by its nature, can easily be impractical. Nonetheless, evaluate your needs very carefully.

We can generalize two broad kinds of liveaboards: the "non-cruising liveaboard" (the more common of the two, the first is primarily located at a slip, only leaving for short excursions) and the "cruising liveaboard" (who is chronically under way). There is a hybrid called the "one-day-I'm-gonna" liveaboard who is stuck at a slip with a day job and either a working boat, or a boat that is in pieces waiting to be put back together. He is always planning that adventurous journey, that great escape. Many non-cruising liveaboards have no desire to leave the dock; some have boats not designed to ever leave the dock.

Those liveaboards have no need for an engine—a floating raft will suffice.

Of each of the two main liveaboard varieties, there are two broad subsets: those who want Netflix, and those who don't. While this is a great oversimplification, the point is that there are those liveaboards who demand a regular connection with civilization and entertainment, and those who wish embrace separation. When it comes to choosing a boat, its amenities, and home port, knowing honestly what your desires are is critical.

When I bought my boat, I expected to do a great deal of reading and far less TV watching. It turned out that while I was at my slip, I did a great deal of TV watching, Internet surfing, and telephone calling, maybe as much as I would have done had I still lived on land. This is who I am, a e-addicted fool (e-mail, mobile phone, streaming media and computer), and only at sea did I manage to avoid these connections (although I still used my cell phone when close to shore).

Know yourself and your hopes, dreams, and aspirations. Are your goals realistic? Is this going to be your dream boat, or a way of getting started in this lifestyle? This doesn't need to be your last boat. Remember that if you have a boat with systems you don't use, you still need to maintain those systems. Can you put off those expenses for a bit? Do you want to? It seems that almost every liveaboard talks about leaving to go cruising, but few ever seem to go.

If we are talking about cruising, will your time away from land be weeks or months, or merely days? Will you always have access to land and provisions? If you are away from civilization, you will need a boat designed for safety and stability, and with adequate storage for provisions. Offshore safety gear, including communication gear and life rafts, is expensive. You probably want multiple backups of systems and spare parts for every major system, and you'll want to make sure that your crew is up to the challenge of undertaking this lifestyle.

Non-cruisers have their own set of decisions to make. They use floating accommodations in much the same manner as a landlubber uses a house. There are many options for floaters; some want a floating home that also works as an operational boat, and many others don't. Since floating accommodations don't need to do much other than float and be comfortable, there are often economical solutions that will satisfy a floater's specific needs.

Most of the chapters included in this book are geared toward the needs of the liveaboard who is looking for an operational boat, and comfort and amenity issues as well as safety and sanitation issues are equally applicable for all types of boaters.

The Steps to Living Aboard

I'm very fond of the couples that I meet in the oceanside bars who have been planning for decades to become liveaboards upon their retirement. These are couples that have often gotten the most out of their lives, with their kids and jobs and homes and families, and now are planning to live their dreams. I know a man who tells a story about how he has been thinking about his perfect boat for the last 40 years, and is now buying his first boat. What a great feeling that must be.

Choose Your Boat Wisely

Based on all of your tangible and intangible needs and limitations, you'll need to choose the right boat. There is a detailed chapter on this topic, and you should take plenty of time to examine many options, visiting as many boats and talking to as many people as possible.

Buy Your Boat

Once you've decided on your boat, you need to develop a strategy to acquire your boat. You'll need a thorough understanding of the buying process so that you can avoid unwelcome surprises and be sure that the experience of taking ownership is as pleasant as possible. We have an upcoming chapter on this subject as well.

Move Aboard

Now that you have the boat, get on it. Sounds pretty simple. To do that, you'll obviously need to have identified a place to keep your boat (see "Choosing A Marina") and have prepared the boat and yourself (see "Preparing To Live Aboard" and "Families, Children, and Pets"). This isn't brain surgery, for moving aboard can be as easy as taking a pillow on board a floating surface and going to sleep.

Depending on your budget, needs, and desires, you will want to equip the boat with the amenities that will make your life comfortable (See "Amenities"). Then follow the rules of the road, taking care of your environment and fellow boaters (see "Safety and Sanitation" and "Government Oversight").

In addition, this book includes a detailed discussion of potential costs of boat ownership, boat operation, and living aboard (see "Costs"). You should carefully consider what you can afford and make decisions accordingly. I know many cruising liveaboards, some of them aging couples, who don't have any health insurance. I know others who only own two shirts and two pairs of shorts. And we all know others who live like royalty on the water. How are you going to live?

The allure of living aboard, fed by blogs, online videos, fiction, movies, and TV, is universal. The lifestyle is usually shown as romantic and carefree. Indeed, life on a boat is often *the* metaphor for someone who has "made it" (or alternatively escaping life on land). People reach for achievements symbolizing achievement all the time; yet there are plenty of stories about couples retiring, buying their first boat, moving aboard, going on their first long cruise . . . and upon landfall, a spouse (or the couple!) decides to abandon the boat life. [Note that these boats may often be acquired economically.] Your success depends on balancing preconceptions with reality. Those who manage to do this, rarely want to turn back. Yes, there will be the clinking of drinks at sunset, but there will be gruesome toilet malfunctions as well.

Perceptions of Life Aboard

Liveaboards are perceived by the general public as being rather unique individuals. Or insane. Many government officials perceive liveaboards to be polluters damaging the environment; likewise, many liveaboards, who constitute a group so diverse and unorganized that it cannot properly defend itself, believe that the government uses them as environmental scapegoats, often seeking legislation to curb live-aboard activities or ban liveaboards altogether rather than target the more egregious acts and actors.

Some permissive marinas allow their liveaboards to use the dock as their garage, scattering storage containers, bikes, tables, chairs, and barbecues—once I even saw junk cars—throughout the docks. The public, government officials, casual boaters, and marina owners look at these few as a representation of all liveaboards, perceiving them to be dirty, unkempt, and disruptive. At my marina, which many liveaboards call home, the docks are spotless, and marina management cares deeply about the condition of the premises. No boater, liveaboard or otherwise, is permitted to use the docks for anything other than expressly permitted purposes.

Your land-based neighbors and coworkers, not to mention your family, might think you're crazy. Or they might think this is a pretty cool thing to do, but even then they will conclude their thoughts with statements such as, "Well, *I* couldn't do it." Either way, you will be on the "other" side. Better to get used to the idea soon; living aboard is very foreign to the general population. The lifestyle is by its very nature different than the norm.

Terminology

Even though this is a book on living aboard, I feel we need to mention a few key terms that every boater (including a liveaboard) needs to know. It surprises me how many prospective liveaboards start looking for their perfect boat without even understanding the meaning of key words. The following is a small list of general terminology. Also, we will take the time to walk through a sample boat spec (specification) sheet and review the definitions of the terms contained on that sheet as well as a brief discussion as to why those specifications are important. (Take no offense if you already know these words. Just skip ahead, if you'd like.)

General Terms

It is common for boat shoppers to find listings that use nautical lingo to describe a boat's layout, accommodations, and amenities. Here is an example of a random listing found on a used boat listing service:

Starting forward is the master head with stall shower to port and marine head to starboard. Moving aft is the large master berth to port with storage beneath. Going aft through a privacy door is the spacious salon area which accommodates diners seated on both settees. To port is a full length L-shaped settee which converts to a double sea berth. To starboard is the other full length settee. Just aft of the port settee is the large galley with sinks near the centerline. A custom shelf folds up between the sinks and bulkhead. To starboard is the guest stateroom with large double berth. Aft to starboard is the nav station. Large spacious cockpit and helm.

This description uses terminology that is quite common for boating, and it is essential for boat shoppers to understand the meaning of these words. Let's start out with the rooms of a boat:

Berth:	A bed or other place to sleep. In this case there are two double beds and a settee that converts to a full double bed. A sea berth is a bed that secures the sleeping person(s) so they do not fall out of bed when cruising.
Cabin:	Any room for gathering of crew or passengers.
Cockpit:	Also known as a bridge, depending on the configuration. A place from which the boat is steered and controlled.
Galley:	Kitchen
Head:	Bathroom and toilet (master head is the equivalent of the master bathroom).
Helm:	Steering station
Nav Station:	Stands for Navigation Station, comprised of a desk/chart table, radio, and often a GPS readout and other electronic equip-

ment.

Salon:	Living room
Settee:	Bench seats
Stateroom:	Bedroom
V-berth:	A berth that is pointy at one end, typically found in the bow of the boat.

Structural layout and related terms:

Bow:	The front of a boat
Stern:	The back of a boat
Forward:	Moving in the direction of the bow
Amidships:	In or toward the middle of a boat
Aft:	Moving in the direction of the stern
Port:	While facing forward, the left side of the boat as well as the area to the left of the boat
Starboard:	While facing forward, the right side of the boat as well as the area to the right of the boat
Beam:	The widest part of a boat

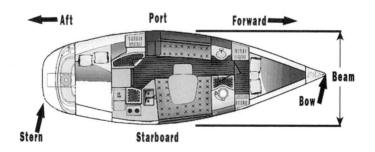

Draft: The maximum depth of a boat

The Listing Sheet

If you want to buy a boat and are given a sheet of the boat's specifications, you should be familiar with every one of the terms on that listing sheet. Further, a buyer would be a fool not to have some understanding of how those specifications will affect the ownership and use of that boat. The same applies for the description and understanding of what equipment is offered with the boat.

A good example of the impact of these terms would be the experience of a guy named Bob (an acquaintance of mine not named Bob) who was looking for a 38-foot boat. Bob fell in love with a Hans Christian 38' sailboat. The listing sheet confirmed that the boat's length was 38', and offered information such as the boat's beam of 12'6", draft of 6', displacement of 27,500 pounds, and LOA of 46'. Bob went off and ran the numbers and learned that a 38-foot boat will cost $6,300 annually at his marina. Although this was a little tight for him, just over $500 per month, this seemed OK. He found a slip that could handle a 38-foot boat and Bob was ready to go—that is, until he bought the boat and pulled into his marina.

The marina told Bob that there was no available slip for his boat, since its overall length (LOA) was 46 feet. The marina continued that Bob would need to be put into a significantly larger slip and that none was available. Bob was forced to find an alternative, less desirable, marina that charged him for a 50-foot slip. The boat could not stay in a 38-foot slip, since its extreme overhang would have been highly dangerous if the boat were docked bow in (the bow toward the dock), and just as menacing to passing boats if docked stern to (the stern toward the dock).

Bob did not know that LOA stood for "Length Overall," or that some marinas charge based on a boat's LOA, particularly if the LOA is very different from the boat's stated length. Turns out, the Hans Christian has a bowsprit that sticks way out in front of the vessel and hardware projecting off the stern; this would be a danger to boats crossing the bow or people walking by on the dock. Bob had a problem. Moreover, even if the marina could have handled the 46' LOA, they might elect to charge Bob for either a 46-foot boat or the size of the larger slip (such as a 50-foot slip). Bob now owed $8,300 annually or $691 per month, a pretty significant monthly increase from the $500 per month he had expected to pay.

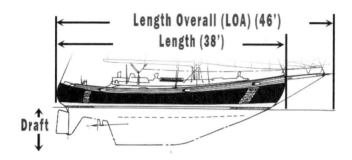

The most important document for understanding a boat is the listing sheet. Every boat manufacturer provides detailed specifications. Some of these terms are essential to the comfort of the boat and others significantly impact the use, enjoyment, and livability of the boat. Other specifications, such as beam, may impact both comfort and operation of the boat. What follows is a listing of common categories on spec sheets. Some of these categories apply only to sailboats, but most apply to all boats.

As an example, let's look at the specifications for the Hunter Marine Passage 420, a 42-foot center-cockpit sailboat (most of these terms are the same for both powerboats and sailboats).

Specification		Meaning
Length	**41'1"**	**Length of the hull of the boat, typically the stated length**

Important Because: A boat's stated hull length is critical for calculations of interior space and the number of feet for which many boating expenses will be charged (such as hauling and launching). Also, this is the length that you, as the owner, will get to tell other people when bragging about how big your boat is. In this case, the boat is a 42-foot craft, but her actual length is much closer to 41 feet.

LOA	**43'5"**	**Length Over All (includes all hardware)**

Important Because: This is how long your boat really is, including all of the hardware and railing, which might stick far in front of or trail behind the boat. Some marinas will charge you based on LOA (they definitely will if it is notably different than a boat's stated length).

LWL	**37'10"**	**Low Water Line, or the length of the boat at the waterline**

Important Because: The maximum speed of a displacement hull boat (a boat that moves by pushing through the water, as compared with a boat that "planes" on top of the water) is calculated by the distance of the hull at the waterline. This is called "hull speed." The formula for a boat's maximum speed is 1.34 times the square root of the LWL. A boat with a LWL of 37'10" will have a maximum hull speed of approximately 8 knots.

Beam	**13'10"**	**The maximum width of the boat at her widest point**

Important Because: The wider the boat, the more living and storage areas in the boat. Beam, while an important measure of comfort, also might be a factor determining which slips at a marina you can be offered.

Some boats get very wide in the middle but are very narrow in the bow and stern. A boat that keeps her width farther forward and aft is said to be "beamy" or to "carry her beam." Powerboats tend to carry their beam not only far forward, but all the way to their sterns, meaning that their width is maintained throughout, making the entire boat much more spacious. Particularly for sailboats, a beamy boat is often not a performance or racing-oriented boat, but will be much more comfortable for living aboard.

Draft   6'6"   The distance from the waterline to the max depth of the boat

Important Because: More draft may correlate to greater stability. Many powerboats do not ride very far down in the water, while sailboats, particularly performance sailboats, will ride very far down. If a boat is too deep for its given environment, it will run aground and risk major damage, injury, or sinking. Pay attention to your specific cruising area to determine the maximum advisable depth of the boat. The more draft for a sailboat, the better the performance (ability to point to the wind and resist cross-tracking) from a stability standpoint.

Displacement   19,500 lbs   The weight of the boat

Important Because: Displacement is one measure of stability. Lighter boats require less horsepower, be it wind or engine, to move the boat to their hull speeds. Heavier boats are more stable but require more horsepower to move.

Ballast   6,700 lbs   The weight of the boat at its bottom

Important Because: The more ballast relative to displacement, the lower the boat's center of gravity and the greater her stability. Ballast also keeps the boat upright.

Mast Ht.   58'5"   The height of the mast

Important Because: A sailboat-only category, this is the height of the mast as measured from the waterline. Depending on your cruising area, your mast needs to be limited to a certain height to navigate bridges and obstructions. The higher the mast, the more opportunity to increase sail area and, as a counterbalance, the more ballast that can be added to increase stability.

Sail Area   875 sq ft   The total square footage of sail area

Important Because: Obviously, another sailboat-only category. The greater the sail area, the more horsepower can be generated by a given boat. Horsepower can be calculated by sail area and displacement.

I	**47'9"**	**Sail measure, jib height**
J	**16'2"**	**Sail measure, jib base**
P	**45'5"**	**Sail measure, main luff**
E	**19'3"**	**Sail measure, foot of the main**

Important Because: Sailboat-only categories, important for sailmakers.

Headroom   6'6"   Headroom

Important Because: Do you want to have to bend over to avoid bumping your head when in your home? Didn't think so. Practically, you might want to be sure that the headroom is maintained forward and aft and is not just a high point in a downward-sloping ceiling.

Fuel Cap.   50 gal   Total fuel the boat can carry

Important Because: Your maximum range under power can be calculated by either engine hours or range at particular RPMs. This is a key element for planning purposes.

Water Cap.   145 gal   Total water the boat can carry

Important Because: Important for cruisers and boats not running a direct connection to city water or using a watermaker. This water is available for showers and washing (and possibly drinking).

Holding Tank   45 gal   **Total number of gallons Capacity for sewage**

Important Because: This is the total tankage for sewage.

Note: *Manufacturers of holding tanks and boats advise that the tank be kept as close to empty as possible under normal conditions.*

Water Heater   6 gal   **Total amount of water held by the water heater**

Important Because: Bigger water heaters mean potentially longer showers, although they take up space and use more power. Many cruisers calculate their shower time not only to conserve hot water, but also to conserve all water and power.

Std. Diesel   56 hp   **Number of horsepower of the engine**

Important Because: Even though a displacement-hull boat cannot go faster than its hull speed, a stronger engine makes the boat far more responsive and controllable.

CE Classification   A   **A rating for the type of usage a boat is able to endure**

Important Because:

A = Ocean (over 40 kts of wind/seas greater than 13 feet)

B = Offshore (34-40 kts of wind and seas of up to 13 feet)
C = Inshore (22-27 kts of wind and seas of up to 6.5 feet)

D = Sheltered Waters (11-16 kts of wind and seas of up to 1.5 feet)

A boater would be a fool to think that every A-rated boat is safe at sea and capable of crossing oceans. I am aware of 33-foot boats that are A rated, with relatively light displacements. Stability is a combination of overall displacement and ratios such as ballast to displacement. Some of these boats will have very little overall stability. Additionally, crossing oceans requires extensive experience, and even more so with a lighter boat. I've done an ocean voyage in a heavy-displacement 55-foot blue-water center-cockpit boat and the ride was quite uncomfortable, for we were flying off of waves and getting soaked by water coming off the beam. The ride in any smaller boat would have been very dangerous.

Finally, what makes a good blue-water cruising boat is not only heavy displacement and adequate length to handle heavy weather and waves, but also significant storage and equipment, fuel capacity, water capacity, and safety gear.

The listing sheet discusses the layout of the boat as well as the systems and equipment aboard. Take all the time you need to understand every single word!

The most that I ever learned in a day about the inner workings of my boat was the day I visited the factory that manufactured it. The amazing folks over at Hunter Marine offered me a personal tour and took the time to answer all of my questions. Most boat manufacturers offer this service; you should be able to develop a close relationship with yours as a source to help you with problems. Many of the best manufacturers are small companies that will welcome your questions and would greatly appreciate a visit.

Now that we know what things mean, and hopefully are getting to better know ourselves, let's go find the perfect boat.

V-berth Used For Storage

Aft Stateroom

My Boat
The Morning Fog
1981 Hunter Marine 33
Cherubini Design

3

Choosing Your Boat

I recently ran a web search for my next hypothetical boat and entered in some criteria that I care about. I came up with 696 boats that fit my needs, 60 in my geographic area. At times like this, there seem to be too many boats to choose from. However, when you boil them down and learn what you are looking for, there can be too few choices. The time you spend learning your preferences and needs is critical to understanding your range of options and ultimately to your final selection.

The proper choice of a boat is one major area in which novice buyers screw up. Because they don't take enough time to understand their needs or alternatives, they end up making unnecessary and unseen compromises. That's unfortunate, given the fact that a little extra time and objectivity can eliminate years' worth of regrets and costs.

Obviously there are prerequisites to purchasing a boat, such as knowing how much you can make as a down payment (your financing company will tell you their required minimum amount, often 20 percent) and how much money your financing company will be willing to lend you. You might want to ask them about their policies for lending money for older boats (more than 20 years old) or non fiberglass (wooden, composite, steel, aluminum, and ferrocement) boats. This is important to know before proceeding. You'll want to have them represent and ultimately put in writing that there is no prepayment penalty. Finally, have your financing company issue you a pre-approval letter, which is a letter telling potential boat sellers that you are a serious buyer who would qualify for financing if the lender approves the terms of your deal and choice of boat.

Once you know your financing company's guidelines, stop worrying about the *process* of buying the boat and focus on *choosing* the right boat. This requires focus and energy and is often a very difficult, frustrating, and time-consuming process, but it is more than worth it! Choice of boat is paramount for liveaboards: This is not a temporary location where you will be spending your time. You don't get to cook your meals somewhere else, or sleep somewhere else, or host friends somewhere else. If you are a cruising liveaboard, you need to be able to adequately store everything that you will need during your excursions while still being safe and comfortable. Boats are designed and built with the *normal* recreational boater in mind, *not* the very small number of liveaboards, and you should be careful to match your needs, wants, hopes, and dreams with that of your investment.

Speaking of investments, in general, boats are not good ones. Not only do boats depreciate in value, but the difference in value between a boat that is 19 years old and 20 years old may be significant, because many financing companies will not generally lend money for a boat that is 20 or more years old, and insurance companies are unwilling to insure older boats. You may find that you own a boat you cannot one day sell, which makes your boat virtually worthless.

Adding electronics and fancy gear to your boat won't help in maintaining value, particularly now in the world of handheld devices and apps (my $3,200 GPS chartplotter of just a few years ago can now be roughly (not perfectly) replaced with a $49 device app). Installed electronics immediately depreciates, in some cases to zero. This isn't like a house (on land) in which a $15,000 kitchen renovation might bring about $35,000 in increased market value in the right circumstances. On a boat, a $2,000 radar system might bring an increased market value to the boat of $500–$1,000. That's an immediate net loss of 50–75 percent. Then, after just a couple of years, the electronics, even if valuable when separated from the boat, will bring no market value increase at all to the boat.

Another liveaboard reality to chew on: A casual boater gets to do his repairs at a comfortable pace, and has no immediate concerns if the boat cannot be occupied for a few weeks/months, or might even have to be moved to the hard (put on land) while significant repairs or improvements are being made. Obviously, this is not the case for a liveaboard. There is no place you can go to hide from the repairs. There is no vacation from the problem, and living on a boat while situated on land is torture to a liveaboard.

Before I purchased my boat, I wouldn't have believed that many liveaboards would let more than a few nonessential problems slip in disrepair. Now, however, it makes perfect sense. If we varnish the interior of our homes, we have to endure the fumes when we eat our meals and go to sleep. So what do we do? Stop varnishing.

In short, you can't easily undo your mistakes. Choose right the first time.

Boats DO Grow On Trees!

There are a lot of things that don't grow on trees, such as money. Money does not grow on trees. But boats do.

My father taught me an important real estate lesson: Houses grow on trees, meaning that a better deal will *always* come along, even if that deal does not exist today. When you think that a great deal is passing you by, don't be nervous, because there is another one coming. Sad as it is, someone will pass away tomorrow and their relatives will need to sell the house. Someone will become divorced and be willing to do anything just to get out of their investment. Someone will like you enough to make a deal. Someone will need to be relocating for work and might only have two weeks to find a buyer. Someone will . . . well, you get the point. Houses grow on trees. The marketplace creates an infinite number of them and they are constantly ripening.

If anything, boats grow more quickly than houses. They are luxury items for most people—although not us. When finances get difficult for boat owners, they sell their luxury items in order to preserve the more essential elements of their life. When an owner sells, he frees himself not only of boat payments, but of the obligation to pay for insurance, storage, engine maintenance, winterizing, hauls, washing, paint, and so on.

Even more significant is the incredible amount of competition to sell boats, which drives costs down. In the old days, before the Internet was so prominent, a boat buyer was locked into the information provided to them by brokers and dealers located in the buyer's geographic area. This information may or may not have been accurate, and a boat buyer, unlike a real estate purchaser, had no access to "competitive" or "comparative" similar sales. These days a boat buyer has access to lots of very relevant information, and additional by-request information (such as mechanic reports, photos and so forth) is available often within moments. For instance, we know the asking price of every other similar boat in the country (and much of the world), and we know how much similar boats have already sold for. Boat brokers and owners price their boats with all of this in mind. You can get this information, commonly available to boat brokers directly through websites and service providers.

So be patient, my liveaboard brothers and sisters. Relax and enjoy the ride. Don't panic. A better boat is right around the corner. If you remember that, and learn to believe it, this process will be less stressful and more fun; you will be a much better negotiator knowing that you can walk away from any deal and still have terrific options. And you will be more emotionally willing to take the time necessary to choose for yourself the best possible boat.

Including and Excluding Boats

To narrow down your choice, you will need to both *include* boats and *exclude* boats. These are not mutually exclusive ideas; a prospective buyer should employ both methods to find the perfect boat.

Establish prerequisites for the perfect boat (such as a specific beam, headroom, number of staterooms, sail or power, etc.), as well as specific things that you do not want for your boat (such as boats that do not meet the above criteria, are located in inconvenient geographic areas, have been used for chartering, and so on).

There is one important word of warning (there will be many more, but let's start here): When you decide which boats to include and exclude, try not to focus on "accessories." Good accessories do not make a good boat. A good boat is a good boat whether or not it has a good radar system. Unfortunately, a bad boat does not become anything other than a bad boat just because it has radar. A pile of poop, when placed in a basket of flowers, becomes merely a pile of poop in a very stinky basket. You won't even notice the flowers. Don't buy yourself a basket of poop.

Many boat buyers, primarily novice ones, will create a spreadsheet of their "needs," which might include lists of "dream" accessories. Example: "I need a windlass, chartplotter, lazy jacks, radar, watermaker, and so forth." If you find a boat with all this gear, will it be a good boat? Who knows? Will it be a better boat because it has all this gear? No. Could it be a bad boat? Yes.

It is very important that you focus first on choosing the right boat. Don't exclude a boat because it does not have all of your dream equipment. Narrow down your choices based on the factors that *can't* be changed, rather than the accessories, which can. Your life and well-being depend on the condition of the hull and deck and seacocks and through-hulls; the condition of your engine is far more critical to a boat's resale value than almost anything else. The condition of the electric wires, overall plumbing, and septic system is unbelievably important, and having to replace one of these systems can take a significant number of hours and cost quite a bit of money. Pay attention to what is important, and expect the boat's owner to have either done the same or discounted the boat accordingly (many boaters expect to expend approximately 10 percent of a boat's value on maintenance on average each year). Be particularly wary of safety issues, as a fire on a boat can be far worse than a fire in a house. Remember, it's a boat and a boat first, even though having a watermaker might seem like the coolest thing.

Then, after you have identified your finalists, you can factor comparisons between the boats, including their accessories, into your final decision in your attempt to best match your desires as well as try to get the most for your money. Accessories can help you narrow down a collection of good choices.

The Factors

Let's start out by conceding that a canoe would likely be the most economical boat we could live in—that is, unless you keep losing your paddle. Then maybe a rowboat (which secures its oars) would be better. I once slept in a rowboat, bent into a gap between two fixed seats, one seat driving into my back and the other jammed into the back of my thighs. It was one of my less enjoyable nights aboard a boat.

You can sleep anywhere, but anywhere is not necessarily acceptable or comfortable. It is very easy to make choices that sound truly wonderful and romantic and then end up feeling as if you're on a camping trip that won't end. Now, that rowboat might have been acceptable to someone, right? Who am I to tell someone else what comfortable or acceptable accommodations are? For better or worse, we get to make our own decisions. For me, I want to be sure that I can stand up in my home, and storage is more important to me than boat performance, although I absolutely want my boat to be operational. I have other requirements as well.

There are a million boats out there for sale, and "new" used boats appear every day to replace every boat that sells. Set up your criteria for what you demand of your boat, and then begin to exclude boats.

Power vs. Sail

Most of the time, your preference is in your heart. Sailors want sailboats. Powerboaters or fishermen want/need powerboats. The decision is often part of your personality.

Sailboats are slow and quiet, with unlimited range under sail, provided there is wind. They require manual labor to operate. A sailboat that is the same weight as a powerboat will typically have a lower center of gravity because of the keel and ballast; the counterbalancing between the keel and the mast will often give the sailboat greater stability under difficult conditions, both at dock and at sea, than a powerboat of similar displacement. While the rigging and sails can be expensive to maintain, a sailboat in good overall condition has much less operating expense than a powerboat.

Powerboats are typically faster than sailboats and a bit louder. They do not have an unlimited range, and range and expense are dependent on fuel usage. While there is no rigging to maintain, the greater number of engine hours usually translates into a higher engine maintenance requirement. Many powerboats are extremely susceptible to wind and weather because of their high windage (exposure to wind—the whole boat acts as a giant sail) and higher center of gravity, and can be uncomfortable under trying conditions. Also, the higher the center of gravity, the more the boat will roll. Unlike a sailboat, there is minimal counterbalance.

The greatest advantage of a powerboat is that at the push of a button the boat can go to its desired location quickly, while a sailboat might have to weave its way to a location slowly, depending on wind direction and speed. Powerboats are also ideal for fishing; they have the ability to trawl, they offer comfortable seats, and they have added storage for bait and catches.

I am a sailor, but have always been jealous when meeting my powerboating friends at one of the Boston Harbor Islands. They would leave after me, pass me, and already be anchored and settled with drink in hand by the time I would arrive. As to comfort, I lived in much tighter conditions. Still, I preferred my sailboat: I spent typically less than $100 in fuel in any one season, even with fairly heavy time away from the docks, and my limited engine use kept engine maintenance to a minimum (usually limited to the beginning and end of the boating season).

As far as liveability goes, powerboats are typically much more comfortable than sailboats. Powerboats carry their beams farther forward and aft, making the interior much more comfortable throughout. Powerboats tend to come up higher out of the water, often creating standing headroom throughout the entire interior, sometimes with multiple living levels and an open flat deck. And the living quarters and galley tend to be so much bigger in powerboats that it is common to find sofas, big TVs, lamps, and carpets in the salons, and full stand up refrigerators in the galleys.

As far as space and storage goes, this is highly dependent on the boat. Typically powerboats do have much more room in the living quarters and staterooms. Depending on the configuration of the engine room, there might be more room down below as well. The fact that a sailboat is pointy in the bow and sometimes the stern, tends to significantly limit a sailboat's storage and living quarters.

Center-cockpit sailboats are able to preserve more of a sailboat's living quarters then aft-cockpit boats. They typically allow for a stand-up aft stateroom that often resembles that of a master stateroom in a powerboat.

A quick comment on powerboats: Fuel is expensive, and a performance 40-foot boat can easily burn $1,000 or more of fuel on a weekend trip from Boston to Martha's Vineyard and back. This detail, seldom mentioned at boat shows, often comes as a surprise to many new, unsuspecting boat owners. There is, however, a wide fuel efficiency spread, and other slower, similarly-sized boats may be much more fuel efficient. Take the time to know what you are getting into.

Regardless of whether you are a sailboater or powerboater, failing to learn the different types of boats and layouts of all boats will make it impossible for you to truly know what your options and choices are and what is available. I guess that's why I love boat shows so much. It's like exploring.

Wood vs. Fiberglass

Fiberglass is strong, versatile, and easily repaired. It is light relative to its strength. It doesn't leak when you first put it into the water, and an accident does not necessarily junk your whole home. Fiberglass is relatively maintenance-free. Finance companies are willing to lend money for fiberglass boats, and insurance companies are willing to insure them. Most boat buyers prefer fiberglass boats, so when the day comes that they decide to sell their boat, there will be a much wider audience of people who might be interested, and therefore higher preservation of value.

So the question is: Who in his right mind would want to buy a *wooden* boat?

One advantage to wooden boats is that they may be cheaper. An old wooden boat may be available for far less than a comparably sized fiberglass boat. Consequently, you get more space for the money. Wooden boats tend to look and smell nice, and even an inoperable boat might be an excellent choice for someone who does not want to leave the dock or perform much maintenance.

Wooden boats (or wooden components on boats) require more care than fiberglass boats. Also, you might not be able to finance the purchase, get the boat insured, or sell the boat. But let's just say that if you want a boat that you do not plan on selling, and love to work on boats, and are great at what you do, and are careful, and don't need insurance, then a wooden boat might be perfect for you. Because of the difficulties in financing wooden boats and acquiring insurance, it is sometimes possible to find amazing deals for wooden boats, particularly those in some state of disrepair. If you don't plan on operating the boat, but have enough cash to buy the boat outright and want to avoid insurance payments, an old wooden boat might provide you with the perfect floating home for a fraction of the money.

Note that some travel lifts will not haul wooden boats because of the stresses that are placed on the hull. So make sure that you have the facilities at hand to allow you to take care of your home! As another word of caution, many marinas require that their tenants carry insurance, which might be difficult to acquire for a wooden boat.

New vs. Old

Boat values do not remain stable or appreciate. Boats depreciate, some faster than others. Go to an online resource such as www.yachtworld.com and examine the decrease in price per year. Remember that even though these are all asking prices and not actual sale prices (your broker can tell you the sale prices), the results are obvious.

You get more value with a boat that is not a new boat—provided, of course, that the boat has been properly maintained. In addition, if you are lucky enough to purchase a boat that has already been used by a person who is the same "kind" of liveaboard as you are (see "What Kind of Liveaboard Are You?"), you may find that your startup costs can be substantially reduced. For instance, if you want to be a non-cruising liveaboard that likes coastal amenities, and you find a boat being sold by the same kind of liveaboard, you may already find your boat equipped with a 110-volt system, inverter, charger, broadband, installed satellite system, good speakers (inside and topside), spreader lights, and so forth. These may have been add-ons on a new boat, but these costs, as well as the time and labor of installation, have already been borne by a prior owner.

Many new boats, even from highly reputable companies, have quirks and bugs that need to be worked out; sometimes they leak from fittings or seams on deck. While manufacturers do everything they can to avoid these types of issues, they are not uncommon. Aging, and using a boat and its engine and systems, will work out many of those bugs.

If logic dictated, very few new boats would be produced. But lots of new boats are produced—lots and lots, despite the fact that there must be a million used boats for sale at any one time.

Some people—enough to keep all of the boat manufacturers in business—do not want to buy a used boat. The choice of new versus old depends not only on your preference but also on your budget. If you can elect to buy a new boat rather than save some cash by buying a one-year-old boat, then you are likely more able to customize for your specific needs and are not as cost-sensitive.

Boat manufacturers know the value of a new boat sale. That's why they might help you secure lower interest rates and provide various promotions to help lead you toward a new boat. Boat retailers do the same thing, and often will take your used boat in trade. Still, at some point—maybe not with a boat that is one year old but perhaps one that is slightly older—a significant financial savings will be realized by purchasing a used boat. These days warranties are often transferable, allowing an owner of a used boat to be protected by the same warranties as the boat's original owner. Many manufacturers provide customer service for the new owner of one of their used boats to the same extent as if the boat had been purchased originally from the manufacturer.

Still, many people do not want to take ownership of a boat that has been used or lived in by someone else, and that is fine. By buying new, they get to customize and break in their boat their way. What a wonderful benefit—coming, of course, at a premium. Depending on your manufacturer, there might be a great deal of potential customization, some as great as having a boat custom built. Keep in mind that the value of a new boat will decrease the most under the first owner's watch, so resale value may not necessarily be proximate to purchase price.

One last issue of note: Remember that purchasing a used boat that will at some point in the owner's tenure become twenty years old is a financial risk, given that many financing companies will not finance a boat more than twenty years old, and insurance may be difficult to acquire, as well. While the market value may be substantially diminished for the seller, the right buyer might be able to capitalize on this lower-priced boat.

Budget

A person's budget can be one of the most frustrating wet blankets on any lifestyle. I'm the kind of person who likes to live n the financial edge because I love the toys that money can buy. As my bankrupt uncle used to say, "With a great credit limit, who needs a budget?"

This topic is important to your short- and long-term happiness. For the most part, boats are expensive to buy, own, and operate. Boats can even be expensive to sell. Understanding the costs of boating is critical to knowing what you can afford. This of course depends on your needs and goals, as well as your location. There are some very economical solutions to acquiring a boat; liveaboards who decide not to use the boat as an operating craft thereby save operating costs. I've dedicated an entire chapter to the costs of boat ownership. Preliminarily, potential liveaboards do need to understand their budget before actually making the jump, and a good understanding of budget will work miracles for establishing the criteria for including and excluding boats.

If a boat is financed, many financing companies will require that the buyer make a down payment of 20 percent of the cost of the boat. There are fewer creative solutions for financing a boat than there are for purchasing real estate. Small economic cycles aside, boats generally go down in value (a lot), while houses and real estate generally go up in value. Thus it is quite possible for a boat owner to owe a lender more than the boat is worth, which is a huge risk for the lender and a paralyzing dilemma for a boat owner who wants to sell. As a result, lenders care much more about the equity a boat owner has in his boat than a mortgage lender cares about equity in a house. This is not like a house or piece of real estate where a borrower can get a second and even third mortgage, or put a lesser amount down in exchange for paying mortgage insurance, because most boat lenders aren't foolish enough to hold a second lien on a boat that may not be worth even as much as the first lien—at least not without some other collateral.

Accordingly, if you choose to finance a boat, your lender will often require certain terms and conditions in your insurance policy; these terms may also limit boat usage. And unlike lenders for real estate, financing companies of boats often want to know that you have experience as a boater, because their collateral could so easily be damaged.

One more point on insurance: Since lenders require that a boat be insured, if the boat owner violates the terms of his insurance policy, the insurance will be lost. That means that the terms of the loan will also be violated, and a lender could at that time ask for the entire balance of the loan to be paid off with your next payment. An example of this would be if the insurance policy prohibited the boat from being taken out more than ten miles from the coast, or prohibited any use in hurricane-prone areas during hurricane season (even in calm weather). If the insurance company finds out about any improper use, particularly if you suffer any loss during that improper use, your whole financial world could come crashing in, causing you to end up with a damaged (or sunken) boat, no insurance, and a lender asking for the immediate payment of the entire balance of the outstanding loan.

Ignoring costs of a boat's ownership and operation, you will need to have at the ready 20 percent of the cost of the boat, plus the applicable sales tax (which may or may not be able to be financed). If you need to have your boat delivered, that will cost money (sometimes a lot of money). Insurance costs money. Surveys cost money, and in addition to the survey, you will need money for the haul and launch so that you can properly examine the condition of the hull, through-hulls, rudder, and any other gear located below the waterline. That means that for a $100,000 boat, you might need upwards of $28,000 just to complete the purchase and take ownership.

Then you will bear registration fees immediately, and your marina will likely charge you money up front for a slip in which to keep the boat. Then, if you have anything that needs repairs or improvements, you will need to address those issues soon after you take ownership.

I hope you were expecting all of these costs. If not, it's a good thing that you decided to read this book. I was not prepared for all of these costs, and was shocked when I got into severe trouble during my maiden voyage, which ended up costing me several thousand dollars just to deal with an emergency at sea and the repairs that followed.

There *are* upsides. Unlike all of those other boaters out there who are incurring the same costs as you for their boats, you don't bear the costs of a landside residence. If you are a cruising liveaboard, maybe you don't even own a vehicle, and there are other savings you will receive as well. And you will eventually own an asset that will have value. Most importantly, you get to be a liveaboard, with all of the benefits that provides.

Big vs. Small

I spend quite a bit of time in Los Angeles. While I enjoy my toys, I don't take the same pride in material possessions as do many other people in L.A. For instance, I drive a Toyota Highlander: simple, pretty cheap, relatively fuel-efficient. That's who I am. Before I met my wife I was shocked to learn how many women in L.A. would not date me because my car at the time (a Corolla) was not "adequate." This as not a question of interpretation. I once asked a woman out and her response was (and I'm not kidding), "What kind of car do you drive?" When I told her, she not-so-politely refused.

Some people have a similar attitude toward boats, and are impressed with size. Of course there is a very practical component to boat size: You are going to be living aboard, and headroom, storage, and a comfortable living area are all very important. But in addition to practical factors, boat size means status. While knowledgeable boaters are impressed with differences among boat manufacturers, the general public is impressed with size and shininess. Even if extra boat length is not needed, many desire it. After all, we all want to look great pulling into a marina. And if you are the kind of boater who wants to impress the world, length is of greater importance. Freud would be proud.

Almost universally, liveaboards seem to agree that no one should subject himself to living in a boat smaller than 30 feet (this may be *the* only thing that liveaboards can agree on). This is, of course, an attempt to set a minimum comfort level. There are many liveaboards who do, however, live in smaller boats quite comfortably. When you think about how large a boat you should acquire, it is best to at least heed the sentiments of my friend and trusted boat technician Chris Birch, who advises liveaboards to acquire the smallest boat they possibly can fit in, and take the money saved, which is significant, and invest in a landside facility for storage. Ironically, many liveaboards over time begin to express similar sentiments.

Storage, which is one of the biggest problems for liveaboards, is often presumed to be more plentiful in longer boats. This is not always true, and many smaller boats, particularly with newer designs, have significant storage as well. For sailboats, some boats that are designed with comfort in mind will intentionally sacrifice performance and quality of sailing in exchange for a more luxurious living space. For instance, an Island Packet 34' sailboat has as much storage and living area as do some boats 12 feet longer. While the trade off is the diminished ability to sail in light air and toward wind, liveability is greatly improved. These are compromises that only you can decide on; do so knowingly and thoughtfully.

Many liveaboards have told me that if they had a magic wand, their boats would be smaller and lighter. Boaters often buy boats that are too big for their needs, and get caught up in that image thing, and in doing so, end up incurring higher maintenance, storage, and operating costs. Every linear foot of a boat brings added expense. And as the corollary to that, every foot smaller results in a significant cost savings.

I should mention that boat manufacturers are getting better and better at designing their layouts with liveability in mind, and are figuring out how to do this with less sacrifice of the boat's performance. Powerboats, however, have not been subjected to this same trade off, since many have always been geared toward comfort and liveability.

Space and Storage

When you talk to liveaboards about what they have given up for their lifestyles, you tend to hear stories about the lack of space. It seems as if liveaboards enjoy every other aspect of their undertaking, but regret not having certain of their possessions aboard.

Liveaboards do give up many of their possessions, at least while they are living aboard, and permanent liveaboards give up certain possessions forever. This includes obvious things like furniture. In a sailboat, furniture (like the settee) is built into the boat. In a powerboat, there might be room for a sofa and the like, but space for furniture remains quite limited. This isn't like living in a small house, where the attic might provide ten times the storage space of even a large boat.

In my experience, furniture is not the biggest loss. The biggest loss is of the more precious possessions: things like artwork on the walls, photo albums and books, grandmother's china, a guitar and amp, or that closet full of clothes and shoes. Sentimental stuff.

Bear in mind that possessions are left behind for various reasons. Would it be possible to find space for the photo albums? Probably. Would it be advisable to bring them aboard? Probably not. At least not the originals. Water damage can happen at any time. Condensation can occur everywhere there is moist air. And salt air will erode anything it touches. Technology is certainly helping us with our storage problem when it comes to photographs, music collections and more; but technology does not fix the core problem - liveaboards have very limited space.

Liveaboards might choose to pay for storage facilities. Mine cost slightly more than $125 a month. If I had had a good friend or relative with an empty room, I might have tried to impose my possessions upon that person as well. What are you going to do? Sell stuff? Store stuff? Lend stuff to others? It's part of the liveaboard plan.

There is an upside to this storage thing: it is impossible to buy anything else. Spending sprees are no more. There is no room for furniture or wall space for artwork. And since everything on board must be properly secured/stowed before cruising, there is an incentive to limit unsecured possessions. My relatives and friends were all told that gifts should be limited to beer (in cans) and wine, trips to restaurants, and other things that do not take up any space. For everything that is added, something must be removed.

Ultimately, liveaboards often move aboard to escape some aspect of civilization, and then we bring civilization aboard with us. This includes having mail delivered to the boat, and overwhelming the limited living space with guitars and skis and clothes and stuff. [Note that there are alternatives, such as post office boxes, services that provide an address for cruising liveaboards to use for mail and vehicle registration, and so forth.] For those who try to use the boat as a fully functional apartment on the water, the experience can become anything but an escape. To make the lifestyle all that was anticipated, the "stuff" should be kept somewhere else, since keeping it aboard both detracts from the experience and imposes a major restriction on the use of the boat (it takes more time to leave the dock if stuff needs to be stowed properly before heading out). In addition, too much clutter aboard imposes a major safety issue, as nooks and crevices of the boat are filled with things that need to be removed if there is suddenly a need to get to or inspect key equipment such as seacocks, hoses, and wiring.

Technician Chris Birch's are even more radical than most when it comes to some of the other amenities on board that are often regarded as essentials. For instance, Chris argues that you should consider removing the shower from the boat. With no shower, you get an entire locker with significant space, since the entire cabinet where the water heater once sat can now be used for storage. You can always take advantage of the showers provided by your marina. Chris argues further that the marine head should be removed, along with the holding tank, and replaced with a five-gallon bucket with a toilet seat lid. His justification, which is very well thought out, is that a lot more space is gained, including all of the space where the holding tank rested, and a primary system which produces odors and difficulty is removed. I think that this approach is too radical for me and most other liveaboards, but this is something to think about, for the advice is an example of how, in one fell swoop, one may resolve many of the challenges of life aboard—including costs, space, and odors—with a simple yet dramatic change in lifestyle.

Storage issues should be carefully considered and planned. Some liveaboards will keep their belongings in storage to make sure that the lifestyle is for them, or to ease the transition until a permanent commitment to the lifestyle can be made. If there is more than one person aboard, careful consideration of locker and drawer space should be made. If you like shoes, how many pairs should be brought aboard? I don't know, but probably less than the number that are kept currently in your house. If there is any relief to this dilemma it is that condensation will cause all of the shoes brought aboard to get really moldy anyway, so it will be good to have some extra pairs in storage.

Use

So, if you want to sail across the ocean, you need a boat that can sail across the ocean. If you want to host social gatherings, you need a boat that can handle social gatherings. If you are expecting to be hosting booze cruises or sunset cruises on board, you will need a boat with the capabilities and amenities, as well as the safety precautions that will make your boat successful in its endeavor.

If you want a boat that can sail across an ocean, don't buy a boat designed for booze cruises. If you want a boat that will see almost exclusive use coastal cruising on weekends in good weather, don't waste money on a boat designed for transoceanic journeys. Most liveaboards rarely, if ever, leave the dock. You can buy an amazing amount of boat for your money if you decide that you do not need a working engine.

If you know what you need, and choose and buy accordingly, you can use your budget effectively, efficiently, and wisely, and maximize the amount of boat for your money.

Despite the fact that this makes perfect sense, this is one of the rules most often breached, particularly by novice boaters. Boaters screw this up because they either: forget or don't know what they expect to be doing with the boat, have unrealistic expectations, are not honest with themselves, get caught up with name-brand manufacturers or status, or just fall in love with the wrong boat.

Equipment

We've talked about how boat buyers should focus primarily on the boat and not on the boat's equipment. That doesn't change the reality that a boat gets real attractive when it sports the equipment you're looking for.

Boaters have a wide variety of equipment choices, whether it be for safety, navigation, comfort, fun, communications, or other purposes. Unlike living in a house, there is no such thing as a "standard" equipment package. I know several liveaboards (me, for instance) who do not have a refrigerator, only an icebox, and I know others who would never consider living this way. Even in the freezing cold winters in the Northeast, I know liveaboards (me, again) who do not have central heat, but only use bulkhead heaters and/or space heaters.

Are there things that you absolutely can't do without? Bear in mind that there are typically solutions and equipment configurations to solve any given problem.

Examples of different types of extras might include:

Safety

High Quality Anchor
Life Raft
MOB
EPIRB

Navigation

GPS/Chartplotter
Radar

Comfort

Refrigeration
Central Heat
Air Conditioning
Lifeline Cushions

Fun

Hammock
Deck Chairs
Media Center
Stereo/Speakers

Communication

Single-Side-Band Radio
VHF Radio
Satellite Systems

Other

Generator/Solar
Inverter
Battery Charger
Windlass
Laundry Machines

Remember that all of this gear can be added after purchase, and that your most important responsibility is to select the absolute best boat possible, irrespective of the extras. Furthermore, these days technical innovation is happening so quickly that there can be many ways to solve a problem. Educate and discipline!

Comfort

While comfort is subjective, if you have a general idea of what you need and expect for comfort, it would make your boat search far more efficient. Comfort factors into every aspect of a boat, whether it be something as obvious as headroom and overall space; a boat's general configuration; the number and location of ports and hatches (for light and air); space in the head, galley, and cockpit area; deck space and configuration for spending time topside; or overall comfort of the cushions and mattresses.

Don't skip any of these details. This is your home and you will have to live with your choices. There are, of course, compromises that are made. Since boats have a finite amount of space, every inch of space that is being used for one function cannot be used for any other. Your needs must match that of the boat's design.

In addition to spatial and design compromises, there are practical compromises. Boats designed for heavy-weather cruising might have a galley in a smaller, circular design so that the cook would be safe and secure during heavy weather. This, just like all other factors in a boat, is a compromise. A faster boat will sacrifice comfort. A more comfortable boat will sacrifice performance and speed, as well as the ability to perform in lighter air. A powerboat that rises high out of the water is more affected by wind and may have a higher center of gravity than other similar displacement boats, and therefore will be less comfortable in rocky conditions. A deeper draft boat might perform better, but will be unable to go to all of the places that a shallow boat can go.

Boats with wider beams, particularly those that carry their beams farther forward and aft, will be much more comfortable than narrower boats, although they too might sacrifice performance. A classic example of such a boat is the sailboat made by Island Packet. The Island Packet is a very stable boat, with a heavy displacement and ballast, and also carries its wide beam throughout. The boats are all extremely spacious and comfortable, but are notorious for their lack of performance in light air. Island Packet owners joke about having to turn on their engines in order to tack in light air, below 10–15 knots. (Incidentally, even 8-10 knots of wind will have *my* boat at or near its hull speed.) In return for a beautiful and comfortable boat, an owner often gets a boat that might perform below her peers. This is the most common problem I see with novice liveaboards' first boats, a mistake that results in significant discomfort and rarely happens again. Nonetheless, everything is a trade off.

A center-cockpit sailboat offers a full stateroom with a queen-sized bed aft with standing headroom, which is not possible with a traditional aft-cockpit configuration. The center cockpit also places the crew up and out of the water and protects them from the elements while sailing. Powerboats provide a wide variety of cockpit configurations, including a possible indoor helm.

The more boats you visit before you make the leap, the better will be your picture of your comfort choices.

Quality and Finish

These are the final touches, including things like that extra (ninth) coat of hand-buffed varnish, marble/Corian counter tops, things like that. These are the luxuries that you want, but you don't need them and you can save money shopping for boats without all of the niceties. Or maybe they are very important to you. To each his own.

We're not going to take any time on this. If you want a perfect boat, you can evaluate those perfect boats that are perfectly constructed and finished, such as Oysters and Hinkleys, among others (as examples of sailboats). While my favorite aesthetic boat is the Hans Christian, my strong owner preference is for the boats that are more simply constructed with less wood and varnish, making maintenance far easier. Many boat owners don't need a perfectly finished work of art, but love terrific boats that are more cost effective, often equally loaded with the same exact equipment and systems. Still, how can anyone take perfectly varnished brightwork for granted? It's just that not all of us want to maintain it or pay for it.

Location

There are thousands of boats for sale in just about every corner of the country and the world. Nevertheless, as you refine your search and begin to understand your exact needs and wants, you will ultimately decide on a final make and model of boat, and you might find that your ideal boat is not available in your area.

Particularly with the invention of the Internet, It is now common for boat searches to involve trips throughout different geographic locations. If you find that the boat you are seeking is not in your area, you have two choices: You can wait for new boats to come onto the market, or you can expand your search by boat type or geographic location.

Before you get too excited about distant boats, speak with a company or captain that moves the type of boat you are seeking. Talk to them about their process, timing, and costs. Keep in mind that boat delivery can be quite expensive, in the thousands of dollars. When I was looking at boats, the prices I was quoted were far outside of my budget (I received a $5,000 quote to deliver a boat 200 miles). As a result, my search was limited to local purchases, which was not that difficult, given the extensive boating culture in the Northeastern United States. At the same time, many buyers in other parts of the country expect to have to ship their new boat great distances— buyers from Canada will often shop for their boat throughout much of the United States.

Resources

If you decide to engage a broker, as discussed in much greater depth in the next chapter, you should expect your broker to work diligently to identify great boats. Not good boats, but *great* boats *for you.* The identification of appropriate boats is, after all, one of the primary reasons for a broker's existence. If a broker is not following your guidelines or requirements, or it looks as if the broker is representing less than satisfactory boats as ideal purchases, then you are dealing with either a bad broker or one who only wants to close a deal and is not looking out for your best interests. Bad brokers will easily waste all of your time, and you will likely settle for a less-than-ideal boat.

In many ways you no longer need a broker in this Internet day and age. In the old days brokers and boat dealers, as well as advertisements in publications, were the only ways of finding and identifying prospective boats, and buyers were limited to this small universe of identified boats. Today, the Internet provides buyers with an incredible ability to search through and learn about every available boat in the world. I would encourage every boat shopper to spend a great deal of time on what is probably the biggest site, www.yachtworld.com, as well as other boat listing sites where you can search through thousands of boats with many different criteria in any geographic location. It's a great way to spend a night in.

Also, don't forget to read the magazines and reviews. Look at the pictures, read the stories, and ask questions of the wide audience of liveaboards both in person and on the Internet. With a little time, you'll get your answers.

Robert Doty's *Candide*
Rob's salon (above) is his office (computer),
dining room, and entertainment center
(TV and rack stereo system).
Note the cramped galley (below)
for safe meal preparation while under way.

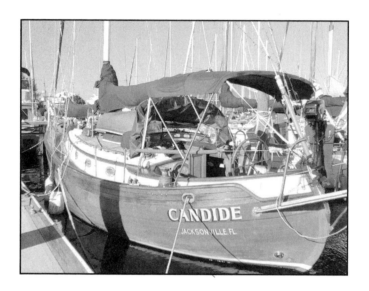

Robert Doty's *Candide*
Hans Christian Traditional 38
Jacksonville, Florida

4

Buying Your Boat

At this point, with luck, you have chosen your perfect boat. Remembering the rule that boats do grow on trees and that if the purchase of this boat doesn't work out, surely another better boat will come along soon, let's figure out what you need to do to take ownership.

Do You Need A Broker?

You might already have your own broker; perhaps one helped you locate the boat. The seller may be using his own broker. So there may be one or two brokers in the picture already. While using a broker is not essential, it often makes very good sense.

Brokers serve several valuable purposes—at least, the good ones do. Sometimes they are the voice of reason. A peculiar thing tends to happen when you find a boat you like—emotions take over: love, expectation, hope on the positive side, and fear on the negative side. The fear of losing the dream boat that you have fallen so dearly in love with is a problem because it could result in irrational decision-making. Funny, it takes months or years to decide if you want to marry someone, yet mere seconds to decide to become permanently wedded to a particular boat. Neither may be a very good financial investment.

A good broker will work to balance the inherent conflicts of this situation—the love of the boat versus the practicalities dictated by your choice of boat and by the buying process. A good broker will speak for you so that these emotions do not conflict with your discussions and negotiations, and he will make sure that you understand all of the terms and complexities of your endeavor.

A good broker should do other things as well: He should make sure the boat meets your needs, is in acceptable condition, ensuring you are protected contractually, and that you are getting what you expect to be getting—such as a boat with a clean title, and the equipment that you think the seller is going to be including as part of the purchase.

It is important to take a moment to discuss a broker's allegiances and responsibilities. In the United States a broker, unless engaged solely by the buyer, works for the seller. Just like the seller, that broker primarily cares about making the sale, and you should understand and believe that the broker will be less than forthcoming with you if he has been instructed to keep information from you. And your secrets and confidences will be revealed. Some sellers' brokers, particularly the bad ones or those who are only looking out for themselves, will work to make sure that you pay the highest price possible. This type of broker is your adversary.

A broker might also be a *dual* agent, owing allegiances to both the buyer and the seller. Being a dual agent is not just a title but a legal status, with the broker owing obligations equally to both parties. It is important that you ask questions to determine the role of the brokers involved. If you don't, then you are allowing the broker to only work for the other side. To be clear... a broker who is not explicitly for the buyer is only looking out for the sale.

Brokers come in all shades, from very good to very bad. Most are average; all are conflicted. It is your job to try to figure out whether the broker can be trusted entirely, for it's absolutely vital for you to be able to trust any broker that you employ. You're looking for the very best. Some brokers will represent every party fairly, while others, like used car salesmen, are looking to move their inventory. Many good brokers work very hard to match boats with the right buyers, and are seeking to represent and price a boat accurately—and are striving to ensure that the final transaction is fair to both parties.

Unlike the ethical code for real estate brokers in the United States, there is no inherent obligation of the seller (and seller's broker) to reveal voluntarily all of the material problems with the boat you are investigating. The good brokers believe that it is in all parties' best interest for the buyer to have the most information as early as possible. Even a dual broker will not reveal to the buyer the seller's secrets, such as the bottom line price, the seller's personal circumstances, or any defects in the boat, even if known to him. The dual broker is supposed to at least keep both parties' secrets. This is in contrast to a seller's broker, who has an obligation to reveal all of the buyer's information to the seller, but not the reverse. While a dual broker is potentially much fairer, this is still not like engaging a partner. And a bad dual broker will be no different than a seller's broker, seeking the best price and most favorable terms for the seller (the higher the price, the more he gets paid), though he will appear harmless, like a wolf in sheep's clothing, the worst of all adversaries.

You can handle this situation in any number of ways, but first you need to understand it. The bad brokers are interested in selling something, and will use a variety of sales tactics to do it. Your first defense is to understand the potential conflict between trying to sell a boat and fairness. You have to use your judgment to determine whether you feel that you can trust the seller's broker. Definitely don't reveal everything to any broker other than an exclusive buyer's agent, especially your highest price, and don't express all of your love for the boat in a visible manner. If you do, you will likely find yourself paying more than you otherwise would have.

Information is valuable, and every party will capitalize on any information that they have about you; similarly, if you heard that the seller was getting divorced and was willing to sell the boat for any amount of money, you might choose to open the negotiations far lower than you otherwise might have and be less willing to make concessions. Consider engaging your own broker to help you identify the right boats (you'll need to do this *before* being introduced to a boat), who will have allegiance to you as the buyer. This may be your best solution if you are an emotional or unsure negotiator. The nice thing about having your own broker is that the seller will be paying for him, as any commission will be paid out of the purchase monies paid to the seller. In other words, it costs you nothing.

Common advice is that it makes sense to always engage a broker. It is like having a best friend who is not allowed to ignore you and your interests, someone you can confide in and reveal and discuss your strategy with. This is someone you need to trust, and it's best not to go through this process alone, particularly if you are a novice buyer. If you are an experienced buyer, a broker is still recommended so that you can focus on the boat and not the logistics. At a minimum, the buyer's broker can help the buyer to remain objective and focused on the goal of acquiring the right boat. A broker's greatest value is helping a buyer to understand the flaws of the boat, particularly the problems revealed by the surveyor. You might hear about some deck delamination or blisters on the hull, and the broker, being part of this industry full time, should be able to give you an idea about costs of repair and the scope of the problem (if it is a problem at all). It's a valuable expert opinion that you don't have to pay for.

Even though there is no requirement to reveal all material defects in a boat, the law in the United States puts some limits on what the broker can say or do. The law calls the broker a "fiduciary," which requires the broker to preserve the integrity of the deal. Brokers can't lie. If you ask them a question, you have to be told the truth. Any monies that they hold in escrow must be held in trust and cannot be provided directly to their client unless released by you. Finally, the broker (in conjunction with the lender) is required to make sure that you are buying what you think you are buying. In other words, the broker and lender must ensure that a boat has no other claims or liens against it by other third parties. It is the broker's job to be sure that all mortgages are paid off and that you are taking a boat that is "free and clear of all encumbrances" (to use a legal phrase), and that you are holding a title which is "clear and marketable" (to use another one).

I would highly recommend putting together a list of written questions to ask the seller in advance, concerning any history of past damages, material problems that the seller knows of, condition of the structure and equipment, identification of things that do not work or that work improperly, and other questions that are relevant to determining the value of this particular boat. You need this information, and it is most frustrating when you find out things later that the owner of the boat knew and didn't reveal. Get the answers back in writing and make their accuracy a condition of the offer. If you ask a question and are told something that is known not to be true, you do have some recourse, including recovering any costs that you expend to reveal the truth. More than likely, however, you will be told the truth and can more properly evaluate the boat.

But as I said, there *are* bad brokers out there. If I had fewer scruples (or if I were willing to get sued) I'd list a few of the Boston brokers that are walking disasters. This one bad guy was trying to help me buy a boat, knew what I wanted, and took me to see six boats that couldn't have been farther out of my price range or more inappropriate for me. As a novice buyer, I was starting to think that there were very few boats out there and that I'd have to make my choice based on the boats that I was being shown. His sales tactics were high-pressure, including the use of guilt, telling me that I was wasting his time and that he couldn't make a living from customers like me. Luckily for me, he didn't. I changed brokers. Note: he's still out there.

Because of the wide variety in brokers, it is important to use word of mouth in order to determine the broker's reputation. Find out if the broker is a member of one of the top associations in the United States—the Yacht Brokers Association of America, Florida Brokers Association, California Brokers Association, or Northwest Brokers Association—all of which have standards related to broker ethics.

Important: Even buyer's brokers only get paid when you buy a boat. Like it or not, they, like the seller's broker, want to work with serious buyers who are going to make offers and consummate deals. They have financial obligations and are trying to make a living, and they face the inherent conflict of making more money with a higher purchase price. It is easy for even a buyer's broker to approach the Dark Side and not provide the advocacy or level of service that you are paying for and deserve. Consider keeping your top price a secret even from your buyer's broker. Be aware, and work with those you trust. If you tell the broker what kind of boat you are looking for, expect to see boats that fit your profile. Ask lots of questions, expect to have the broker teach you things, and most importantly, expect and demand that the broker tell you when a boat is the wrong boat. If the broker fails at any of these requirements, get away from that broker. He cares more about himself than you.

Finding a good broker is like striking gold. I know of a few wonderful brokers and the value added is immense.

The Buying Process

Pre Approvals

While we are about to explore the boat purchasing process, one critical thing to do in advance is be certain that you can acquire financing and insurance. Financing companies will give you information based on which boats they might or might not be willing to finance, and will often provide you with a letter of acceptance in advance so that you can proceed comfortably, demonstrating to yourself, the brokers, and the seller that you are not wasting anyone's time. Insurance companies will also be able to let you know whether or not you are insurable based on your boating background and experience.

Without this information, not only might you be wasting everyone's time, but you also might end up falling in love with a boat, having an offer accepted, and then paying a substantial amount of money for a survey only to find out that you are unable to proceed.

Making an Offer

Every used boat has a stated "listing" or "asking" price (except those on eBay or at auction), which is established by the seller or seller's broker. This is really just a starting point to attempt to gain interest and commence discussions. Concessions are made from that price, which means that the price represents the most that a seller thinks that he will be able to get for the boat. It is higher than the price that he thinks he will get. Many new boats have a fixed price set by the manufacturer, which the seller (in most cases the dealer) may not be permitted to negotiate. However, there are usually factors that may be negotiated; these include added accessories, trade-in value, and other incentives.

While this isn't a book on negotiating techniques and strategies, I would advise you to start with the premise that everything is negotiable. Telling a buyer that something is "as is" or "non-negotiable" is merely a negotiating tactic. The seller typically wants—often quite badly—to sell the boat, and the discussions and negotiations are really a game. The seller doesn't want to lose a legitimate buyer and you don't want to lose the boat. If you stop playing the game, you will lose. It might be a game that no one really likes, but it is the only way you will get the best deal. Don't tire of the game, and remember that it will end soon enough.

Your job is to develop a strategy to acquire the boat of your dreams for the best possible price. Maybe offer close to your best price first and communicate that this is the maximum price within your budget. But if you do that, making future concessions will prove you to be a liar, which will open you up to even more concessions. Maybe start very low and work up. Start too low and your offer might be considered offensive and you might lose your credibility with the seller and the brokers. Ask about the seller and know that any information you receive will be valuable. Is the seller trying to buy a new boat? Does he desperately need the money? Maybe he now has two boats and is desperate to get "out" of one of them. Maybe there is a divorce and the court has required that the parties sell the boat. Information is power (and in this case, money). Maybe the seller doesn't really care whether the boat is sold and plans to use the boat if it is not sold.

Remember that this is a game—or a dance—and the seller will always want you to think that the situation is not desperate, that there are others interested in the boat. Why? It scares you into thinking that you might lose the boat. Remember, the seller is often dying to sell the boat in almost every imaginable scenario. While you are scared to lose the boat, he is scared of losing you.

Note: The use of the phrase "as is" is often a seller's way of saying "there's lots of stuff wrong here that I don't want to fix. So offer with caution." It might also be a way of saying, "I won't fix stuff. What you see is what you get, so only offer what the boat is worth." Don't be intimidated into thinking that because you made an offer on a boat that is reportedly "as is," you need to incur any shortcuts in deciding whether to purchase the boat, including omitting a thorough survey. When you find something wrong, you will find that "as is" doesn't mean anything at all.

You want the seller to think that while you love the boat, your life and happiness don't depend on whether or not you end up owning that particular boat. Keep looking at other boats while you negotiate. A very famous book on negotiating, called *Getting to Yes, Negotiating Agreement Without Giving In* by Roger Fisher talks about making sure that you always have another option (known as the next best alternative)—remember, there are millions of other options, and even if today no option is evident, tomorrow one will be. It is not cause for an emotional breakdown if you don't end up with the first boat that you love.

Use your buyer's broker to help discuss strategy, and then be calm and calculated as you advance through the process. And be sure that even your broker does not know your highest price, and you want to be reluctant to make concessions from the initial discussions. That will make your broker a better negotiator.

A couple of final thoughts: First, there is a value to goodwill—it is nice when the seller wants to help and get to know the buyer, and this will only happen if the seller doesn't feel as though he or she has gotten screwed. If the deal is amicable, many owner/sellers will gladly meet with the buyer to teach the buyer about the ins and outs of the boat that has been purchased. There is quite a bit to be said for this, although despite the promise, few buyers and sellers ever really stay in touch.

The second thought relates to the offer itself. It is important to be sure that your offer does not give away all of your protections. Make sure that your offer either makes the deal contingent on your getting adequate financing and an acceptable survey, or provides you with sufficient time to secure financing and a survey before requiring you to go forward with the transaction. This is standard in some forms of offers and not in others (the Yacht Brokers Association of America, YBAA, form contains this provision).

Also, the offer should contemplate the complexities of the survey, the most important thing that you will do in the boat buying process. Does the boat need to be hauled so that the surveyor can check the bottom? (Many surveyors will want the boat hauled several days in advance so that the hull adequately dries.) If so, the haul and launch will need to be scheduled. The boat will need to be sea-tried (motoring the boat in a waterway to check engine operation and other equipment). Who will captain the boat during this time? Will the engine need to be commissioned and decommissioned? Is the boat insured (particularly if the purchase is occurring off-season)? While all of this is at the prospective buyer's expense, it is important that these issues, including timing and logistics, be negotiated and agreed to up front. Don't just focus on the price of the boat.

Having an Offer Accepted

Sometimes offers and transactions get a bit complicated. There might be delivery terms, logistical problems for surveys, and things like that. Although the day that the seller finally tells you that your offer is accepted is a truly wonderful day, you do not have time to celebrate—except maybe for a glass of wine, as there is always time for a celebratory drink: you have work to do. Work very diligently to secure your financing, and have a surveyor hired and surveying very soon after the offer is accepted. You need the information that the surveyor has, and so do your financing and insurance companies.

There is a deadline in the offer, a date by which you must complete your obligations. Standard forms have different terms for it, although the YBAA calls it "acceptance of yacht." You might have only two weeks to "accept the yacht," and that period of time is very valuable. Get that survey report quickly and start calling around for quotes for fixing certain problems. Find out how much the repairs and desired improvements would cost, and don't trust any one person. Learn everything you can about the boat and be sure that all of the logistics of boat ownership are in order. The scope and scale of any problems must become known to you right away.

The period after an offer is accepted and before the deadline for accepting the transaction is a very special and important time for a buyer, and the time belongs entirely to you. The seller cannot walk away from the transaction, but you can. It is important to use this time wisely—and the clock is ticking.

Your most important concern is that you are buying what you have offered your money for. You need to hire a very good surveyor very quickly.

The Survey

I made two substantial mistakes when I bought my boat: First, my choice of boat was not ideal for a four season liveaboard in Boston, and second, my surveyor was "distracted" (yet recommended by the broker).

While there is a wide range of competencies, it is absolutely critical that you find a good surveyor. This is by far the most important part of the buying process. A good surveyor knows boats, all boats, inside and out. A good surveyor knows every system and type, and common problems associated with every make and model of boat that he surveys. He will have done the research on your boat's make and model before arriving for the survey. A good surveyor will be honest and ethical.

Further, a good surveyor *will not care* whether you actually purchase the boat. The problems of the boat must be uncovered, and you need to know every single problem that exists. Not only might you be able to have the price adjusted to fix problems, but also your safety and the safety of your mates depends on the boat.

The problem is that many surveyors get much or all of their business from the recommendations of brokers. The surveyors know that if they become known for being too hard on boats and end up causing deals to fall apart, brokers will no longer give them business. So some surveyors soften up and end up trying to appease the brokers. This can be devastating to you. Don't let it happen. Seek recommendations from fellow boaters, marina management, and Internet e-mail groups. You'll hear the best surveyors' names repeated.

When I first started writing this book, I was prepared to advise that no matter how inconvenient, a buyer should never hire a surveyor recommended by a broker. *I* did and got screwed so badly that the surveyor returned all of my money for fear of getting sued for quite a bit more. My surveyor's biggest problem was that the boat fell apart on the maiden voyage (I'm not exaggerating), so that there was no defense for his ineptness. Moreover, my surveyor signed off on gear that, just three weeks after the survey, literally crumbled in our hands (the *emergency tiller*, specifically mentioned as functional safety gear in the survey, had rusted through and crumbled when the steering system's *rudder stops* fell apart and the rudder jammed against the hull - I had never even heard of an emergency tiller or rudder stops). That surveyor's negligence could have easily cost me and my hired captain our lives. By the way, my surveyor is still surveying boats in the New England area. I regretted that I was not litigious and didn't sue for all of the damages that I incurred, as well as the expenses to fix the things that the surveyor had signed off on as being in good working condition. [The surveyor's defense was that he didn't get much sleep the night before.]

John Procter, former president of the Yacht Brokers Association of America and a boat broker who I truly respect, was concerned that my advice that no buyer should ever work with a surveyor recommended by a broker was a bit too strong. John believes that it is a disservice to rule out what is possibly the most knowledgeable source of information available to a buyer. While agreeing with my cautionary note, John believes that boat buyers often have little access to information such as the reputation of surveyors. He suggests it is more important to understand the potential motivations of the broker and surveyor. John adds that good brokers want good surveyors, as it is good business to want the client/buyer to get the best advice possible.

Let's take a second to talk about boat owners. Every boat owner is *handy* when provided with electric tools and silicone, and can drill a hole in anything. The blind use of a drill, however, without any thought behind the ramifications of the hole, is not an acceptable boating improvement. Anyone who has been around boats has seen some insane "improvements" that are a testament to how genuinely absent-minded, lazy, or downright stupid boat owners can be.

A good friend and local liveaboard had a leaking diesel fuel tank. Instead of cutting the old tank out, he decided to put a new tank in his starboard lazarette. Aside from losing some storage area, he saw no downside to doing this—that is, until there were some engine problems a year later and he hired a mechanic who came by and couldn't get to the entire starboard side of the engine because the only access was through the lazarette. Not only that, but the fuel and oil filters could no longer be changed, the oil level couldn't be checked, and the impeller couldn't be changed—and now we all know that the boat owner did not perform any routine maintenance in more than a year. The mechanic left in a state of shock, knowing that now the new tank would have to be drained and removed, making it impossible for essential boat maintenance to be performed in a reasonable period of time. A surveyor is charged to find this kind of stuff, whether it be this big, or much less obvious.

Other boat owners like to add through-hulls, sometimes beneath or near the waterline (remember—a boat owner with a drill…). Through-hulls *above* the waterline, to say nothing of those *below*, must be completed properly and with care. As will be discussed in the "Climate" section, many boats, of which a significant number were liveaboard homes, sank in Seattle during a snow/ice storm because the through-hulls placed just above the waterline were pushed below the waterline by the weight of the snow. You need a surveyor who will notice this type of potential problem.

Boat owners like to install their own gear, sometimes not taking the time to properly seal the installation or use the right tools to do the job correctly. Some boat owners do their own electrical work, using wire nuts and household-rated wires. These wires will crumble, for they cannot survive a marine environment. This is "the easy way out," and a surprising number of boat owners do their fixes while cognizant of their shortcut, thinking that at some point in the future the wiring will be completed the right way. It often never is—until at a later point by the unsuspecting buyer.

You need to know this stuff. If it is a sailboat, not only do you need to know the conditions of the lines and sails, but you also need a surveyor who will go up the mast to check out the spreaders and rigging.

My advice is to do what is necessary and pay what is necessary to be sure you get a thorough survey. A good surveyor should want to explain the problems of the boat to you. Consider carrying a video camera to record explanations so that you get the fixes right in the future. Get a great report and then learn everything you possibly can.

Also, never discuss the survey results with the seller without first having the opportunity to read the report and think very carefully. This time of contemplation is invaluable.

Post-Survey Negotiations

Brokers and surveyors like to remind potential buyers that "there will always be problems with every boat," and "there are always opportunities for improvement." While true, these statements can be offered with either of two intentions: one, to explain the reality of boats; or two, to mollify the buyer's reaction when receiving the survey report. Some problems truly need to be anticipated, and some problems might actually be expected to be transferred to the new owner.

The real question is whether the seller and broker have been forthcoming and offered full disclosure and whether the buyer considered the problems when he made the offer. When you decided how much to offer for the boat, you took into consideration all of the facts that you knew. Every problem that you find out later, regardless of how big or small, is something that makes your offer too high. While nitpicking is annoying, and you might find an unreceptive audience if you come up with too many cost adjustments, that is merely a negotiating strategy issue. *You are theoretically entitled to a cost adjustment for every single problem that you were not aware of and did not anticipate, especially for any issues that materially affect the value of the boat.* Even the nit picky problems will take time and money to fix—and many small problems will become bigger problems once things have been taken apart.

When it comes to raising issues with the seller about problems, emotions take over. Buyers don't want to feel as though they are nickel-and-diming the seller, and sellers do not like to feel as though a buyer is constantly trying to renegotiate a deal that has already been agreed to, or be told that their repairs and improvements were not done correctly, or that the boat has not been maintained perfectly under their watch. Additionally, structural and engine problems *do* occur and a seller may be just as shocked to find out about the problems as the buyer is. Moreover, buyers are often already emotionally bound to the boat, and feel frustrated about having to take the time to identify another boat. The buyer does not want to have wasted valuable time and money for the survey, for he knows that walking away from this boat and making an offer for another boat will require spending money again for another survey. And lastly, the buyer does not want to have the seller get mad at him for asking for concessions at this point in the process. Therefore, many problems are never raised and compromises often occur at this stage.

This may be the wrong result for the buyer, as even minor problems will often end up costing as much as or more than a new survey would have. Do not be so emotionally bound to a boat, which is replaceable, that you end up buying a bad one just to conclude the buying process. Feel comfortable raising issues. The seller does want to sell you the boat and would feel equally frustrated if you walked away. Don't be annoying; be practical. Remember that your offer did not anticipate the problems that you, at your own expense, were able to identify. Be tactful, smart, and strategic. Use your broker for guidance and for communicating with the seller.

Being told of problems known to the seller after your offer has been accepted is dishonest, particularly if you asked the right questions prior to the offer. The timing of when you are told of problems might be indicative of a dishonest seller. Sellers shouldn't receive high marks for being honest, but should be graded lower for any problems known to them and not revealed to you before you made your offer. While you appreciate having this information, (i) it is always information that you should have been told anyway, (ii) it is important for the seller and broker to tell you first so that you are not surprised in the survey and don't waste your money and time, and (iii) it does not impact your right to walk away from an unsuitable deal. Remember that you have the power (and the money) here, and everyone else needs to keep *you* at the table.

Various negotiated solutions might be satisfactory, including a cost adjustment. Bear in mind that if you are financing the boat, a cost adjustment will not be immediately realized by you for any boat you are financing. It will only be realized by you in lower monthly payments, and you will still have to find the cash out of your own pocket and the time to make the repairs. Maybe you could get a cost adjustment and have the finance company provide you the difference in cash to make the repairs. Another option would be to have the seller make the repairs. Be careful of this option, since it is in the seller's best interests to spend as little money as possible, for he will never have to see the boat again. You can make a condition of the repair your right to have your surveyor oversee the repair and sign off at the conclusion of the work. (Sellers usually don't like that.)

Always remember that you don't need to answer right away when presented with a solution. You don't want to buy problems that really weren't yours in the first place. Trust me when I tell you from personal experience that this can be financially devastating. Demand excellence and a fair deal.

Remember that all boats are theoretically sold "as is." Give that phrase no credence. You will be stuck with what you buy no matter what (absent malicious circumstances). If you plan to live aboard the boat soon after purchase, repairs and maintenance can be more than a mere inconvenience. In that case, be even more prepared to walk away from maintenance problems rather than take them on as your own.

Insurance

Should you get insurance? If you are financing the boat, you will not have a choice (marinas typically require insurance as well). Financing companies want to know that if anything happens to their collateral, they will not be out of pocket for the entire value of the loan. Moreover, some marinas will not allow you to berth your boat in their facilities without insurance.

Insurance companies generally require a survey when the boat is first purchased, and they might even require ongoing surveys periodically thereafter. Pay attention to the needs and wants of your insurance company. If there is ever a problem, and at some point there will be, you want to make sure that your thousands of dollars actually bought you the peace of mind that you paid for.

Insurance is typically significantly higher for liveaboards than for non-liveaboards. I've heard different justifications for this, but it is the way of the world. At least remember that you will not have to be paying homeowner's insurance as well, so it will not hurt as badly, but it will still hurt.

Insurance companies typically have "use" clauses that limit how, when, and where you can do certain activities. You might have a company that will not let you go offshore more than ten miles, or that will not let you sail more than a few miles off of the Southeastern United States during hurricane season. Make sure that you acquire insurance that provides coverage for your type of activity.

As mentioned previously, your insurance company might not provide insurance for certain types of boats. Wooden boats and older boats, among others, are considered higher risk and might not be permitted coverage at all. Or the rates might be overwhelmingly high. Know and understand the insurance company's preferences and concerns before it is too late and you get stuck paying obscene premiums.

Financing

Financing is pretty simple. A financing company hands the seller some money to cover the amount of the purchase price that you don't pay. If your boat is pretty typical and if you have a job and can make your payments, there will be many companies lining up to do this for you. If the boat is insured and you pay a nice-sized down payment, the financing company's risk is fairly limited. In return for their loan, financing companies get a pretty good rate of interest for their money, significantly more than a typical home mortgage would offer. They make quite a bit of money off of you.

Most finance companies require the buyer to make a down payment of 20 percent of the cost of the boat, and will have the boat appraised to make sure that the boat you are buying is worth approximately what you are paying. This appraisal not only protects you, but it also protects the finance companies from fraud. The maximum term for most boat loans is twenty years. Finally, since you are living aboard, interest should be tax deductible just as if the residence were on land. Regarding tax treatment, you will need to consult your tax advisor.

Financing companies, just like insurance companies, will not lend money for all boats (again, old boats and wooden boats, and especially old wooden boats). There will be other limitations and conditions as well. Just as for your insurance policy, get to know what their rules will be before you spend too much time looking for a boat for which you will be unable to acquire insurance or financing.

Remember that in general you are personally liable for your loan. If you forget to pay your insurance premium and you hit a rock, you will have to repair your boat out of your own pocket and will still have to make all of your payments to the finance company. If your boat sinks and you don't have insurance, you will still have to make potentially twenty years' worth of payments even though you no longer own a boat—that is, unless the finance company wants its money all at once for your violating the terms of your loan.

You may also be liable for any balances due in the event that either (i) you sell your boat for less than your outstanding loan balance, or (ii) your boat is repossessed and auctioned off. For instance, if the boat that you purchased for $100,000 (with a down payment of $20,000 and loan of $80,000) is sold at the end of four years for $60,000, and after four years your loan balance is $70,000, you will owe the finance company $10,000 out of your own pocket (in addition to the brokerage commissions).

As one final thought on financing, there might be options for acquiring a loan other than going to a company to lend money specifically for the boat. You might be able to take money against real estate, such as by way of a line of credit or home equity loan, or you might seek a personal loan. The advantage of a line of credit or home equity loan is that you might be able to secure the funds at a lower interest rate, and the interest should continue to be tax deductible (deductability is subject to certain limits). Personal loans often provide for higher interest since there is often no stated collateral, and the interest on such loans is usually not tax deductible. Boat loans often charge a higher interest rate because boats are viewed both as a luxury item and a high-risk loan because of the decrease in a boat's value and potential for damage/loss.

The Closing

So you've decided on a boat, made an offer, had the offer accepted, completed a survey and final negotiations, secured financing and insurance, and are now ready to proceed. Congratulations. All you have to do is "close" the purchase and sale transaction.

Closing is very simple. You give the seller the rest of the money, and the seller gives you the title and the keys. Or at least the keys, as it can sometimes take months to get the title back from the Coast Guard if the boat has been documented with them. Easy as pie.

Brokers exist for closings. Literally. It is the broker's job to make sure that every single thing required of either party is done. In the boating world, unlike the real estate world, it is common for both parties and the finance company to deal directly with the broker. In other words, the broker gets the keys from the seller, title from the seller or the seller's lender, payoff information from the seller's lender, down payment from the buyer, certificate of insurance from the insurance company, money from the financing company, and signed documents from everybody. Once the broker gets everything, the broker simply sends the buyer the keys and sends the title either to the buyer or the finance company. My broker calls it "closing by FedEx."

All done, right?

Almost. Many financing companies want to make sure that your boat is properly registered or documented (or in some areas, both) with the state and/or federally in the United States with the U.S. Coast Guard. While the buyer could very easily take care of this himself, some financing companies don't want to take the chance that something could go wrong (of course, they make money by doing it as well). Accordingly, your financing company might charge you a fee or hire a documentation company to complete your desired form of registration or documentation, or might even require that your boat be federally documented.

Things *can* go wrong during the closing phase, and it is extremely important to you (as the new owner) and your financing company that everything is done correctly, so that you actually own and can use the boat you just paid for, and so that your financing company adequately secures its first lien against the boat.

Problems have arisen when past boat loans are not identified or paid off, or in situations in which a boatyard or marina might have an existing lien against the boat. Sometimes identifying these outstanding liens is as easy as calling the marina or yard storing the boat. I have been told of a situation in which a boat that was purchased was sitting in a yard with an outstanding maintenance bill of several thousand dollars, and the yard would not release or launch the boat until her past bills were paid. The new buyer must have been surprised, although probably not as surprised as if the buyer had just purchased a stolen boat! Sometimes even the seller doesn't know of a prior theft. We want to actually own what we pay for.

The benefits of using documentation services are that not only is the boat properly documented or registered, but often the company provides other services such as title/lien checks to attempt to identify any of these unexpected liens.

That's it. Congratulations. You are now the parent of a beautiful new (maybe used) boat. Don't forget to cut the umbilical cord and take her out to do what she was meant to do.

"Only a fool tests the depth of water with two feet."

African Proverb

"If you wish to drown, do not torture yourself with shallow water."

Bulgarian Proverb

Home, Sweet Home!

5

Choosing Your Marina

As a liveaboard, you have the opportunity to choose your location, as well as the atmosphere and environment in which you want to live. You get to choose your neighbors and marina staff, amenities, distance to conveniences and entertainment, and such considerations. After your choice of boat, your choice of location is the most important factor in determining whether you will enjoy your lifestyle. Luckily, given the mobility of your home, you have the freedom to change location as desired. Nonetheless, it is a far better strategy to first figure out exactly what you are looking for. And then of course, you need to find it.

Since there are alternatives to marinas, this chapter may be incorrectly titled. Marinas are, however, the most common setting for liveaboards. Other options for liveaboard locations include living at anchor (on the hook) or on a mooring (on the ball). I know cruising liveaboards that live *under way,* refusing to ever pull into a marina, and when not cruising, living exclusively on the hook. I tried to live at a mooring for a bit, but at that time I was working in the corporate world and found it very difficult to get to land well-dressed and dry. At my mooring there was a water taxi, so I wasn't subjected exclusively to my inflatable dinghy, which leaked a significant amount of air through every seam (my friends thought that my pumping up my dinghy while underway was my favorite hobby). Still, after only a few days I realized that this mooring lifestyle was not an acceptable one for me. The hardships were just too difficult: the long travel back and forth to land, my water tanks holding less than a week's worth of water for showers and washing dishes, regularly running the engine to charge the batteries, and things like that. For me, this was the equivalent of a never-ending camping trip.

For cruising liveaboards, hundreds of books have been written dealing with the issues involved in living away from a home port. Among other concerns, there needs to be a constant focus on water conservation, energy creation and conservation, weather observation and preparation, food provisioning and storage, and more. Cruising liveaboards also deal with many different ports, some international, and therefore need to be very aware of those issues as well. Also, there are security concerns on the high seas requiring knowledge and adequate planning. In contrast, at this point your discussion of life aboard is primarily directed toward those liveaboards who are connected to the land.

Marinas—In General

Marina living can mean anything at all, and marinas can be found anywhere there are boaters. Some marinas offer many social amenities, others none. Some are rural and quiet, others urban. Some are primarily boat storage locations, others are designed for heavy recreational use. Some promote living aboard, others prohibit it. Some are geared toward transient boaters, others have tight communities rarely invaded by outsiders. Some marinas are staging grounds for long-term, long-distance cruisers, while others typically see only coastal day-trippers. Some marinas are even limited to members only and resemble country clubs, with highly prestigious memberships and five-star restaurants and golf courses. And there are unlimited variations of each.

My marina, located just outside the city of Boston, focuses on the social aspects of boating. It supports liveaboards and hosts them all year round, even during the cold winters. This marina, sitting in the shadow of Boston, is a short walk from many of the conveniences of city living, including hundreds of restaurants, professional basketball and hockey, concerts, and festivals. Less than a five-minute drive away one finds a movie theater, a supermarket, and other shops. My marina has bathrooms and showers that are cleaned daily and a heated pool that is open during the summer and is under a tent on special occasions during the winter. This marina also throws several open-bar pool parties throughout the year, maintains a very responsive staff to assist with any problems, promptly pumps out boats on request, and makes sure that the docks are clean and safe. The marina also provides telephone and cable jacks to each of the slips, provides a shore power connection (the amp service depends on the slip), and provides city water throughout the facility. Just as importantly, the marina is also very well-protected from the elements and only a very short cruise away from open water.

The downside of the marina is that it is loud, being surrounded by downtown Boston with its major streets and highways, and sees lots of boat and car traffic. In addition, all of these benefits come at a cost, and while mine is not as expensive as *some* marinas, it is far more expensive than most. But it was, for me, a wonderful location for living aboard; I worked in downtown Boston, and enjoyed the short walk from my boat to the subway.

Factors for Consideration

Of course, we need to break down the factors that any liveaboard needs to consider when choosing a marina. Make sure you are methodical in your choice; take the time not only to see the list of services that a marina provides, but also to inspect the facilities, speak to marina management and their employees, and walk the docks inspecting the condition of the boats, slips, and amenities.

Also, be sure to talk to the residents. Are these your kind of people? And does the marina support liveaboards, or merely tolerate them? Some marinas do not permit liveaboards at all! Do you want to have to sneak around (known as being a "sneakaboard")?

Find out what the boat owners think of management and the services provided, and get the lowdown. If you ask people about their biggest complaints, you will find that if given the opportunity to speak, most people will enjoy elaborating on their problems.

Location

General location is one of your most important decisions. If you want to live near Boston, then this particular location needs to be the beginning of your search. If you work in Boston, not only do you probably want to live in or near Boston, but you will also need to be in a location that makes the commute manageable.

If you decide that you want your boat to be operational, you should have reasonable access to your cruising grounds. If you enjoy ocean cruising, then you should be sure that you have acceptable access to the ocean. Many liveaboards live in the shadow of Seattle on Union Lake. While boating on the lake is very nice, it takes about three hours negotiating the locks just to get to open water, and of course the same amount of time to return (although the locks don't open at rush hour, so the wait can be longer).

Atmosphere

Some marinas are like social clubs—I've lived in two of these. Everyone knows everyone else's business; we witness each other's lives, good days and bad; and we imbibe cool beverages regularly with our neighbors. In these marinas, the quiet neighbor is not only out of place, but he is out of his element. Social marinas often have lots of people on the docks and boats on nice evenings, particularly during the weekends, and the community feeling is often wonderful (and quite the soap opera).

Other marinas are quiet. If there are people on the boats, you don't see them or hear them. You might see some light sneaking out of different boat windows in the evenings. The sounds are perfect—for some—with wilderness noises and the sounds of boats lightly clinking in the lapping waves. Deer might approach this type of marina, standing off at the edge of the parking lot, looking on in approval. Everyone is nice and keeps to himself. There are some wonderful marinas like this in rural areas, where a passerby will smell a wood-burning stove and see candles and lights in the boat windows. There is a terrific romance to being a part of that.

There are liveaboard marinas that might as well be cut right out of suburban and city neighborhoods. There are marinas that cater to blue-collar boaters, weekend warriors, zippy powerboats, sailboaters, partying kids, fishing, retirees, and everything in between. You have to find yours.

While some marinas can be luxurious, others can be downright rough. There are quite economical marinas known for their tough atmospheres and personalities, where you will find firearms on board, fire hazard boats, drinking binges, and unemployed boat owners. One marina that I visited featured several sunken boats, still underwater off of the main pier (I wonder if the boat owners are still being charged for their slip fees?) and many of the boats looked as if they could be ignited by the hint of a spark. In a conversation with one of the members of that marina, I was told that the television show *Cops* had filmed past episodes there, with fugitives arrested aboard several of the boats.

Much of the atmosphere will be created and enforced by marina management. Marinas pick and choose their tenants just as apartment buildings do. They develop and enforce guidelines for behavior and set a culture in their image. A marina that makes the effort to throw parties throughout the year is looking to make sure that the boaters know one another, working hard to create a tight community. In contrast, a marina that only has two garbage cans for fifty boats, and allows the garbage to overflow everywhere, is clearly not catering to the luxury (or clean) boat owner and management. Such a marina might be seen as leaving the boat owners alone, a positive factor for those who want to be left alone, but might not be responsive to other important issues.

Well-Protected

During my interviews in preparing this book, when I asked about choosing a marina, every single interviewee talked about finding a marina that is well-protected from the elements.

This unanimous response demonstrates the importance of living in a well-protected location. As a liveaboard, you have no other place to go when the weather is difficult. Most casual boaters only show up when the weather is perfect, and would rather sit at home watching TV waiting for that beautiful, sunny day. You, however, and all of your possessions, don't get to leave. If you have a spouse or significant other, or children, your time in an unprotected marina will likely signify the end of your days as a liveaboard (if not also as a boat owner). And if you have a pet, as I do, your pet will likely not be very happy either.

There are lots of formulae to help people figure out how big the waves might get, such as wind direction, wind speed, and fetch. Obviously if you are in an unprotected windward location, your comfort will be diminished. Even small motion can feel magnified over time. What would not bother a casual boater might begin to drive you, or at least your guests, crazy. If even under normal conditions your boat doesn't move around all that much, under heavier weather conditions it might. And heavy weather is always going to come again soon.

I spent some time at a popular marina on a local harbor. My boat always moved around more than I wanted, but one night a storm kicked up and I found myself in the v-berth, bouncing violently. The next night was more of the same, and by the third night, my cat and I left to find a motel room. The experience was horrible.

Also, when judging how well-protected a marina is, don't forget to pay attention to the wakes generated by other boaters. If boats zip by outside of the marina, generating wakes felt inside, you might want to find another marina. I've seen experienced liveaboards get thrown about and injured when, without warning, a boat speeds past. This is your home, and you're not always holding onto something for safety. Wakes can cause damage and hurt people. Be wary of exposing your home, as well as your and your companions' well-being, to these conditions.

Amenities

Many marinas give their boaters more than just a slip. Some offer showers, bathrooms, and laundry facilities. Some even keep their showers, bathrooms, and laundry areas clean and working! Great marinas have them cleaned every day. As a liveaboard, you might want to make sure your marina provides you with these facilities, and maintains them, since there will likely be some point when either your shower or head is inoperable for any number of reasons: Maybe your systems have been winterized in cold weather climates, maybe there are mechanical problems, maybe your holding tank is full, or maybe you've run out of water and don't have time to fill your tank before showering.

Other amenities offered by marinas might include providing city water on the docks and electrical hookups for shore power (be sure to check to make sure that the amperage you desire is available). These are often essential for liveaboards. Some marinas also provide telephone jacks and cable/broadband hookups (fewer as reliance on cell phones, unlimited data plans and wifi takes over the world) and wireless service, great amenities for the liveaboards who seek these types of benefits. With that said, wireless service is often considered as essential as a rest room.

Some marinas provide a lounge and a TV, offer small libraries, or have swimming pools, game rooms, and other forms of entertainment. Some marinas might even provide dock boxes for each boat's use in order to ensure that the docks are clean and uniform in appearance.

I don't know if parking is considered an amenity, but if you have a car, hopefully you'll have someplace nearby to park. Some marinas charge for parking passes and others offer free parking for slip owners. There are marinas with regular shuttles that take their boat owners to trains or local attractions or to downtown locations, either around rush hour or at other regularly scheduled intervals throughout the day.

Conveniences

Some marinas are like mini self-sufficient cities. They have restaurants, grocery stores, provisioning stores, marine stores, and haul-out facilities. Other marinas are located in the midst of such conveniences, or are only a short walk away. What about mail delivery? As a liveaboard, you should ask about and be comfortable with the location of the nearest grocery store, post office, movie theater, laundromat and dry cleaning (if not offered by the marina), and other conveniences.

Rules

Marinas have rules. These might relate to conduct or guests or noise. Some marinas are more lenient than others, allowing boaters to use the docks for the storage of equipment and even bikes, sheds, and junk. Others maintain absolutely spotless docks. Not all marinas will allow satellite dishes to be mounted on the dock, a major inconvenience to some liveaboards. Be sure to become familiar with the rules of your potential marinas to be sure that your lifestyle and needs are accommodated.

Culture

Marinas have styles and cultures. Some marinas cater to sailboats, and others, powerboats. Some are designed for luxurious vessels or affluent boaters and others are not. Some marinas promote socializing and/or partying and others pride themselves on their quiet atmospheres. And like any community, there will be significant differences in opinions, personalities, and styles; some marinas are gay-friendly, gun-friendly, or golf friendly. Further, one trait that affects us all: Some are liveaboard-friendly and others are not. Your enjoyment depends on being in a community that you can enjoy and that can enjoy your presence.

Service

You depend on your marina staff for many different things. If you need something from the marina, will they be prompt and responsive? Will they be thorough and careful?

There are high-priced marinas right here in the Boston area that are known for their terrible service. One major marina is actually *famous* for its lack of responsiveness. To make matters worse, it is owned by a highly bureaucratic corporation, so anyone the boaters complain to just passes the buck to someone else.

Perhaps cleanliness and prompt maintenance fit most appropriately into the service category. That includes not only the bathrooms, but also any community areas, barbecue pits and tables, and the like. The garbage dumpsters or cans should be large enough to handle the population of boaters, and the area around the containers should be kept clean, to help prevent odors and cockroaches and other unwelcome pests. Failure to keep this area clean may also be a violation of local health codes.

Security and Safety

Security is a serious concern. I once lived at a marina very close to bars and clubs on a boardwalk overlooking the marina, and some nights when I'd get home from work, drunk bar hoppers would be sitting on the boats! Peace of mind would suggest that the marina not only maintain some form of security, such as keypad entry systems, but also ensure that a security system is functioning, and if the system is failing, employ guards to protect the boaters and their boats. This means that the doors should not be routinely propped open and strangers should not be permitted to wander the docks at all hours. I have seen gates that could be opened by simply reaching around to the inside.

Boats are highly susceptible to being broken into and stolen, and their equipment is often easy to remove. Ask whether the marina has experienced security breaches or any other problems from the surrounding community. Security cameras are now so easy to install and economical that an effective marina surveillance system should be expected.

With regard to safety, be sure that the marina takes care of its property. If a marina is located in an area with freezing temperatures, how will the management handle snow and ice on the docks and piers? What about the risks of the water freezing? Does the marina provide bubblers or something to keep ice from forming around your hull?

In addition to general safety, every boat owner depends on his or her neighbors not only to be responsible members of the community, but also to maintain their homes and use their equipment in a safe manner. Fires are notorious for spreading from boat to boat. Some marinas allow the boats to fall into a high state of disrepair.

As we've mentioned previously, liveaboards come in all types, including the fugitive/hiding-from-the-law type and the type that keeps his boat in a highly flammable condition. Make sure that your safety and security are protected in every sense.

Costs

Marina costs vary widely, although hardly any marinas are "cheap." If you are sensitive to costs, you might find that one marina might offer you a cost within your price range while still providing the level of amenities that you need as a liveaboard. You do get what you pay for, but you might not want or need all that you get. Strike your balance. We'll explore costs now.

Transient Dockage - May 1st to Oct. 31st	
Dockage Per Foot	Per Day
vessels under 50 feet	$3.25
vessels 51 to 100 feet	$3.50
vessels over 100 feet	$3.75
Stern –to- berthing	$2.75
Casual Dockage / Per Hour	$15.00
Electric Service	Per Day
30 amp 120 Volt Single Phase	$20
50 amp 240 Volt Single Phase	$25
100 amp 240 Volt Single Phase	$45
100 amp 208 Volt Three Phase	$45
Summer Seasonal Dockage - 31st 2004	
Dockage	Per Foot
vessels under 30 feet	$135
vessels over 30 feet	$155
Electric Service	Per Foot
30 amp 120 Volt Single Phase	$20
50 amp 240 Volt Single Phase	$25
100 amp 240 Volt Single Phase	$40
100 amp 208 Volt Three Phase	$40

6

Estimating Costs

Many people consider boating a rich person's activity, at least with regard to casual (pleasure) boating. I don't think that many people envision lobster or commercial industry boating to be luxurious (even though modified lobster boats can make really terrific liveaboard homes). Nonetheless, casual boating is perceived as an activity for people with surplus income. When it comes to owning a 30-foot (or longer) boat and getting to spend time aboard, the general public, and the government, feel as though the boat owner has benefited from the fruits of society, liveaboard or not.

I have always enjoyed having my friends drop by, even if many of them loved me a bit extra for my boat. Liveaboards are popular and spoiled: People would bring me food and beverages and spend the day in my "house" at the dock or cruising the islands. In my many years living on dry land, even my dearest friends were reluctant to bring me food and drinks just so they could sit in my living room. The boat, however, is a different story.

Whether or not my boat is a luxurious craft, floating nearby the islands *is* luxurious, and that opportunity is perceived as a special activity reserved for the elite few. The person without boating experience, or who has not done a little research, wouldn't guess that a boat capable of providing that kind of enjoyment need not cost $100,000, but can be acquired for mere thousands or even hundreds of dollars. Of course, you get what you pay for, but there are some wonderful opportunities throughout all price ranges.

Anything that is perceived to be luxurious and high-class will often be an easy target for taxes, surcharges, and inflated expenses (note, for example, the luxury tax). Boating is highly susceptible to that generalization. It's too bad that the government and general public don't get to know me specifically, because then they would know that I'm a pretty normal guy not blessed with the fortunes of the few—I count my jellybeans like the majority of us.

Relative to land-based houses, things break and deteriorate much more quickly on boats. Boats rock and move; there are stresses on the hull and deck with every movement. Water damages everything, and salt air contributes more damage, whether at sea or shore. At sea, there is a whole other world waiting to hurt you and your boat, including dumb boaters doing dumb things, rocks and debris sitting just below the surface, lobster traps so poorly marked that they are just waiting to foul your prop, and drunken crew and passengers that don't understand or respect a boat's systems (think putting garbage into the toilet and trying to flush it down).

I once had a simple sail problem and needed to have an inexperienced crew member keep the *Fog* pointed into the wind while two of us went forward to try to unsnag a furling line. The crew member couldn't keep us pointed into the wind despite my many attempts to teach her to aim at a certain fixed point on land (the scary part is that she has a driver's license). The failure to get that line unsnagged quickly, ended up tearing my headsail, causing more than $400 in damage. It could have been much worse, for my friend and I were almost thrown overboard by the thousands of pounds of force on the luffing sail.

For me, that $400 was a big deal. For some powerboaters, spending $400 in fuel is a light weekend. Still, it's all relative and things break for many reasons, or no reason at all.

Some people who do not own a boat, joke about how much they love it that their friend owns one, because they can boat for the small weekend cost of some food and beverages. They appreciate the luxury of boat ownership and have decided to pass the costs off to their friends while still getting to enjoy the best parts.

Some days we get a lot for our money. Other days we get very little. But no matter how we look at costs, it is imperative to understand them. I know there are publications that elect not to discuss costs in a realistic way since, as one magazine editor told me, they vary so widely from boat owner to boat owner, and situation to situation. Yet another person at a well-known publication told me that the reluctance to discuss costs was tied to an internal policy of trying to avoid discussion of specific topics that could scare people away from boating, and thus, the purchase of the publication.

Cost Spreadsheet

The best way to handle a discussion of costs is to walk through an example. I have tried to ascertain average costs at a few of the more-popular marinas in the New England area. I spoke as well with marinas in Southern California, Northern California, and the Pacific Northwest and know that these costs are reflective of many of the popular urban boating centers. Rural and less-populated boating centers will be less expensive.

Despite the difficulties of putting together a general spreadsheet with all of the potential variables to assist you in your decision making I feel it is essential that I provide a basis from which you can begin your research. Percentages and costs will vary based on an infinite set of circumstances, including location and service providers. Your financing company may require a different down payment percentage than I have assumed. You may see line items and costs that do not apply. Good for you: delete them from your spreadsheet. Particularly if you have limited means or want to get a good grasp of the potential financial impact, please take time to create your own spreadsheet so that you can avoid unpleasant surprises.

When I was living in San Francisco, overall the most expensive city in my experience (even more expensive than New York City), every local newscast on TV finished with a segment introduced this way by the announcer: "Now here's one more reason why the Bay Area is the greatest place on Earth!" Despite the high costs, the population of the San Francisco Bay Area believes that they have bought a slice of heaven for their money.

Living aboard is no different. In exchange for your money, you get all of those benefits that you had considered earlier, including things like freedom, sunsets, lifestyle, getting rocked to sleep, and getting to enjoy the sounds and smells of the sea. These aren't just a list of nice things, but truly hold a special meaning. Many of us stop everything we are doing to watch a spectacular sunset. Some of us throw parties in storms, and toast Mother Nature. Only by carefully considering the costs compared with the benefits can you make a final, educated decision about whether this is financially, practically, and emotionally right for you.

Bear in mind that this spreadsheet does not include such expenses as food and alcohol, costs of an automobile, going to movies (and renting movies), and other costs—this is not a total budget for you and your life. If you have a child in college, you'll still have to pay college bills. If you owe child or spousal support, don't forget to make your required payments. I don't know your individual situation, so your financial needs are yours to determine. And if you like going to fancy restaurants, your luxury is only yours to know. Together, however, we should do a pretty good job of covering the costs of boat ownership, certainly an estimate that is able to be compared to the costs of other lifestyles.

Before we get started let's talk also about the issues of opportunity cost and depreciation. Opportunity cost means the cost of lost opportunities as a result of your chosen path. For instance, if you are living aboard and do not choose to own any real estate, you are foregoing any price appreciation. Maybe you don't care. But it is a cost. Even more dramatically, if you own a home, or at some point would have owned a home, you are trading an asset that would have likely appreciated for one that will depreciate.

In recent years, some marinas have sought to raise money by selling *property interests* in their boat slips, just as if the slip were a piece of real estate. There are various ways to do this, but the most common structures are similar to either a condominium or a cooperative (co-op) association. These structures allow for the slips to be bought and sold, potentially with some restrictions, and the marina continues to require the slip owner to abide by marina rules and by votes of the marina, condo, or co-op board. Just like condominium fees for real estate on land, there are condo fees or association fees, which provide payment for management, taxes, improvements, upkeep, and maintenance.

Another structure now in use is one whereby a marina sells *share certificates* to boat owners. Shares, sold at market value, allow for the exclusive use of a designated slip when the share owner is in the marina. The certificates for larger slips cost more. In this model, the *shares* are really a part ownership in the marina, and when the share owner is away, the marina can rent out the slip as though the slip were vacant. The money generated is used to offset fees of the share owner, and generate profit.

While more susceptible to market adjustments (since these slips, like the boats in them, tend to be luxury items), share certificates allow the potential for capital appreciation and tax benefits. In addition, these investments, if purchased for a reasonable amount and assuming that marina fees are not too high, will allow for the acquisition of a valued and worthwhile asset. Some of these deals, however, are overpriced and carry a great deal of market risk.

Of course, there are also cost offsets to the expenses of boat ownership. If you are paying rent on land, then maybe you'll conclude that you don't incur any immediate opportunity costs and, in fact, might ultimately save quite a bit of money. If you are a renter on land, you may be paying renter's insurance, which you will no longer have to pay. When you pay your boat insurance, the impact of the cost is not as significant as it would have been without any offsets. If you decide to become a cruising liveaboard, you may find that many of your former expenses—such as automobile and marina costs, your cable and utility bills, the cost of daycare for your children, and things like that—could be entirely avoided. Your specific circumstances will differ.

We'll compare a few different choices, including:

Old Woody / 40' Wooden Boat
Cost: $10,000

Rafthouse / 40' Rafthouse
Cost: $15,000

Mini Sail / 30' Sailboat
Cost: $35,000

Speedy / 40′ Performance Cruising Boat
Cost: $150,000

Big Sail / 45′ Sailboat
Cost: $150,000

Initial Costs

Let's begin by focusing on how much it will cost initially (out of pocket) to purchase and take delivery of your boat.

Initial Cost Comparison Table

Type of Expense	Old Woody 40'	Rafthouse 40'	Mini Sail 30'	Speedy 40'	Big Sail 45'
Down Payment	$10,000	$15,000	$7,000	$30,000	$30,000

With the exception of *Old Woody* and *Rafthouse*, which cannot be financed, down payment is calculated assuming 20% of the purchase price (most lenders require this).

Tax	$500	$750	$1,750	$7,500	$7,500

We'll assume that our state charges sales tax of 5%. Some lenders will permit the sales tax to be financed and added to the loan balance, while others will not.

Survey	$0	$0	$960	$1,280	$1,440

We'll also assume that *Old Woody* will incur a realistic expense of $14 per foot. Also, good surveyors will want the boat hauled several days prior to the survey in order to dry the hull, which may result in additional costs for out-of-the-water storage. Some marinas might charge high storage costs for this (a local marina charges $2 per foot per day), while others might do it on a complimentary basis. I'll assume a fee of $1 per foot for three days.

Registration/ Documentation	$45	$0	$45	$500	$500

You will typically have a choice of state registration or Coast Guard registration, although the *Rafthouse* is not typically required to be registered, as she does not have an engine. Some states require registration even with CG documentation, but this is the exception. For state registration, costs vary by jurisdiction. Some lenders charge a fee and require that they be hired to perform the registration or documentation services (or they will farm this service out to a documentation service provider). Massachusetts charges $15 for the title and $30 per year. CG documentation will cost $150. Whether done yourself or done by the finance company or documentation service, the fee is typically about $500, which often covers other services as well.

Delivery	$400	$400	$400	$400	$400

If you need to have your boat delivered, there will be fees, whether the delivery is by captain or truck. When I was looking at a boat in Maryland that I wanted brought to Boston by truck, the cheapest quote I could find was more than $5,000, not including the haul and launch. A delivery captain will charge a fee, which will include per diem, expenses, travel, and time, including delays. We're going to assume that every boat will require a delivery fee of $400.

Repairs and Upgrades	$200	$300	$700	$3,000	$3,000

There are always immediate costs, whether they be new linens, safety gear, or immediate repairs. This is a wild card, for the sum could be many times this amount, or very little. Because of my bad surveyor and bad luck, my costs for emergency repairs (all unforeseen) were approximately $4,000. Just for purposes of a number, we'll assume that the new owner will spend 2 percent of the value of the boat for repairs and necessary "stuff."

Total Initial Costs:	$11,145	$16,450	$10,855	$42,680	**$42,840**

Observations: Remember that *Rafthouse* and *Old Woody* are likely uninsurable and may not be able to be financed (so no survey may be *required*). The buyer of *Rafthouse* has decided to forego the survey because not only is she an economical residence, but with no engine, her systems are limited. The owner really just wants her to float. It is foreseeable that other "cheaper" boat buyers such as the owner of *Old Woody* might want to do the same, but if there is any rigging or equipment, as well as an engine, it really helps to have an expert examine the condition of the boat. Variables are involved in the process of boat buying. For instance, a boat purchased on the hard may need to be launched and have her engine commissioned as part of the survey. Then she may need to be decommissioned and returned to land. All of these expenses are borne by the buyer; their terms should be contemplated and agreed upon as part of the original offer.

Other initial costs will be incurred but are more appropriately placed in the monthly payment category—such as slip fees—or in the seasonal category, depending on whether the purchase is made at the beginning or end of the summer season in a cold-weather climate location. For instance, marina costs are often assessed initially for the season, and you will surely be required to provide your insurance company with a hefty check to get started. Paying the amount up front means less future charge, but be prepared for other costs and expenditures to hit, such as costs for provisioning. Some lenders might consider, in addition to financing the cost of a boat, financing sales tax and costs of boat repairs or improvements. They will very carefully consider financing boat repairs, for they often expect that you are buying a boat at a discount and restoring it to its proper value.

Monthly Costs

Some marinas will allow you to pay your slip fees monthly, others seasonally. Clubs may require annual payments. This depends on the type of facility and geographic location. While the average cost may be as stated in the spreadsheet, some of these costs might be assessed initially in a lump sum. My goal is to create a line item for you to consider.

Monthly Cost Comparison Table

Type of Expense	Old Woody 40'	Rafthouse 40'	Mini Sail 30'	Speedy 40'	Big Sail 45'
Boat Payment(P+I)	$0	$0	$270	$1,158	$1,158

Except for *Old Woody* and *Rafthouse*, which were purchased with cash, the remaining loans assume a traditional payoff (including principal + interest) at 10% interest over 20 years. Bear in mind that maximum boat loans are often no more than 20 years, and interest rates tend to be quite a bit higher than for loans of real estate because of the "luxury" nature of the activity and higher risk to the lender.

Insurance	$0	$0	$100	$200	$200

Old Woody and *Rafthouse* are likely not insurable. The other boats assume annual payments of $1,200 for *Mini Sail* and $2,400 for *Speedy* and *Big Sail*. Insurance is typically a bit higher for liveaboards than for non-liveaboards. Also, marinas might require that all boats have insurance, which could create a problem for *Old Woody* and *Rafthouse*.

Slip Fees	$267	$267	$325	$433	$488

Assume $100 per foot for the summer season and $30 per foot for the winter season or $130 per foot for the year except for *Old Woody* and *Rafthouse*, whose owners have elected to stay at a more economical marina that charges $80 per foot for the year. Some marinas charge for the seasons in one lump sum before the season commences, and others will allow you to pay periodically or monthly.

Municipal Taxes	$0	$0	$0	$0	$0

Some marinas pass along their taxes to the slip holders or owners. In these cases, no taxes are assumed.

Utilities	$150	$150	$75	$175	$175

I pay my electric bill for the winter months but am not charged utilities for the summer months. *We'll assume that every boat is subjected to this same cost structure, with our 40+ footers paying higher monthly utilities primarily due to added heating costs, but also the likelihood of higher-consumption equipment such as a/c units aboard.*

	$0	$0	$0	$0

Water

Marinas in water conservation areas, such as islands where fresh water is metered and sold at a premium, will often charge their slip owners for water usage. Water is metered at each individual boat slip, and because of the high cost of water, water use is kept under lock and key. Don't let your neighbor catch you taking a drink from his hose! Most marinas do not charge for water usage, so for this table we are assuming that no boat is charged this expense.

$65	$65	$65	$65	$65

Telephone/Cellphone

I have a cell phone, typical for most liveaboards. Telephone service would cost about the same, *but* since I would end up also having a cell phone, my bill would be doubled. Satellite communications systems offer a wide variety of fee schedules, but since I am a coastal cruiser, I am not in need of any other type of communication system. We'll assume that everyone decides to use only a cell phone.

$20	$20	$20	$40	$40	$40

Internet

I often use marina wireless for my laptop or cell phone, or alternatively use my cell phone's data plan to connect my laptop computer to the Internet via a mobile hot spot connection. Depending on your marina and service providers, you may receive free general wireless as part of your slip fee, or may incur a marina charge. Some marina's charge for their "premium" speed/bandwidth service. We'll assume that everyone wants Internet service, and everyone except for *Old Woody* and *Raftbouse* decides to pay for Internet service whether through their data plan or the marina. There are other options as well (see "Amenities").

Sat/Comm or Remote Communication Systems	$0	$0	$0	$0	$0

For our purposes, we are assuming that our liveaboards are dockbound or coastal cruisers, who make up the vast majority of liveaboards. For those of us who venture offshore, there will be added communication costs, whether it be satellite cell phones and plans, SSB e-mail, satellite telephone systems, or satellite entertainment systems.

TV/Entertainment	$0	$0	$40	$40	$40

I have a simple hoist antenna for reception. There are online entertainment packages (including satellite TV without the dish). We'll assume that everyone except *Old Woody* and *Rafthouse* decides to pay something for entertainment. I am a big fan of Netflix ($10/mo) and YouTube Red (music, etc.). Sky's the limit here, but costs are cheaper than ever.

Parking	$60	$60	$60	$60	$60

My marina charges a fee of $60 per month for parking privileges. We'll assume that all boat owners are subject to this cost.

Storage	$0	$0	$100	$100	$100

I pay a significant amount for a storage container that is temperature- and humidity-regulated and big enough for my furniture and other possessions. We'll assume that everyone has a storage facility except for *Old Woody* and *Rafthouse*.

Total Monthly Cost:	$562	$562	$1,075	$2,271	$2,326
Total Annual Cost:	**$6,744**	**$6,744**	**$12,900**	**$27,252**	**$27,912**

Observations: There are quite a few personal preference items here. Liveaboards who are more cost-sensitive, such as *Old Woody* and *Rafthouse*, are more likely to do without paid entertainment or high-speed Internet, while less cost-sensitive liveaboards might desire some of these amenities. Liveaboards who work aboard may need these types of services.

We're starting to see the cost of luxury, with key differences now occurring—monthly boat payments aside—in marina costs, insurance costs, and storage fees.

How are we doing? Remember the sunsets and water lapping against the hull and trips to the islands. Stay focused, people!

Seasonal Costs

Now let's explore costs that are assessed annually or associated with using the boat during a cruising season. In cold climates, we have a defined "boating season," which means that cold-climate boaters need to prepare their boats for use in the summer and prepare for cold weather in the winter as the temperature drops to a point where "normal" boaters actually pull their boat out of the water for the winter—paying, of course, fees for hauling and dry storage. Liveaboards tough it out, since our boats are our homes, but we still have to protect our engines and water systems from freezing temperatures. In climates that do not freeze, some of these expenses, such as shrinkwrapping and engine commissioning/decommissioning, can be avoided.

Seasonal Cost Comparison Table

Type of Expense	Old Woody **40'**	Rafthouse **40'**	Mini Sail **30'**	Speedy **40'**	Big Sail **45'**
Annual Registration Fees	$30	$0	$30	$0	$0

This is my annual fee, which varies by type of registration and geographic location. Some states require registration even if documented with the U.S.C.G. (CT for example). There is no C.G. documentation renewal fee.

Annual Licensing/ Use Fees	$0	$0	$0	$0	$0

This is a luxury item. I pay a fee of $6/foot for a mooring that I like to use in a favorite harbor. If you have a lobster license, fishing license, or some other type of license, this might be a good place to add those fees as well. We'll assume that no boat owner incurs these types of fees.

Annual Property/ Excise Tax	$20	$20	$75	$140	$140

Another fee in many states—in Massachusetts this fee is based on the value of the boat.

Type of Expense	Old Woody 40'	Raftbouse 40'	Mini Sail 30'	Speedy 40'	Big Sail 45'
Routine Maintenance	$500	$500	$2,000	$5,000	$5,000

An average 40-foot cruising boat has about $100,000 worth of replaceable equipment—engine(s), steering gear, spars, standing rigging, running rigging, plumbing, electronics, electrical infrastructure, canvas, upholstery, docking and anchoring gear, and winches and sails for a sailboat—all of which last, on average, about 10 years. Continuing with rough estimates and averages, every year a boat owner should expect to maintain, replace, or upgrade an average of 10 percent of the purchase price of this replaceable equipment. That's $10,000 per year, even on a boat that had a selling price of less than $100,000. We're assuming that *Old Woody* and *Raftbouse* are not investing in their boats, and that *Mini Sail* is replacing the gear that is breaking. *Speedy* and *Big Sail* are putting $5,000 per year into their boats, but my number is potentially significantly lower than the actual amount being expended. Bear in mind that sail service can cost $400, new sails costing from $1,500 to $5,000 alone; new winches can cost thousands (winch service alone can run $200/winch x 5 or more winches). Engine overhauls can cost thousands, with new performance engines costing $20,000+ with installation.

Type of Expense	Old Woody 40'	Raftbouse 40'	Mini Sail 30'	Speedy 40'	Big Sail 45'
Commissioning Expense	$0	$0	$300	$800	$300

Known as "commissioning" the boat, this is the cost for preparing the boat for use. In a cold climate area this must be done annually in preparation for the warmer seasons. The fee typically includes flushing out antifreeze; cleaning and flushing the fresh-water systems; and changing oil, filters, impellers, belts, and any other equipment that needs changing. This fee can be entirely avoided in moderate to warm climates, although the routine maintenance embedded in this fee cannot. There is no fee for *Old Woody* and *Raftbouse*, as their primary responsibility is to pump fresh water through their systems to replace added antifreeze.

Decommissioning Expense	$0	$0	$250	$700	$250

Known as "decommissioning" the boat, this is the cost to take the boat out of service and, for cold climate liveaboards, to prepare her for the impending cold climate. This fee can be entirely avoided in moderate to warm climates. There is no fee for *Old Woody* or *Rafthouse*, as we have assumed that neither has an operational engine. Their primary responsibility is to pump fresh water through their systems to replace added antifreeze.

Hauls/Wash/Launch	$0	$0	$495	$635	$705

Explanation: Local lifts in my area are now charging between $11 and $15 per foot for the haul, wash, and launch; they will allow the boat to be kept on the hard (on land) for a weekend to allow for bottom painting and out-of-the-water maintenance. We'll assume a fee of $14 per foot. Of course, the two dockbound boats do not need haulouts except on rare occasions. We'll also include a diver at $75 a season to change zincs and scrub the hull.

Bottom Painting	$0	$1,000	$1,000	$1,400	$1,500

Explanation: Some boat owners paint every year, others every other year, and some hold out for five years or longer. Boats exposed to salt water or heavy conditions require service more often. Reduce your number accordingly to the extent that your average cost is diminished. This represents the cost of the paint and the fee charged by the marina (estimating a fee of $20 per foot + $400 in materials for *Mini Sail* and $600 in materials for *Speedy* and *Big Sail*). If you decide to perform this service yourself, you will need to pay the marina for land storage, but you will avoid labor costs.

Winter Shrink-wrapping	$780	$0	$610	$780	$865

This is another cold-climate expense that can be avoided in warmer climates, though it's essential for comfort during the freezing cold months. My shrinkwrapper charges me $17/foot for the frame and shrinkwrap and $100 for the door. One year I did this myself; the equipment and shrinkwrapping gun cost me approximately $135, while the wood for the frame cost another $40 or so. *Raftbouse* does not need to shrinkwrap, as many floating houses contain insulation and thermopane windows just like a land-based house.

Liveaboard Fees	$480	$480	$480	$480	$480

Marinas charge various fees for living aboard in order to help offset the costs of marina amenities (or for some extra revenue). My marina charges a fee of $80 per month during the winter months. Some marinas in Southern California charge $200 per month all year round ($2,400 annually). We'll assume that each liveaboard pays $480 in liveaboard fees ($80 per month for six months).

Emergency Service Fee	$0	$75	$0	$75	$75

Explanation: Two local service providers, SeaTow and BoatUS, offer on-the-water towing and emergency service. I've definitely gotten my money's worth.

Average Monthly Cost:	$151	$83	$443	$834	$776
Total Seasonal Cost:	$1,810	$1,000	$5,315	$10,010	$9,315

Observations: Note the number of costs related to cold-climate living. For those of you who are living or planning to live in the cold climates, now you have more reasons to know why those liveaboards in San Diego are laughing at you (us). Of course, their liveaboard fees are a bit higher.

The other major difference is the amount spent for routine maintenance. Chris Birch, who spends much of his life maintaining, repairing, and upgrading boats, says that while many owners often spend far less than 10 percent of the value of their boats in maintenance per year (as indicated by my table), a 15-year-old boat with all original equipment is running on borrowed time—and the owner may be hit with major expenses. Now we know why Chris likes to recommend that liveaboards trade in their cruising boats and squeeze themselves onto a $5,000 26-foot dockbound boat (with no head)!

Oh, and if you have a dinghy, you'll need to maintain the dinghy as well. And if it has an engine, add that to the list as well.

Are we done yet? Keep the faith! Reminder: margaritas on deck, scantily-clad people, barbecues, interesting neighbors, and beautiful days.

Operating Costs

This section is specific to your lifestyle, desires, and boat type. Will you travel to other marinas that charge you an additional (often outrageous) slip fee? Many liveaboards, and boaters for that matter, never take their boats away from their slip. Moorings in harbors might cost $10 per night, so going away on weekends to other harbors might cost hundreds of dollars per season. Does your mooring or anchorage require a water taxi for transportation? If so, that might cost $5 per trip, or, in one local harbor, $400 per season. What will your fuel costs be? What about purchasing ice for those times when you are away from shore and don't want to run your refrigeration? When you are away from home, you might want to go to more restaurants and bars. They aren't cheap.

I spend about $100 staying in other harbors over the summer—just in mooring fees. Luckily, the moorings I travel to typically include water taxi fees, so I don't have to use my leaking dinghy. Still, I pay about $200 in water taxi fees through the season. I spend about $200 for ice over the season, which is about 40 bags or 3-4 bags per week. My fuel consumption is very low ($100/year), since I enjoy sailing and avoid turning my engine on. I certainly enjoy a good restaurant, and get a bit carried away with steak and lobster, although I'm not going to reveal how much I spend. Luckily, my guests often bring aboard so many beverages that I almost never have to purchase any.   My operating costs, excluding meals, approach $1,000 for the summer.

I know powerboaters who spend $1,000 per weekend just for fuel, never mind food and beverages. I know sailboaters who race and get a new set of $4,000 sails each season. I know couples that host very fancy meals every weekend aboard their boats and pay hundreds of dollars for wine and gourmet ingredients. My marina charges $3 per foot for a transient boat to stay the night, which makes the stay for a 40-foot boat $120 for the night, and I know boaters who visit us several weekends per year (spending upwards of $1,000 just for slip fees for visits to my marina). And I know boaters who never leave the dock, never incurring any of these types of fees. The choices of lifestyle are yours.   Sample numbers might look like the chart on the facing page.

Operating Cost Comparison Table

Type of Expense	Old Woody 40'	Rafthouse 40'	Mini Sail 30'	Speedy 40'	Big Sail 45'
Fuel	$0	$0	$100	$8,000	$500

Just making up numbers here, although the figures in the 30' sailboat category reflect my past expenses. Speedy's numbers might be a bit low.

Transient Fees	$0	$0	$150	$1,500	$1,500

Do you visit other harbors? Participate in flotillas? Do you ever go anywhere? Everything costs money.

Water Taxi Fees			$200	$200	$200

A fee that includes transportation from an anchorage or mooring to a port.

Ice	$0	$0	$200	$0	$200

I assume that Speedy has a generator and fridge. I'm assuming that Old Woody and Rafthouse, being permanently connected to shore power, have typical refrigerators aboard. The others I assume spend $200 for ice.

Other	$?	$?	$?	$?	$?

Fill in your own other expenses.

Average Monthly Cost	$0	$0	$54	$808	$200
Total Operating Cost:	$0	$0	$650	$9,700	**$2,400**

Observations: The biggest wild card here is fuel. If you have two engines and enjoy performance cruising, expect to pay for it. Other fees, such as transient fees and entertainment, can add up as well; their sum is due purely to personal preference.

Special Assessments

There's not a lot I can say in this section except that I wish you the best of luck. Problems will occur, some covered by insurance, many not. I was once out sailing and had my rudder "bounce" off a rock. The rock was a mere dot on a chart and I didn't see it. It happens. The only visible damage to the rudder was a tiny chip. Unfortunately, the impact managed to bend the rudder shaft just enough so that the back of the rudder could no longer clear the hull. I needed to be towed in (free, thanks to BoatUS). After lots of experimenting, which took me half of the sailing season, I found that I needed a new $1,400 rudder.

I've had a headsail tear because of a seized furling line; once, a flood occasioned by a failed bilge pump damaged the cabin sole (floor). I've repacked both stuffing boxes; replaced seacocks, wiring, and plumbing; and after repairing my headsail twice, ended up having to replace it after it was damaged in a storm. (The insurance company covered a bit of that cost, but after they depreciated the cost of the sail and took the deductible, they gave me only about 50 percent of the cost of a new sail.)

You may think my stories are bad; they are not. My bad experiences were plentiful, but none was of the break-the-bank variety. I recently read a story in which another boat owner, on his maiden voyage with his new sailboat, while sailing under a bridge ended up getting pushed by the wind into a low clearance area, causing massive damage not only to the boat, but also to the bridge.

Another cruiser whom I met in the islands tells of having to be towed to a foreign island, not his destination, after mechanical problems. The insurance company denied coverage, and the captain ended up paying several thousand dollars for the tow, several thousand more for the repairs, several thousand dollars for the hotel room, and thousands of dollars for the short-notice airplane tickets. And I am very familiar with the all-too-common situation of a boat that drags anchor in the middle of the night, only to crash into another boat, causing significant damage.

Other special assessments might include new equipment. Boaters are notorious for wanting new toys. A good friend (who rarely cruises) just purchased a $5,000 radar system that he plans to have professionally installed. Another performance cruising neighbor recently decided to upgrade his engines to diesel, a venture that is costing him more than $30,000.

Special Assessments Table

Type of Expense	Old Woody 40'	Rafthouse 40'	Mini Sail 30'	Speedy 40'	Big Sail 45'
Repairs/Damage	$500	$500	$1,000	$2,000	$2,000
This is part of boating. Costs vary widely.					
New Equipment	$0	$0	$800	$2,000	$2,000
If you want new stuff, or if you want to replace existing stuff, you'll have to pay for it and have it installed. If you can do the installation yourself, this number will be less traumatic. Just do it right or you'll be paying for it again (as well as the cost to repair your mistakes), whether it be in the form of a repair or a diminished sale price for your boat.					
Average Monthly Cost:	$41	$41	$150	$333	$333
Annual Special Assessments:	**$500**	**$500**	**$1,800**	**$4,000**	**$4,000**

Observations: The cost of new equipment can easily exceed the number provided, as a watermaker, refrigeration, central heating/air, standalone chartplotter or dedicated properly configured laptop, SSB radio, or any of a thousand other pieces of gear will be more than $2,000 (just for the equipment itself, without any installation costs at all). Theoretically, money will be spent on new equipment during the periods where there are not as many repairs, or in periods when routine maintenance expenditures are down—so the costs are moved around a bit. The bottom line here is that this is difficult to predict, and surprises in this area can be quite expensive.

Savings and Offsets

I like this section because it is where you get money back, or at least don't have to spend what you used to have to spend.

How much can you save? For renters in Boston, these numbers can be pretty significant. My rent was $1,900, renter's insurance was $90 per month, and car insurance decreased $350 a year by moving out of downtown Boston. And my tax deduction for interest payments returned about $100 a month, which was the equivalent of spending $100 less for the boat payment every month, a huge savings—although only realized at tax time.

- Tax deductions - If the boat is your primary or secondary residence, the IRS might let you deduct the interest paid for your mortgage
- Proceeds from sale of house or savings from avoiding rent
- Savings from insurance and utilities and other bills
- Automobile savings if you can do without your vehicle

Conclusions

What conclusions can you draw from all this? I chose to stay at one of the most expensive marinas because I loved the atmosphere and proximity to everything. I chose to have much of the work on my boat performed by professionals so that I knew the work was done correctly. Unfortunately, I learned as I went along and was often shocked at how many checks I was writing.

The Grand Totals

	Old Woody	Rafthouse	Mini Sail
Initial	$11,145	$16,450	$10,855
Average Monthly	$755	$687	$1,722
Total Annual	$9,054	$8,244	$20,665

	Speedy	Big Sail
Initial	$42,680	$42,840
Average Monthly	$4,247	$3,636
Total Annual	$50,962	$43,627

We can draw many conclusions from the above, including that cold climates cost significantly more, fuel costs can be prohibitive, operating boats cost much more than dockbound boats, and luxury has a significant cost both in terms of equipment and choice of marina. I hope it is also evident that it is possible to live aboard throughout many different economic ranges. The spreadsheet is yours to use as you see fit—and the decisions are yours alone to make. Can you reduce these costs? Yes. Some liveaboards, even in cold (snowy) climates, will not shrinkwrap their boats, avoiding that cost. Another liveaboard I know doesn't even perform routine engine maintenance and has never purchased a new piece of equipment. These shortcuts may come back to haunt him later—unless he decides to sell his boat before that point, in which case the new buyer might be in for a surprise. Many liveaboards perform all of their own maintenance in order to save substantial amounts of money. Just do it right.

Some liveaboards live on the hook, and avoid all slip fees, in boats that merely float and haven't been maintained in decades (this is often an alternative to being homeless). Their total costs are near zero. On the other hand, performance yachts that remain under way can spend tens or hundreds of thousands of dollars in fuel alone, never mind costs of crew, provisions, and constant maintenance.

I am a proponent of life aboard, and believe that we pay for brilliant benefits. And while I want to encourage life aboard as an option for everyone, I have attempted to be exceedingly honest in discussing the costs.

(A copy of this interactive spreadsheet is available for your downloading and use at: http://www.livingaboard.net.)

Once you begin to think about the costs, it's time to remember some of the seemingly radical advice of Chris Birch, stated back in the section on "Choosing A Boat," in which Chris argued for smaller and simpler boats. If you were to run the same numbers for a smaller boat, the savings would be significant. Putting a 30-foot boat into my marina as opposed to a 40-foot boat saves $1,300 per year—more if the 30-footer decides to stay in a more economical marina. Every haul, launch, shrinkwrapping, and cleaning would be significantly cheaper for a smaller boat, and still cheaper in a more economical location. And the learning curve would be more manageable. The fancier the boat, the more that can go wrong. In addition, the more complex the gear, the more it costs to repair, maintain, and replace it.

Does this seem like a great deal of expense for a diminished amount of space? Ask my father, he'll tell you yes. Ask me, and I'll tell you no.

Still with me? Great. Then let's get aboard.

Storage overflowing.

Don Stonehill's extra refrigeration
under the salon table.

Twenty years from now you will be more disappointed by the things you didn't do than by the ones you did do. So throw off the bowlines. Sail away from the safe harbor. Catch the trade winds in your sails. Explore. Dream. Discover.

- - H. Jackson Brown's Mother

7

Preparing To Live Aboard

How does a person prepare for life aboard? You are doing it now, by reading and learning as much as you can. Also, visit other live-aboards and ask questions. There are many nuances to the science of living aboard, such as understanding how to prepare your boat for climate fluctuations and the change of seasons. The purpose of this chapter is to delve into the world of actually living aboard, and talk about things that are typically learned the hard way.

Basics

Liveaboards, like all human beings, need shelter and food. At a minimum, our shelter must provide us with protection from the elements, as well as our desired separation from the world. Our food must be safe and edible. We must have a safe and comfortable place to sleep (I also recommend some good tunes). These are basic needs, and any preparation for life aboard should ensure that these and any other personal requirements can be met.

Mental Preparation

Mental preparation for the new lifestyle—for the challenges that you will endure and overcome—cannot be underrated. While nothing can completely prepare a person for something he has never experienced, there is a big difference between making an effort to learn in advance what to expect, and not making that effort—just as there is a big difference between reading about how much space a liveaboard must sacrifice, and moving aboard and realizing the sacrifices firsthand.

The best advice is to find a boat and move aboard for a bit, even if just for a day or two. Perhaps you can offer to watch someone's boat when he or she goes on vacation (these opportunities are more common than you might think). Have you ever been aboard a boat in poor weather? If not, then make sure to try a night of it.

Once aboard, you will probably notice the following:

First, your luggage will probably have to be placed on top of a vacant berth, or if there is room in a locker (closet), your luggage will take up the entire locker. This might be your first exposure to the challenge of lack of space. If you bring a guitar aboard, there will likely be no locker space at all that can contain it. (When I have guests aboard my boat, I am forced to sleep with my guitar.

Second, boats move. Even if properly secured in a slip, they move. If other boats pass by, then the boat moves a bit more. If there are waves or wind or weather, then the boat moves much more. The extent of the movement depends on many factors, such as how well protected the marina and slip are, and the direction of the boat with respect to weather and waves.

Third, boats make noise. Noises aboard your boat will be magnified and will reverberate throughout your boat; noises aboard other boats and upon land will be heard, depending on how far away and how soundproof your boat is. Noise travels well over the water (historians say that one of the biggest tortures of being a prisoner in Alcatraz Prison in the middle of San Francisco Bay was that the prisoners could so clearly hear parties in the city, more than a mile away over the water).

You will hear the water and waves. There will be unwelcome sounds as well, and aside from cars, planes, and trains passing by, you will hear things banging and halyards slapping against sailboats' masts. That sound not only sends shock waves throughout the boat, whose mast is making noise, but also permeate every other boat in the marina. I have seen fellow boaters react violently to this sound after hours, days, or weeks of persistent clanging. While sailboat owners in particular should be very sensitive to this and pull their halyards away from their mast with elastic cords or lines and secure them properly, there are always at least one or two offenders and the impact can be a form of gradual torture. Other things, such as running engines, not only make noise but produce odors and release poisonous fumes.

On this topic, your neighbors will make interesting sounds, whether simple conversation too early on a Sunday morning, the muffled sounds of love, or the sounds of disagreement. Where and under what circumstances these sounds are initiated will determine whether and to what extent they will impose on your lifestyle and space. Some of these noises enhance the experience of close living, while others disrupt and detract from it. Your close quarters will, however, make these noises a certainty.

Fourth, things smell. Odors will come from the water, things that live (or once lived) in the water, boats, toilets, sewage hoses and holding tanks, fuel (particularly diesel fuel), silicone, fiberglass, mold, your mates, and your neighbors. Some of these odors can be managed, and others cannot. If you spill some diesel fuel, you might continue to smell the residue for a very long time. Every so often a neighbor will do something offensive, such as empty his holding tanks into the water, thus creating a flowing layer of horrible putrid effluence throughout the marina. I guess his parents never told him it was inconsiderate to do things like that.

Fifth, with the exception of some rafthouses, boats are not weatherproof. Rafthouses, like land-based houses, can be insulated by a siding and plywood frame on the outside, a thick layer of sheetrock or plasterboard on the inside, and fiberglass insulation filling the three-and-a-half-inch gap between the frame and the interior. Typically, there are at least six inches of heavy insulation at the roof and additional heavy insulation where the ceiling meets the attic. Most windows these days are double-pane argon-filled glass designed specifically for weather (and sound) insulation.

Care to guess how much insulation a boat has? None. It's just fiberglass. Well, that's not entirely true, as there might be two layers of fiberglass on either side of a thin piece of balsa wood or foam core. The ports might be only a thin piece of glass or plastic; hatches are typically made from a single pane of plastic, glass, Lexan, or acrylic, none of which is known for its insulating or soundproofing capabilities.

Lack of insulation means that (in addition to added noise) when cold water surrounds the boat, the interior hull and surfaces will chill. We will talk about this in the "Climate" chapter. When there's cool or cold air, the boat's topsides will chill. When it is cold and damp/rainy outside, everything will chill. This is not only uncomfortable, but it also results in condensation.

You must be mentally prepared to deal with these types of issues. If you have a spouse, or children, they too will need to be prepared. These are some of the prices you will pay, and the sooner you realize that these challenges exist, the easier it will be for you to complete your final mental preparations.

Comfort

We spoke about comfort in the section "Choosing A Boat," including issues such as headroom, layout, and space. These, and many like them, are examples of the types of comfort issues you need to consider and decide on initially when reviewing your choice of possible boats. You also want to be comfortable with your location and neighbors.

Comfort means other things as well. To me, comfort means not only having a great boat, but also feeling warm and cozy. I like to feel comfortable at night when I read and watch Netflix; I like to have a soft place to sit and sleep. No one enjoys sitting in wet clothes or sleeping on wet berths, so comfort also means being dry.

Everything aboard can and will become damp and possibly damaged. Pillows get damp. A damp pillow can take forever to dry and can become moldy from the inside out. Many household pillows will do this. Down blankets and pillows are certain to fail, and as wonderfully cozy as down can be, real down is likely a disaster for the liveaboard lifestyle. Synthetic down might be a more sensible solution; consult with the manufacturer and retailer for more information.

Note: While the Internet is a fine resource for just about anything that anyone could need to know, calling the manufacturer is often the best resource. Got a question? Find the manufacturer's number and pick up the telephone. These people are experts concerning their products and are often very willing to tell you more than you could ever wish to know.

Life Aboard

Essentials Gear for Life Aboard

Your job is to figure out what you *need* to be happy and comfortable. The question is what sacrifices you are willing to make—and you need to be firm regarding any sacrifices that you are not willing to make. Sounds pretty basic, but it is surprising how many liveaboards start out by making unfortunate concessions and then never quite rectify them, misspending their money on amenities that do nothing to erase the sacrifices that are making their lives uncomfortable. There may not have been a bigger culprit at this than I, as I spent my first two years living aboard making many incorrect decisions.

Unfortunately, a liveaboard who uses his or her vessel as an operational boat has a dilemma. For my first two years living aboard, one of my principal mistakes was not understanding that I was a liveaboard *first*, with a corporate day job and suits filling the locker. My cruising was limited, for the most part, to weekday nights and weekends, and I never spent a single night *under way*, although I did spend many nights at anchor. I incorrectly spent money on upgrading the boat as if it were a true cruising vessel, and yet never purchased super comfortable cushions for the deck or salon. And while I had a lot of clothes, I didn't have really comfortably warm and cozy clothes.

I've since learned that I'm a liveaboard even more than a boater— though I *do* hope like everyone else to one day take a boat around the world. I deserve to be more comfortable in my home. I want and expect warm clothes and a comfortable berth and salon.

My essential comfort possessions include (remembering that I live in the Northeast of the United States where the climate can be damp and temperatures extreme):

Clothing
*Wool-lined slippers with a rubber boat-worthy sole
*Long underwear
*Hiking socks
*Waterproof socks
*Rain or foul-weather gear

I want to be sure that I am warm, comfortable, cozy, and protected from the elements.

Salon
*Comfortable cushions
*Candles/lanterns for ambiance
*Stereo/Bluetooth Speakers
*LCD screen smart TV (I rip my DVDs and everything is digital, both saving storage and allowing archiving)
*Laptop computer and cell phone charging station
*Fans and ventilation

Since this is my home, I should be able to watch the news and do my work in a comfortable space.

Galley
*Stove/Pots with locking lids/Rubber hot mitts/Galley strap
*Non-skid plates, bowls, cups, and silverware
*Adequate cookware

It is obviously important that liveaboards be able to prepare food safely under all circumstances. Boiling water sure can hurt when it spills on you in shaky conditions.

Bedding
*Suitable blankets
*Extra sheets fitted for the berths
*Pillows
*Great mattress

Keep in mind that your bedding will get wet. Be sure that the bedding can withstand moisture and can dry quickly.

Deck
*Comfortable cushions and places to sit
*A protective system for sun and a weather protection system (dodger, bimini, and/or canvas tarp)
*Hammock

Be comfortable, cozy, safe, and not trapped inside the boat. I enjoy having outdoor speakers playing music to the cockpit as well, and I like to sit on deck in all conditions.

Overall
*Adequate heating system
*110v shore power with outlets
*Battery charger/Dual batteries with isolated starter battery
*Pure sine wave inverter
*Moisture absorbing paper and desiccant system
*Plenty of fire extinguishers

Again, warm and safe. And dry! The battery charger is important for two reasons: First, you don't want to have to run your engine at dock in order to charge your batteries; and second, for cold-climate liveaboards, your engine will be inoperable during the winter, since it will likely need to be decommissioned for safety. Consequently, a shore power system and charger are essential.

A quality pure sine wave inverter is more important than ever given the sensitivity of electronic gear. Given our general reliance on our sensitive electronic devices, greater care should be undertaken with our use of A/C current.

Having learned my lessons, for my comfort I consider the listed items non-negotiable. While I spent my time buying and installing a new high-powered alternator, battery monitor, lazy jacks, and refrigeration, while all important, I should have invested in the above-listed items sooner and with less thriftiness.

Here are some more interesting bits of advice that are important for liveaboards.

- Use a permanent marker to write on top of the can; label the contents of all your canned goods. The moisture in a boat will cause the paper labels to fall off.

- Get used to wearing the same clothes over again, cutting the amount of clothes aboard and number of times you need to do your laundry. Some liveaboards I know only own two pairs of shorts, one pair of jeans, and some shirts (in addition to socks, underwear, and a few pairs of shoes).

- Take SUPER care when boarding or disembarking with a cell phone or keys in your hand. They will find their way into the drink when you least expect it. Always have backup keys.

- When going to the store, consider buying what can be carried or easily brought to your boat in a cart in one trip. And then be so kind as to return the dock cart to the proper location for others to use.

- Don't rely on paper matches, as they will deteriorate with the moisture and fail when you need them most. If you have paper matches, be sure to put them in sealable plastic bags. But the best options are tools that will create flame without any risk of damage by moisture.

- Showering adds a lot of moisture to the air. Cut the time spent in the shower and use lower temperatures to decrease steam.

- The less time you boil water, the better—this puts moisture into the air *and* uses up stove fuel. The fastest way to boil water is to use a wide pot and only as much water as needed.

- Learn boating etiquette and follow the rules. Asking for permission to come aboard, among other things, is a matter of respect and should be practiced until you *know* your neighbors and their requirements. When joining a party or gathering, bring something to contribute. It is amazing how quickly you will be identified as the person looking for a free meal or drink.

Cruising

It is very hard to speak about the preparation for cruising, since there are so many varieties of boaters, boats, cruising grounds, techniques, etc., and there are some wonderful resources written by world cruisers on their preparation, experiences, and safety. Read as many of these as possible and listen most carefully to the challenges that have been experienced. We'll offer a few specific thoughts about cruising in a couple of chapters, but only as a broad introduction to the subject.

In fact, many liveaboards never take their boats away from their slips; some are even without an operational boat. The rest of us still head out, and even though we are not going too far offshore, there are essential needs for our comfort and the safe operation of our boats. As discussed earlier, this is not a book on boating, but on living, and it doesn't make sense to take up much time with information that is available in so many other places. Nonetheless, a moment on this subject is in order.

Make sure you have a boat that has been fully prepared to cruise safely and reliably, and that you have (at a minimum) the required provisions and safety gear necessary to keep you afloat and alive in the event of a problem.

Regardless of how far you take your boat, some form of a communication system is essential for safety reasons. All systems fail at some point, and a handheld backup radio for communications and weather updates is critical. To communicate with neighboring boats and shore, to call for assistance, information, and advice, you must have a working communication system on board.

A global positioning system (GPS) is essential for any form of cruising, and a basic unit can be acquired economically. A good chart of your cruising grounds is also essential—unless, of course, you are cruising in a body of water with no obstructions.

You must have a horn, extra dock lines (longer than you think you'll need), a good primary anchor with more chain and rode than you will think you will need, and a competent backup anchor. Also important is safety gear such as a manual water pump and wooden bungs to block burst hoses.

Ironically, many boaters have far more equipment on board than they need. With a GPS and a chart, you should know exactly where you are. Chartplotters, autopilots, and radar are all wonderful enhancements that might be essential for some boaters under some conditions, but in general they are not essential, since their functions can be replaced with manual labor, a pair of eyes, and a little conscious thought (although I did an extended ocean cruise recently and couldn't imagine having to take the trip without an autopilot). The advertisements for these products are compelling, designed to make every boater buy gear he might not need. Of course, that's not to say that chartplotters aren't totally cool!

We haven't discussed life jackets, flares, fire extinguishers, throwable life preservers, man-overboard systems, EPIRBs, and other safety gear that is either required by regulations, or highly recommended. Take the time to learn safety requirements and survival needs. All cruising is potentially dangerous and requires a competent captain at the helm, knowledgeable about the boat systems, conditions, and cruising grounds. The boat should be prepared adequately and should be safe not only for the knowledgeable crew, but also for passengers who might have had one drink too many.

Chris Birch's Aft Desk and Office

Solitude is not the same as loneliness. Solitude is a solitary boat floating in a sea of possible companions. - - *Robert Fulghum*

Tara Densler, Elizabeth Starkey, and LeAnn Helms
during a sleepover aboard
Stories She Could Tell
Endeavor 37, St. Augustine, Florida

8

Families, Children, and Pets

Pretty much everyone living aboard can share interesting stories about the lifestyle, experiences and trade-offs, but few stories are as interesting as those of the families, particularly families with young children. These families give up houses and yards, as well as individual space and privacy. They leave surplus clothes, shoes, toys, and other "excesses" of life ashore.

The transition to life aboard is complex enough for a single person; it is quite a bit more difficult when the culture shock is experienced by several people at the same time. Land dwellings offer shelter and privacy behind visual and sound barriers, bedrooms and playrooms where children can develop and grow privately (for better or worse), and sometimes multiple bathrooms and dressing areas. Most boats don't offer these luxuries.

Living in close quarters requires that people like and respect each other. It's probably not the place to go for families that aren't getting along, or for families that think forced communal living will compel everyone to like each other. Respect and tolerance could not be more important. And there will be physical contact, even if it is just trying to squeeze by the same gangway or hallway. Every sound and smell is shared, every mistake magnified, so that every person's problem becomes every other person's problem. When one person listens to music, absent sensory separation via headphones, everybody else *will* participate in the experience.

It is interesting how appealing this sounds to many families, and how appalling it sounds to others. The chemistry and timing must be right. The individuals' close-quarter interests must be compatible. Boats are hard work, and while having a team of people participating in the chores sounds like a blessing for most liveaboards, having less than a team effort is sure to add resentment to the already tight space. Throughout this book, we've talked about how small a boat can be for just one person; add another and the space diminishes. Add a few more and you create a wonderful system of full-contact communal living . . . in a tiny fraction of the space of a commune.

Spouses/Partners

Liveaboard couples talk about how they know more about their partners than they could ever have expected or should ever want to know.

The best liveaboard couples are amazing in their enjoyment of each other's company, as well as how perfectly complementary they are in their roles. Moreover, the best liveaboard couples truly enjoy the liveaboard lifestyle. They, separately and together, want to be aboard, enjoying the sunsets and water and wind and atmosphere.

Those who like to touch and sit together and who are not troubled by the close contact are candidates for this lifestyle. Couples that share interests and objectives, as well as lifestyles, are ideal. Few boats can offer separate accommodations for the private space of multiple people. I have interviewed many couples that have undertaken this lifestyle, several of whom have lived aboard for a decade or more. Their love for each other is palpable and evident in every aspect of the boat. One couple described their relationship as "lovie-dovie"; they were in physical contact with each other throughout much of the interview.

In contrast, another couple never made contact at all while we talked. All the while drinking rum, the couple finished each other's sentences and occasionally barked at each other. But they understood each other, and it was clear to me that while they were very different, each complemented the other. Together now in what is for each a second marriage, this couple is interesting: He has always had a strong love for the water, and she (before they met) had never imagined living aboard. Yet they function as a team, each with specific responsibilities while under way and at anchor, and they have always struck me as a finely-tuned operation.

But in general, couples that need space might not be as well suited to the lifestyle. The truest example of a lack of space is found in the companionways (hallways) of a boat, in which two people cannot maneuver without making contact. This close contact is a part of the experience and while embraced by some, becomes a source of friction (pun intended) for others.

I have lived close to both kinds of couples. The loving couples can be annoying, and the fighting couples can be entertaining—for a little while, at least. Welcome to the soap opera. It is common in the boating world to know a lot about your fellow marina tenants; you are a part of each other's lives and play a role in everything that is going on...the good times and the bad, the love and the affairs, the fights and problems. Nothing really gets by an observant boat owner. Make sure that your partner truly wants this life as much as you, or *more* than you, or else you may become one more source of your neighbor's (or my) entertainment.

On more than one occasion, I have been the one with a loved one on board. Unfortunately, mine was the classic example of a boat with barely enough space for a single person. Watching a movie comfortably together was a challenge, trying to squeeze together on an already too-narrow settee. The galley was adequately sized, but far too small for two people to cook together. And sleeping...

I slept in the forward cabin, a v-berth. With a companion, there was no way to sleep without being in contact at all times, even if it was just our feet being joined tightly as a result of being stuffed in the v-berth. One particular partner wasn't fond of sleeping with feet touching. And she kicked a bit. When she wanted to cook or clean, even in the protected slip, she'd start to get a little queasy with the movement of the boat. And extracurricular activities were a challenge due to the low headroom in the v-berth and the awkward cushions of the settees. It didn't take long before she was asking me to visit in her apartment, and then her trips to the boat stopped.

In addition to both partners wanting to be aboard, each needs to understand the sacrifices necessary to be successful. They should enjoy the simple things in life and not sweat the small stuff. There is simply not enough room aboard a boat for the chronically unhappy person.

It is interesting how many couples plan for years on becoming cruising liveaboards for their retirement. They buy a boat, but after taking their first transoceanic cruise, one person decides that the lifestyle is just not for him or her. On one trip to the islands of the Caribbean, I met a couple that had just made their maiden voyage and, upon landfall, had decided to sell their boat at any price and move back home. I met another man, in his late sixties, who divorced his wife of 40 years when she decided not to join him aboard. He told me that he still dearly loved her, but the boating lifestyle meant more to him; it was his lifelong dream.

I have known single liveaboards who are unwilling to date any woman not willing to seriously consider the lifestyle—and they are content to be single forever if the right person does not come along.

When more than one person plans on moving aboard, honesty is paramount. If one partner wants to live aboard and the other does not, then it is incumbent upon her to speak up. Each must want this lifestyle just as much as the other or it will not work. Plenty of people who really want to succeed engage in this undertaking, only to fail in the end. That's what this whole book is about. Life aboard isn't easy in the best of circumstances. Now imagine having to live with someone who doesn't care to enjoy the lifestyle, and is only living aboard as an accommodation to his or her mate.

Ease in. There is no requirement that everything happen overnight. Visit lots of boats, take trips together, and be absolutely sure that this is what you both want.

Children

Liveaboard children, adopting their family's lifestyle and limitations, are impressive. Kids adapt very quickly, and to me, this has always been a beautiful thing.

Children require certain things: a safe place to live, space to play and learn, adequate supervision, and a good education. Liveaboards who have home marinas often send their children to the local public school or a private school, just as landlubbing families do.

Parents should understand the general perception that bringing a child onto a boat is fundamentally dangerous. In addition, family and friends may cause more stress and volatility. This is often magnified if (as is common with liveaboard families, particularly cruising families) the child is home-schooled.

The issue here really is the unknown. When I first decided to live aboard, two people were particularly worried about me—my parents. They knew, however, that their slightly eccentric son was going to be okay. At least I think they did. Years of experience had trained them to accept that I don't always take the easy or most traditional path in life. Now imagine *two* sets of parents (and if there are kids, grandparents) worried to death about the safety and well-being of their floating family and the innocent and helpless young ones. Most people don't understand boats or living aboard, and certainly not cruising or home-schooling. More people than just the new liveaboards will be suffering culture shock.

A second issue involves isolation. While there are many other liveaboard families and children, finding them might be a challenge. Again, particularly for those cruising families, the children spend quite a bit of time growing up without companions. Depending on age, home-schooled children might miss the school dances and proms, sports and sporting events, and traditional interaction with classmates (the good kids and the bad kids).

The age of the child matters when it comes to adapting to the lifestyle. It is generally believed that the younger the child, the better. As infants, children will adjust to life aboard as if it is their natural environment, growing into the lifestyle, understanding the safety issues and requirements. Slightly older children are a bit more of a challenge, having already been presented with open spaces for playing, streets with lots of kids, and notions of privacy. Imagine living with a two-year-old child in a small, inescapable box, particularly one unfamiliar with the box but rather accustomed to open playgrounds. It is even more rare to find those families that have moved aboard with their teenage children. Teenagers have already built their own social circles and networks; they are dating and going out and often want to maintain a physical and emotional distance from their parents. On land or at sea, teens are the biggest challenge.

At the same time, parents of teenagers who have grown up aboard report that they are generally impressive people. This is based on my interviews but lacks scientific objective data. Having avoided many of the bad elements of society, having had close supervision and responsibilities, they are reported to be very bright, polite, and helpful. Parents of children who are home-schooled also report that their children are able to become highly educated because of the one-on-one tutelage.

The Transition

Giving up loved possessions is scary, but the biggest fear is always the fear of the unknown.

When a child is involved, the challenges discussed throughout this book are no longer mere inconveniences; they are barriers which must be quickly overcome. Keeping things like milk and juice aboard requires reliable refrigeration. Adequate safety gear is no longer something that can be upgraded over time. More space is no longer a luxury but a requirement. Kids need toys. Babies need clean baby stuff. Teenagers need space.

The transition to life aboard is part culture shock and part new occupation. But time cannot be wasted, particularly if the boat will be under way. Adequate communication is essential. Assigning roles and responsibilities to those who can perform is important, if for no other reason than to make sure that every family member is involved in the process of being aboard.

Several families have reported that the process by which they moved aboard involved having every person perform certain tasks on the boat or in preparation for the move. The *team* effort began as soon as the idea to move aboard started to become a reality. In one case, the family told me that everyone got to decide on the boat that was chosen, and the vote had to be unanimous. Even the eight-year-old had a right to veto the boat choice.

Family Safety

If you plan on bringing children aboard, take care to outfit the boat completely and correctly for safety.

Things change when there are children aboard. Unlike a house, a boat cannot be made entirely childproof. There are fuel and propane, candles and lanterns, outlets, pumps, and switches. And then there is the giant moat surrounding the boat. Docks can be slippery, with hazards strewn throughout. There are lines and chains and…well, you get the idea. Where do you start?

I would suggest starting with the biggest safety risks: Figure out how to keep the children aboard. In addition to general safety gear, which must be employed while cruising (such as life jackets and harnesses), it is common for boats with children to add metal bars to the stanchions and lifelines, as well as adding netting so that children (as well as pets) cannot slip and fall off the boat. The idea is to ensure that there are no gaps between the lifelines, minimizing opportunities for a fall overboard. Unfortunately, not all overboards can be prevented and I have seen plenty of boats with climbable netting that hangs in the water anticipating this very event.

Many parents require life jackets whenever the child is on deck when the boat is under way and harnesses whenever there is a greater risk. Some parents require life jackets at all times on deck or dock and often help encourage compliance by themselves wearing jackets such as inflatable models that provide more range of movement than traditional ones.

Storage areas in a boat often cannot be locked, as access to those areas in an emergency must not be hindered. Just as in a house, knobs can be installed to limit access to those who understand the release mechanism. In speaking with liveaboard families, I learned that these types of solutions were rarely employed. Education remains the primary safety device.

One word of caution: In my role as an attorney, I can tell you that, just as for those families on land, if a hazardous condition is created or not alleviated, and if that hazardous condition potentially puts a child in harm's way, many states in this country would consider this to be equivalent to *child neglect*. Neglect can even put you in jail *(e.g.,* criminal neglect or manslaughter). Some conditions could even accompany an allegation of *abuse.* It is a crime for an owner to fail to have done all things reasonably possible to protect children (as well as your crew) aboard.

There are amazing differences among families, creating various unique approaches to the lifestyle. I see great camaraderie and love aboard these vessels. There are terrific articles in magazines, the Internet, and e-mail forums; I would encourage you to read them and take a trip to the marinas to meet families and ask questions.

Roles and Responsibilities

Take some time to think about roles and responsibilities. Every family, land-based or otherwise, establishes expectations of each of its members, and certain people take on certain chores and responsibilities. This is typical.

When cruising, however, these roles are not "soft." There *will* be problems, and when those occur, each person must be at his strongest for the sake of the crew's well-being as well as the integrity of the boat. Consequently, there must be a captain, and the captain must be able to give orders that will be followed. Captains and crew will of course establish their own system for working together while under way, but there will be times when one person needs something of another person very quickly. In emergency situations or other occasions when time is critical, such as docking, one person will need to e completely in charge and the other crew members must allow that to happen, and follow the orders that are issued. This requires acceptance as well as respect; it is critical to boating safety. In other words, companions need to act more like *captain* and *crew* than *lover* and *petulant children*. While there are natural differences in the manner in which spouses communicate, everyone should understand that the speed and precision in giving and following orders could be far more important than thoughtful, patient, and clear communication.

The importance of a finely-tuned crew is noted in the simple and stupid things that happen, such as when a crosswind causes a docking boat to merely *touch* another boat, causing thousands of dollars in damage. Out on the docks, there are major problems all the time; sometimes the problem will be yours. Under stressful conditions I tend to bark out orders (I do add the word "please" to orders when I remember). I've had good crew and bad crew...but when the crew is your family, they are impossible to fire and don't like to get barked at.

In my experience with families, these roles are exceptionally clear. One person takes the helm, another helps with the lines. The cooking, cleaning, and maintenance routines are so organized that they appear choreographed. I would encourage you to understand the roles that need to be filled in order to be safe. However you decide to divide the responsibilities in those instances, acting in a cohesive way is critical.

Many liveaboard families make sure that each member of the family and crew understands how to operate the boat in the event that there is ever a person overboard or some other health emergency. Every member needs to be taught how to use the communication equipment; and I've seen preteen children doing man-overboard drills with their parents.

Many boaters establish their own procedures for the tasks of boating, procedures for leaving the dock, returning, setting anchor, picking up moorings, periodic cleaning, maintenance, and the like. All members of the family are incorporated in the tasks. It's not uncommon to see a boat and crew preparing to be under way: The family scatters to perform their respective functions, checking the oil and belts, stowing away loose articles, manning the helm, releasing the lines, guiding the boat out of the slip, and so forth. It is like a football team breaking its huddle. Skilled families can do this practically without a word ever being spoken.

In the event that you decide to become a cruising family, these roles will extend to the education of the children, as well as procedures for watches (when someone is responsible for paying attention to conditions and surroundings). While the cruising lifestyle is generally outside the scope of this book, there really are terrific resources that are must-reads if you are seriously considering this. Because of the freedom of the liveaboard lifestyle, including the option for cruising, many liveaboard children are home-schooled, a system that takes a dedication and commitment. Liveaboards on the Internet report that a few home-schooling programs have received high marks, and if I have been swayed, it is in my belief that many of these programs are not only legitimate, but also provide children with real educational advantages. The requirement is that the parents commit to these programs and dedicate the time necessary to fulfill them.

Pets

Speaking of companions aboard, I enjoy pets, and have a cat (Max The Cat) that has become quite accustomed to the liveaboard and boating lifestyle. [*New Edition Note:* Max passed away in 2006. He was an amazing liveaboard pal.] Max had only gotten seasick in the slip once, a situation that I mentioned previously in which the boat was flying about violently in a storm. During cruising, he typically looks like hell for about a half hour, gets seasick, falls asleep for several hours (totally dead to the world), and then wakes up refreshed, healthy, and feeling bit too fine. He would run forward and aft, scaring me to death that he will fall overboard (remember that I am a sailboater and the boat often sails heeled over at a steep angle). Time to get the leash out again or lock him down below!

There are many interesting approaches to cats and dogs, but there are primarily three things that your furry friends need: food, a place to relieve themselves, and exercise.

I mounted a gimbaled food bowl in the galley (kitchen) for Max, and that worked well. Our collective problem was that the kitty litter, which is small and sand like, was not only being moistened and tracked around falling into every crevice, but was extremely difficult to clean, particularly once the litter became wet. My imperfect solution was to take a piece of vinyl flooring and create a sealed container around the litter that would catch a bit of it. I'm sorry to say that I've never stopped finding kitty litter throughout the boat—particularly where one would least expect to find it.

Both dog and cat owners have reported success in training the pet to use a rest room consisting of a piece of outdoor carpeting with a rope tied to it (I used a carabiner). In the case of cats, litter is applied over the carpet until the cat becomes accustomed to using the carpet, and then the cat is weaned off of the litter. The carpet is used and then dropped off the transom of the boat while under way to clean itself. It can be reused with no further need for supplies or mess.

Pets need exercise. Aboard my boat there was very little room for Max to run about, and he started to walk the docks as though he owned them. Max, a highly independent cat, soon started wandering off the docks and into the highly urban, traffic-filled region surrounding the marina, ending up on such national landmarks as the U.S.S. *Constitution* and the Bunker Hill Monument. After calls from neighbors, the Parks Department, and the Historical Society, I tried and failed in my measures to curtail the wandering.

A leash seemed to work well, until Max tried to jump to the dock. The leash tightened and down into the water he went. Luckily I was there when this happened, and despite a few scratches, both cat and liveaboard owner were fine.

Max hit the water a few more times as well, once when a neighbor's dog surprised him, and another time during circumstances unknown. If you don't know, cats (unlike dogs) have hair that works like a sponge. Max once managed to extricate himself from the water and appeared at the top of the companionway about 20 pounds heavier than when he left just a few minutes earlier (he was retaining water). Despite my many efforts to catch and dry him, he remained elusive and sopping wet for a full day, soaking everything he touched. Moisture has a tendency to get into the living space, and on this day Max was a major source of moisture.

Many cat owners drop heavy ropes with knots off parts of the boat to allow a cat to climb back out of the water if it falls in, and drag a long line behind the boat while cruising to provide a fighting chance for a cat in the event that it goes in while under way. I don't know if there are any examples of this working and could only imagine fouling my prop with this technique. Not for me.

Dogs present other challenges. One family in my marina has trained their dog to use the foredeck as his bathroom. I have always found this to be a bit off-putting, but since this family did some extensive cruising, this was the only acceptable location for this activity. The family would clean the waste whenever they noticed it and hose the urine off daily.

One last thought about pets: Some countries have very strict limitations on the importation of animals of any kind. If you do any international cruising, be absolutely sure that you know and understand the policies and procedures of your inbound destinations. A mistake in this regard could end up unexpectedly quarantining your pet for an extended period of time or the duration of your stay.

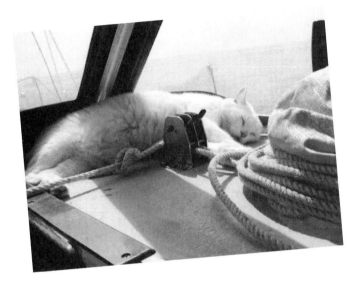

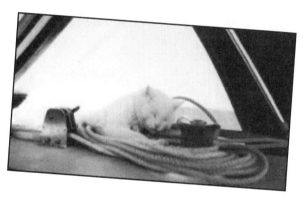

Max the Cat Sleeping While Under Way

Self-Tracking Dish for Cable TV

Entertainment Center Aboard (circa 2004)
Don Stonehill's *Shiloh*

9

Amenities

This is my favorite topic. I like toys. I like my Netflix, television and the Internet. I work from wherever I am, love to write, and therefore need my laptop computer and a power source at hand. I love music and demand a great sound system. There are amenities that I don't need, such as a landline telephone.

Our boats are our homes and we should be as comfortable as we want. If we deprive ourselves of certain luxuries, it should be by choice—and most of us do not want to adopt a lifestyle that resembles camping. Liveaboards who enjoy a minimalist lifestyle may decide to employ fewer of these amenities, or none at all. It is the freedom to decide for ourselves how we want to live that makes our lifestyle so special.

If you want to do some kind of hobby aboard, you probably can, provided that you are able to operate within the space and structural limitations of your boat. I have seen a 50-foot boat with a full-sized hot tub in its v-berth, although in order to make this tub operational, special jets had to be added to remove the water from the tub within seconds in the event that the boat ever needed to quickly get under way. I've seen basketball nets installed on deck, disco balls placed on masts, and a lobster boat modified to look like a prehistoric Flintstones-like cruiser. I have a good friend who has a full jewelry manufacturing studio aboard and another with a small machine shop. Boaters are only limited by their imaginations; just bear in mind that if you get *too* creative, you may find that no future boater wants to take ownership of your masterpiece, no marina wants to berth her, and no finance or insurance company is willing to come near her.

Every day, technology opens up new possibilities in satellite communication, navigation, and comfort. Digital music has gone mainstream (and virtual), providing liveaboards (and lubbers alike) with immense choice, no risk of damaging original copies, and wonderful economy in physical storage space. You can now make phone calls from anywhere on the globe, as well as accessing e-mail and the Internet.

Periodicals, blogs and newsletters offer terrific ideas and examples of what is possible and available, but despite my love for toys, few, if any, are necessary. Boaters have been cruising the world for centuries without GPS, chartplotters, radar, or inverters. A $100 handheld GPS will give you the same exact position as will a $5,000 chart plotting/radar system; and now assisted GPS on phones and other devices makes utilizing chartplotting software and charts even easier and cheaper than ever. Yet even today, cruisers who strive to conserve energy, as I do, write or listen to music by lantern until going to sleep. Whenever away from the slip, I shut down the general power systems (except for refrigeration) just a couple of hours after dark, offering light only from lanterns and sound only from conversation—with a few exceptions, such as a Yankee baseball game on the radio or some background music for stargazing.

The biggest challenge in discussing amenities is that there are too many alternatives to speak about. I've tried to pick a few of the more popular ones. If you want more choices, just hang on the forums and you'll see possibilities that you'd thought couldn't possibly exist. Get catalogs issued by major marine and electronic retailers, including West Marine—catalogs that not only show many products, but also provide lots of advice. Catalogs from other retailers, including electronics stores, often provide more specialty options and product choices. The ancient mariners must be rolling over in their graves. Whatever happened to celestial navigation?

Entertainment and Fun

Music/Stereo Systems

As a music lover, I believe that good speakers should be a staple aboard every boat. Luckily, there are a few options for providing music in boats of any size.

Space and sound quality are two major considerations for the type of system you choose. Space is often solved with the purchase of a car stereo type of system, which is often a fine option. Rack systems are no longer common and CDs are less and less common. Car stereos work well because they are designed to house many features in a small space and operate on 12 volts and very low amperage.

The most common music player now is the mobile phone, iPad-type of device. The music can reside on the device itself, or in the "cloud." My entire music collection resides on both Google Play. I am careful to keep the majority of music on a local drive as well for when I lose reception, although the phone can store quite a large number of selections.

There are downsides to Bluetooth, particularly in proximity. The device and speakers must be close and best unobstructed and taking calls from the device turns off the music (or turns the speakers into a speaker phone). I don't like interruptions, so I run the sound wired from my navigating computer or plugged into my mobile device. Pretty easy.

Sound quality is typically not an issue, since the listening environment is not acoustically ideal. A properly powered amp or speakers will improve sound quality even at low volumes and will last much longer. Take a trip to your local store and you will notice that different speakers will sound dramatically different. Listen for muffled sound and bass and treble frequencies, and make the best choice for you.

Still, the most popular speaker for on-deck music are Bluetooth speakers, which can be battery operated, or operated via 12v, and brought anywhere aboard. While I do wire my speakers at the helm (as discussed above), I do have a portable Bluetooth speaker for music nearby to whereever I'm working or for whatever island or beach I may find myself enjoying.

Don't forget that, condensation is likely to form *everywhere* within a boat, including inside the stereo and speakers. Even if your system and speakers are located away from water sources, moisture and salt air can still damage the units; consequently, it is often a good idea (but certainly not necessary) to buy units designed for the marine environment. In the alternative, some portable speaker systems (such as mine) are not designed to last forever anyway and are viewed like a general consumable.

Many liveaboards want to have speakers in both the salon/living quarters and on deck although there are times when music is not intended for one or the other location. This is an advantage to a wired system with a simple speaker selector switch. It is also possible with a car stereo system to take advantage of the speaker fader to put sound in the front speakers, rear speakers, or a combination. That is how I set up my former system—my salon speakers were on the *front* speaker selection, and my deck speakers were on the *rear* speaker selection. I could put the sound down below, up top, or both. *On a cautionary note, don't forget where you set the sound, or you might inadvertently be sending music throughout the marina when you think it's off—soon to be followed by an angry knock on the deck at 3 A.M. This has happened to me on more than one occasion.*

Satellite radio technology, which suits liveaboards—particularly those who cruise—is common, but not as prevalent as I might have thought it would be when it first rolled out. Satellite radio requires a special antenna and receiver, and in return, provides HD-quality sound anywhere with more than one hundred commercial-free stations, including genre-specific, news, sports, and entertainment stations. The advantage to this type of system is that you will receive clear reception throughout your cruising grounds, whether coastal or offshore. The disadvantage is a slightly higher initial cost for equipment as well as a monthly subscription service cost.

MP3 music and digital movies (such as MP4) have truly changed the world. In the old days, meaning as recently as only a few years ago, music was distributed and carried in a traditional format, primarily on CDs, that were capable of storing approximately 70 minutes worth of music. New generation CDs can now hold over 600 minutes. Another choice, particularly one when a car stereo or other device can take an SD memory card, is to place the music collection on the memory card or USB with the capability of holding tens of thousands of minutes of media including movies and more. Amazing, considering that just a decade ago, when the first edition of this book was coming out, I still had boxes of music and DVDs taking up a significant amount of space aboard.

Many car stereo systems can be purchased with detachable faceplates in order to make the system less valuable if stolen, although while theft of audio systems used to be a big problem, now the bigger problem is the theft of iPhones and other similar devices. Also, remote and amplified antennas will often do wonders for improving radio reception in more remote areas. It is advisable to place the system at the navigation station or salon in order to protect the unit from weather, as well as to provide increased security.

One more important point to consider is that the location of your stereo could pose a difficulty in case you need to immediately address a problem and/or communicate with others (*e.g.*, a boat looks as if she is going to hit you, a boat is trying to hail you, you need to give orders, there is a man overboard, and so forth). Many boaters typically require that their VHF radio be on so they can communicate, particularly when in traffic. In either circumstance, it is critical to be able to cut the volume of music at a moment's response. Many systems now come with wired or wireless remotes; if the stereo is located away from the helm, it's important to use a remote control to ensure safe communication with those aboard and on other crafts. It is often only $80, money very well spent.

Television and Reception

When I started life aboard, I purchased a 9-inch television with a VHS player that could work on 110 volts with shore power or 12 volts while cruising. I paid quite a bit more to get the 12-volt system and never (never ever) watched TV away from dock. I used two elastic bungy cords connected to eyebolts to ensure that the TV was kept securely in place. My small TV took up a lot of shelf space.

Today there are a ton of amazing, space saving options: flat screen LCD screens, smart systems, tablets, mobile devices and laptop computers are all great options. Many screens will take any input, including HDMI inputs allowing larger communal screens and improved sound. My favorite add-on is the Google Chromecast system allowing all of my devices to broadcast their content to the big screen. I have carried my Roku smart system around with me for years. Many smart TVs even include a built in Chromecast and direct access to an incredible variety of media channels. Some No wires, no problem.

The downside to using many of these viewing monitors is that they typically work on higher voltages and therefore cannot be used when 12 volts are all you have (though an inverter could solve this problem). Careful evaluation of your options may provide for some great solutions.

It is an option is to purchase a TV antennae tuner for your laptop computer, often connecting through a standard USB port (very economical and available everywhere). All of the systems that I looked at will work on any computer with a USB port and allow the use of picture-in-picture, so you can use the computer and watch TV at the same time. With an Internet signal, you can bring in a wide variety of content and even subscribe to television services (YouTube, DirecTV and others) delivering live television and cable channels directly by subscription without a dish or box.

Cable TV requires that there be a cable hookup at the slip as well as cable service. Some marinas still offer this hookup although fewer and fewer as the years pass and options increase. Even if your marina has the hookup, getting service might still be a challenge. In any event, cable service requires a monthly fee (unless your marina provides cable to all slips) and stops working once the wire is unplugged.

Reception over the airwaves requires an antenna and a broadcast signal. Even in downtown Boston, I was only able to watch three channels, and only two of those reliably. There are a variety of marine antennas available, some designed to be mounted on elevated parts of a deck, and others designed to be hoisted up the mast. Some antennas are powered and others aren't. It is possible to purchase a signal amplifier, in both 12-volt and 110/220-volt systems. Some antennas are designed to double as an am/fm antenna, as well.

Satellite systems are the most versatile method for TV reception, permitting excellent reception away from transmitted signals and offering hundreds of television stations, CD-quality music stations, and data transmission services such as e-mail and Internet.

A satellite system requires an antenna (such as a dish or mounted signal receiver) and a decoder (to translate the signal). The decoder consists of a receiver and, for most networks, an ID card that has been registered with the company offering the service. There is a subscription fee for the use of this service. While some receivers and cards are offered on the black market, this is theft, and the service providers are always searching for illegal units and disabling the contraband systems as well as periodically filing complaints against users.

The satellite dish needs to be mounted pointing toward the incoming signal, which is easy if you only want to use the system while at dock and the marina allows you to mount the antenna on the dock. This task is far more complex if the antenna is mounted on the boat, since any boat movement will change the relationship of the antenna to the signal. A boat under way, at anchor, or at mooring will certainly make a fixed dish useless.

This problem of movement is solved with either a self-tracking system or a tracking mount designed to rotate the antenna so it remains fixed at the proper heading and angle. While a fixed mounted system can be quite economical, a tracking system's initial costs can be extremely high. The advantage is versatility.

Regardless, the current direction is wireless, subscription and Internet dependent.

Modernizing the Viewing Experience

While I enjoy live network viewing from time to time, most of my live viewing is now accessible directly from the Internet. ESPN, March Madness (NCAA basketball), and so forth are now available for free over-the-air viewing. Most of the primary networks provide their content as well, but with a slight delay.

In the U.S., we are still seeing a transition in allowing direct-pay licensed content through the Internet. In other words, HBO, Showtime and other premium channels no longer require a cable plan, just like other services, such as Netflix, Amazon Prime, Hulu and others.

Many liveaboards still enjoy watching videos or DVDs. Video tapes deteriorate (more so at sea, being susceptible to damage from moisture) and take up more space than DVDs. DVDs can be brought aboard in a storage book and their cases can be discarded, which allows hundreds of DVDs to be aboard in a minimal space.

Video and DVD players are quite economical, although care should be taken that your unit operates on the available voltage.

For just a few bucks (mine cost $24.95), I acquired software which I use to rip my DVDs and place them onto USB thumb drives. Each thumb drive holds 20+ movies and takes up no space whatsoever. (My thumb drives are entirely resistant to moisture when I store them in a plastic bag with a desiccant.)

Books and Reading Devices

The adoption of eBooks has also been quite a revelation for liveaboards. Books are heavy, bulky, and don't take kindly to moisture. Now, for those of us willing to abandon the tactile experience of turning a page, huge collections of reading material can be brought with us at all times. New books can be purchased instantly and read within seconds. Apple, Amazon, and Barnes & Noble are at the forefront with some pretty great devices. My iPad, iPhone and Android devices can handle any format with free apps from each provider.

Apps like Zinio are brilliant for magazine reading—allowing subscriptions to be delivered directly to the device as well. In other words, I no longer receive physical magazines, but now read all my periodicals the moment they are released, right on my device, wherever I happen to be.

Communications

Most liveaboards want telephone service, and many want Internet and e-mail. In addition, for those liveaboards who head out cruising, second to safety equipment there is nothing more important than being able to communicate reliably.

Telephone Service

There are now several methods of telephone communication: cell phone, landline, Internet (VOIP), and satellite. Ship-to-shore service is another option that provides telephone capabilities and other services.

By far the most common telephone for liveaboards is the cell phone. Its advantages are that you can use it both on and off the boat, the cost is about the same as landline service, plans often allow for Internet and e-mail access both on the phone and when connected to a computer, and long distance is typically free. Cell phones can also be charged and operated with any 12-volt connection (car adapter). Consequently, they are terrific replacements to the traditional telephone. The disadvantage to cell phones is that they cannot be relied upon as your sole means of communication when away from land, since there are locations on and near shore where there is no signal. Just off shore there is often no signal at all.

Many marinas still offer landline telephone service to individual slips, although this is becoming less and less common as boaters opt for alternatives to landlines. The advantage to landline service is that the signal is typically high quality. For me, my best quality is when I use a Google Voice number that rings both my cell phone and my Google account. When the cell signal is low, any wireless makes the call successful. My phone, for whatever reason, does not properly use data when calls get weak. Maybe in the next generation of the phone will this be improved.

Voice-over Internet protocol (VOIP) is revolutionizing communications, permitting global communication for a very economical monthly fee. Any Internet connection will work and free or extremely low cost telephone service is available. I use Google Voice and Skype regularly (Google Voice is free and Skype is free for IP calls, but extremely cheap for calls to non-Skype telephone numbers), and for business use another VOIP provider that also allows calls on any device, computer and Internet connection.

Satellite telephone service comes in two versions: regional and international. Some regional satellite plans provide the equivalent of cell phone service out to approximately 200 miles off shore in North, Central, and South America and much of the Caribbean. For the cost of the phone, approximately $500, you can subscribe to a plan offering a reasonable monthly fee and per-minute usage.

For a bit more money, some newer technologies offer reasonable global voice and data service. For several thousand dollars your boat can be equipped with satellite telephone service that allows you to select various service plans, or merely pay a per-minute charge. Technology is no longer a barrier to communications; cost of equipment and service is now the only legitimate obstacle to reliable global communication. And for a bit less money (free), you can connect with others over your existing internet connection using instant messaging, including text, VOIP, and video calling.

Radio Communications—VHF and SSB

For any liveaboard taking a boat out for a cruise, radio communication equipment is a requirement, not a mere amenity. With economical radios available, all boaters can now radio for help.

There are two kinds of radios: very high frequency (VHF) and single-side-band (SSB). VHF radios are economical, easily installed, and reliable over short distances. SSB radios tend to be quite expensive, require complex installations, and, in return, offer communication over far greater distances—often several thousand miles.

Many boaters, including myself, advocate that anyone who heads into coastal waters should have not one but two VHF radios aboard in case the boat loses power or a radio fails for one reason or another. One radio should be a handheld, or be otherwise capable of operating independently of the boat's electronic systems.

For VHF radios, range is a function of antenna height (primarily) and power (secondarily), since VHF communication range is line of sight, and typical fixed radios can communicate over 5–25 miles. Antennas are placed at the boat's highest point (sailboaters tend to put their fixed VHF antenna at the top of the mast) in order to achieve maximum communication. VHF radios often include a variety of extras, such as global positioning system (GPS) locators, emergency beacons, weather reports, and loudspeaker systems. Many VHF radios can monitor multiple frequencies simultaneously and provide a remote microphone/speaker so that one unit placed securely down below can also be operated from a remote unit located at the helm or different part of the boat.

Handheld radios are good not only as a backup, but also for local communications or communications when not near the fixed radio (such as from the local restaurant near the marina). Some VHF radios can be connected to an external antenna so that, even with a lower power transmission, the radio can achieve better distances.

Spend the extra money (it's not too much) to buy a radio that is waterproof and capable of taking a beating. This is such a critical piece of safety equipment that its failure could turn a dangerous situation into a life-threatening one.

For cruisers going offshore, a SSB radio is important, for it offers reliable long-distance communication. The radios can be expensive and installation may be extremely expensive. The advantage is that once it is installed, there are no additional fees—and communication capabilities are greatly enhanced. In addition, SSB radios can permit e-mail/data transfer as well as receive weather faxes.

Internet Access and E-mail

The ability to send and receive e-mail is no longer considered an amenity; it has matured into a full-fledged requirement even for those who wish to otherwise escape civilization. There are many different alternatives available at dock, with fewer in open water, although many of these options are quite reliable and, even in distant waters, are now quite economical.

Higher speed *wired* connections are often available through telephone lines (called DSL connections) or the *coaxial/fiber* cable that provides your boat (and houses) with cable TV (called broadband). Marinas have largely moved to wifi systems but still wired solutions are available in many markets. These systems require a computer with either a DSL or cable modem and require that your marina provide you with the proper connection (telephone or cable). Your local telephone or cable provider will need to offer the specific service you are requesting, as neither DSL nor broadband is available in all locations that provide telephone or cable TV service. Monthly fees can range, but in some areas can exceed $50 per month, not including rental or purchase costs for the modem—often provided by your service provider. The advantage to these systems is their extremely high speed, and the fact that they are on steadily when connected. The primary disadvantage for liveaboards who cruise is the slightly higher expense and the lack of service once the wires are unplugged or when the subscriber is away from home port.

Some exciting wireless options are currently offered through your common device. My iPad and cell phone connections are sufficient to do pretty much anything I could want to do, even watch a live sporting game or Netflix movie. In addition, many cell phones can work as a modem, and for the purchase of an inexpensive cord or Bluetooth connection can provide a liveaboard with full Internet access on any computer.

The primary drawback to using a cell phone has been limitations in coverage areas and that they have tended to transmit and receive data at slower speeds than wireless although these days mobile data moves at a remarkably fast speed and sufficient for most of the average person's needs.

Many marinas offer wireless networks for their tenants. The marina creates what is called a wireless hotspot, and boaters are provided with the information necessary to connect to the marina's high-speed wireless system. Some marinas are providing this service for no additional charge, while others are offering subscriptions to their boaters. This is appealing to marinas, for high-speed Internet is a valuable service that can be offered with no additional lines to install or maintain.

Other options are available for e-mail access offshore, and Internet access is now becoming available even in more remote conditions. For a fee similar to many dial-up services, e-mail services may be performed over SSB radio. Satellite services generally also provide e-mail services, with costs either on a subscription basis, amount of data basis, or combination of the two. Costs for any of these services have become quite economical.

Conveniences

It's the conveniences and toys that make a house into a home. Or is it love? I forget.

Refrigeration

It's refrigeration that allows beer to taste better, and butter and milk to keep. Those who like to barbecue need a place to store meat and vegetables—and while we all know the value of refrigeration, it is the moment our iceboxes are no longer cold when we really appreciate how wonderful refrigeration was.

The easy cure for refrigeration is to not buy things that need to be refrigerated, and learn to like your drinks at boat temperature. I've been asked to recommend the drink called BT Rum Tango, or Boat

Temperature Rum and Tang (invented by my marine tech Chris Birch). Mmmmmmm. And learning to enjoy a cup of coffee with no cream will help, as well. On many occasions I have dropped a bag filled with items into the water for cooling down. Mother Nature's refrigeration is always available and rather economical. This is a perfectly reasonable option, even for many liveaboards, requiring no modifications to the boat, no electrical draw, and no cost—except, of course, for ice.

For those of us who buy things that need refrigeration or require our drinks to be colder than boat temperature there are a wide range of options for refrigeration. Many coastal/day cruisers use an icebox, or an insulated box that they put ice in to cool the space, with a drain in the bottom running to a through-hull. Depending on the outside temperature and insulation, some of the better iceboxes can maintain wonderfully cold temperatures for more than a few days without adding any additional ice.

Liveaboards, particularly on smaller boats or those with budget constraints, may use a countertop electric cooler or an insulated, portable container that uses 12 volts and acts as a portable refrigerator. Some of these can keep goods frozen, and some can even make ice, albeit in small quantities. Many of these units are very satisfactory options, not always fairly considered by liveaboards who are thinking of adding refrigeration to a boat. Another thing that makes these units appealing is their versatility—they will work wherever there is 12-volt current, such as in a vehicle, so a day trip off the boat can be accompanied by refrigerated food and beverages. The advantage is that there are no installation costs and the units are highly portable. The disadvantage is that the coolers drain more than five amps, have a moderately high initial cost, do not have much capacity, and take up boat space.

Stand-alone refrigerators are another option. There are models that work either on 12 volts (designed for boats) or 110 volts (some boat units will work on either voltage). Depending on the available space in the boat, as well as the needs of the liveaboard, units can be small or large. While 12-volt units can be expensive, 110-volt units can be extremely economical and offer quite a bit more internal space than a cooler. The disadvantage to 110-volt units is the large amount of space they occupy. For liveaboards who stay in their slips and have access to shore power, the 110-volt unit can be a highly economical solution, for it can be purchased at any home appliance store and often costs less than a quarter of the next nearest option. Care must be taken when preparing the unit for cruising, since this can be quite a mess if it were to fall over at sea (I know this firsthand). Also, 110-volt units do not work away from shore power without an inverter or generator, and either system will have a significant electrical draw.

There are two other options, both requiring conversion of an existing icebox. One is the incorporation of an evaporator, and the other is a holding plate system. An evaporator system, which can be expensive, requires a compressor (which takes up space outside of the icebox, often in a locker) and cools air moving past the evaporator. These units can have a significant electrical draw of more than 5–6 amps when on; they will cycle on regularly throughout the day.

A holding plate system can be expensive but has much more modest electrical needs. The system works by freezing—often very quickly—a container of fluid, which then remains frozen for many hours.

Once again, match the system with your needs. If your cruises are for only a day or two at a time, a holding plate system is entirely unnecessary. If you can spare the space, a stand-alone refrigerator or 240/120/12V cooler can be ideal because of the cost and storage capability, particularly if you stay at dock or take only short-term excursions, particularly if the boat has an icebox to store ice during trips.

Power Use and Creation

For those liveaboards who never plan on leaving the dock, I congratulate you for being able to avoid one of the biggest pain-in-the-butt problems for liveaboards, which is how to ensure that there is enough power contained aboard a boat to perform the most basic of life's requirements, such as starting an engine; operating safety/navigational lights, VHF radios, and GPS; and, of course, running the stereo. Most of us, however, exist to leave the dock.

Liveaboard cruisers need to be conscious of their power capabilities at all times, so that they know the condition of the boat and can easily identify a problem before it is too late. There are so many *most important things* when talking about electrical power. There typically should be two separate battery banks, one reserved for essential functions such as starting the engine and running the bilge pump, and the other for the *house*. There should be a volt meter and ammeter showing available volts and amperage draw, and capable of showing or switching between the two battery banks, so that you always know the state of your batteries. And you must either be able to generate more power (if this is by running the engine, you must have the fuel to do this) or conserve power by understanding the available power and related amperage draw. Particularly for those of you who spend greater lengths of time away, seriously consider a system offering not only an idea of amperage draw, but also providing some idea of the number of amp hours remaining, so you don't wake up to find yourself without power because you ran your refrigeration and air conditioning all night long or forgot to switch your battery selector to just the house bank.

This is the game often dubbed "doing the amp dance." Whether you are at dock or away, you can draw only a limited number of amps. Boat slips often come with either 30-amp or 50-amp service. If you go over, the circuit breaker cuts off, a terrible inconvenience—

particularly in cold or rainy weather. And it's not difficult to go over 30 or 50 amps, particularly when you are running an electric space heater or two, each drawing 10 amps, a refrigerator drawing 6 amps, an electric toilet flush drawing 18 amps, lights drawing 3 amps, a fresh-water pump drawing a few, a bilge pump drawing a few, an LCD TV drawing a few, a laptop plugged in, and so forth. Of course, there are also circuit breakers inside a boat, and they will break when their rated amperage is exceeded. You can be fine one minute and then have a system cycle on and suddenly find yourself in darkness—and worse, without visual or audio entertainment.

There are few systems aboard that do not use electricity, so it is important to know not only how many amps each unit requires, but also how many amps the entire boat's systems are drawing. Systems such as the fresh-water pump, bilge pump, stereo, lights, refrigeration, alarms/detectors, and electronic equipment (such as GPS and VHF) all draw juice and will steadily drain your batteries.

Battery Chargers and Alternators

There are two common ways of charging batteries: You can use a battery charger connected to shore power, or you can run the engine, which runs the alternator, which charges the battery. Chargers and alternators are rated for various outputs, and it makes sense to know that rating so you know how long it takes your batteries to fully charge. If you can identify when the amperage output drops, you can spot a problem. (Note that to avoid damage, the regulator will cut the power as the batteries approach a full charge. This will cause electrical output to drop naturally.)

Speaking of batteries, there are three types: wet cell, absorbed glass mat (AGM), and gel. The problem with wet-cell batteries is that they require weekly maintenance (adding water that is boiled off by your battery charger). Be committed to your battery maintenance schedule before you make this choice. The disadvantage to gel batteries is that they are not compatible with many charging systems. Check twice (both your alternator and your battery charger) before you make this choice. AGM batteries are expensive. Other than that, they are compatible with all charging systems and are completely maintenance free, which makes them the best choice if you can afford them.

There are other, "natural" ways to charge your batteries. It is not uncommon to see boats with wind generators and solar panels. For dockbound boats, these systems are generally unnecessary. They are better designed for boaters with little access to shore power, boaters who can't afford to use precious fuel to charge batteries, and boaters without power generators. (These natural battery-charging methods might be preferred by those boaters who want little connection with land, or by those who wish for a more natural approach.) It is also possible to drag a propeller behind the boat when under way to generate energy.

As additional boating systems, these methods require maintenance and care, not to mention storage space on deck and below deck when not deployed. The best advice is to invest in them as a valuable tool and not merely for the novelty.

Generators/Solar Panels/Wind Generators

Aside from running the engine when away from dock, or using a charger while dockbound, there are three common ways in which energy can be created: generators, solar panels, and wind generators.

Generators, which can produce a wide range of outputs, are suited to heavy electrical demand, typically providing enough electricity to run all the systems of a boat and charge the battery. They make noise and use fuel, but for many liveaboards and cruisers, they are the only way to go in order to permit life's luxuries away from the slip. Generators take up a significant amount of space and often require a separate fuel tank and exhaust. With that said, my Honda quiet portable generator has proven valuable on many occasions.

Solar panels and wind generators, the environmental methods for energy creation, need either sun or wind to work effectively. Many of these systems can create a reasonable amount of energy, capable of running all of a boat's key systems. Many different options are available for each, some requiring a permanent installation, others allowing you to store them away until needed. You will need a regulator to ensure that the batteries are not overcharged as well. Pricing for these units varies widely.

Inverters

Inverters convert DC energy (from your batteries) into AC electricity (110 volts) to run your standard kitchen appliances and conveniences. Since they do draw energy from the batteries, often at a heavy rate, care should be taken to track the electrical draw and remaining power. Do your amp hour calculations before building a system that relies on power conversion. Many inverters also serve double (or triple) duty as battery chargers and monitors.

Inverters can range once again from economical to very expensive. Some require a significant amount of space to be permanently mounted and others fit into a drawer and plug into any 12-volt outlet, which is ideal for power tools, laptop computers, and the like. Carefully evaluate your inverter options, as the sensitive gear we use may find a pure sine wave inverter more friendly. I, for instance, see odd behavior on my cell phone and other devices when charging with anything other than a PSW inverter.

Battery Monitor

For those of us who rely on our batteries away from dock, I don't think that a basic battery monitoring system is a mere amenity—it is essential. There is a very wide range of products available, some that simply show available voltage (volt meters); others that show the amount of energy amperage being created, drawn, or output (ammeters); and still other systems that provide low-voltage alarms or remaining amp hour estimates and even time-to-depletion calculations.

It is important to be aware of remaining voltage in all of the battery banks, and having multiple or dual bank meters allows for easy switching or monitoring amongst the battery banks.

Moreover, some of the fancier battery digital monitors also require electricity to work, and therefore consume amps. Analog systems, while less versatile, require very little electricity.

Water Systems

While many liveaboards might argue that beer and wine are the keys to life, I understand that many scientists still take the position that water is the key. Perhaps we can all compromise on rum.

Water Filtration/Purification

There are two options for ensuring clean and safe water aboard. One is to stock drinking water—typically purchased in one- or five-gallon containers. The other is to install a system for water filtration in combination with a system for water purification.

Liveaboards who wish to drink water out of their tanks will generally filter the water that comes out of the faucet, even if it is drawn from a potable city water supply. Others will *in addition* filter the water that is brought aboard when filling the water tanks. Filters can be mounted on the faucet, installed in-line in the water hose leading to the faucet, or even be filtered after the water has been poured into a pitcher—as in a water-filtration pitcher. The important thing is to filter the water as close to its destination (your mouth) as possible, for bacteria and algae can be present throughout the hoses.

In addition, it is good practice to use a water purification system to ensure that the water and the fresh water system are free from bacteria, algae, and contamination. This will also significantly improve the smell and taste of the water. On a less frequent basis, purification powders/chemicals can safely be added to the water tank as well as other systems used to flush out fresh water systems. Basic systems are economical and important; they should be a staple of every boat.

Water Heaters

There are two typical systems for heating water aboard a boat: a traditional hot water heater and instant hot water.

Typical hot water heaters, such as the type used in a house, heat several gallons of water in a storage tank using either shore power voltage or a heat exchanger, which uses the engine's own heat while under way.

The advantage to a typical *marine* 12v hot water heater is that you can heat water both while at shore and while under way. The biggest disadvantage of a typical hot water heater is the amount of space it occupies, as well as the additional plumbing and electrical labor required for its installation and maintenance. There are also some traditionally designed heaters that are portable and are designed to be plugged into 110-volt outlets—offering a much more economical (and portable) solution—but providing only the hot water that was heated and stored while at dock.

One other under-appreciated option is an instant hot water heater. Instant hot water heaters are wonderful, as they can be placed anywhere and take up virtually no space.   An unlimited volume of water can be heated, and the units do not require a storage tank. Instant water heaters only draw an electrical charge when heating water and, while drawing a significant number of amps, these units usually require 110 volts and consequently are used only at dock. Although the water generated by these units is not scaldingly hot, the units are more than adequate at satisfying needs without costing too much (they typically cost far less than a traditional water heater). They don't require complex installations or take up much space, but neither do they allow you to carry preheated water for later use.

In all my years on the water, I can tell you that I've never needed hot water while under way, and have been willing to sacrifice when at anchor. If anything, I'm pretty content with my little solar shower.

Watermakers

Watermakers are "cool" amenities—really only needed by long-range cruisers who are either safeguarding themselves against running out of a safe supply of fresh water or ensuring more of life's conveniences without worrying about conservation of water.

Watermakers come with a high price tag, require regular maintenance, and generally draw a high number of amps. Watermakers are rated either at gallons per day or gallons per hour. The idea is to preserve electricity by running the watermaker for as short a time as necessary to create the desired amount of water.

There are also manual watermakers requiring a fair amount of labor to produce a limited quantity of water. These are ideally suited for life-threatening situations and are most commonly found in "ditch" kits taken with the crew onto the life raft if they ever need to abandon ship.

Navigation and Safety

Modern navigation and safety gear allows boaters to do some pretty impressive things, such as pinpoint their location to within a few feet.

GPS

In today's world there is never an excuse for not knowing *exactly* where you are. Global positioning systems (GPS) calculate a position based on three or more satellite signals, triangulating exact coordinates. Handheld GPS units are cheap and widely available. GPS can also provide exact coordinates for rescues.

GPS devices come in handheld and fixed-mount units. Some provide coordinates, while others show the boat's location with respect to other points, such as designated points on land, marine buoys, and other landmarks. It is important to use basic GPS units in conjunction with a chart in order to adequately identify the boat's location.

More complex systems and those tied to a laptop provide a "chartplotting" capability, which places the boat onto an image of a computer chart that shows the information provided on a marine chart, such as obstructions and underwater topography. This is essential in many regions as small mistakes can have rather massive consequences.

In all modern GPS units you can set multiple waypoints, which is another way of saying that you can tell the GPS where the captain wants to go, and the GPS will tell the helmsman what course to set in order to hit that point and then the next point and the next, and so on. Many will work seamlessly with a laptop computer for plotting courses and establishing waypoints. Advanced units will tie the GPS and boat's autopilot system together so that the autopilot brings the boat to its next targeted point; the autopilot then might even ask permission to change course to the next waypoint. When the helmsman grants permission, the autopilot changes the boat's course to aim for the next point. This is an amenity that might introduce danger if not used cautiously.

One disadvantage of GPS is that it could go down. A backup navigation plan system is always advisable. Other more common disadvantages of GPS are that the system has, thus far, been too reliable and too accurate. Sailors used to mark locations on charts like diaries but now use chartplotters, no longer keeping the wonderful records that used to so clearly describe their journeys and adventures. More serious a disadvantage also has to do with the GPS's brilliant accuracy: A friend once set his waypoints for a journey by pointing the boat at various buoys, ultimately having his GPS guide his autopilot directly into a midpoint buoy, thus damaging the craft and shaking up a few of the souls on board. GPS (particularly when used with an autopilot) allows users to pay less attention to their surroundings than they should, and we are hearing more and more stories about collisions and other problems that result.

Radar

Radar is a system designed to identify obstructions, including boats and land masses around a boat, particularly when visibility is diminished. The majority of liveaboards will tend to head out for a cruise only when conditions are favorable and tend to tuck in when conditions are not. Consequently, it is rare for typical cruisers to ever need radar for safety. Longer-term and offshore cruisers who could encounter heavy weather, or boaters in areas known for decreasing visibility, such as Maine or San Francisco, should have radar as an advised safety enhancement.

Prices for good radar systems vary widely—and a radar installation requires an antenna and viewing screen. The more power, the better the range of visibility.

Many units are now sold in combination with other electronic gear such as GPS chartplotters, allowing the helmsman/navigator to see the boat's exact position and all obstructions. Such systems can even layer the radar image over a GPS chart for some very cool results. As far as toys go, radar is one of my favorites, although on my boat, which is a coastal craft, I have never encountered a need for it.

One radar-related cheap enhancement that every cruising boat should have is a radar reflector, a piece of equipment put onto a boat to help ensure that other boats with radar can see you. Horror stories tell of smaller craft run down by cargo ships or larger yachts. Particularly when at anchor, it is nice to know that you are doing everything you can to be "seen."

Chartplotters and Laptops

A chartplotter can be a wonderful tool, helping to minimize errors in charting by projecting the boat's image onto an image of a chart that shows depth of water, obstructions, buoys, land masses, and so forth. Channels are often clearly marked; lines are also drawn for past course and future track. Chartplotters, like non-charting GPSs, provide extensive data such as speed over ground and estimated time of arrival, as well as many other interesting pieces of information.

Many GPS units, even those without chartplotting capabilities, can output their position to a laptop computer that with the right software can be used as a highly advanced planning tool and chartplotter. Tablets and smartphone apps are providing some all-in-one chartplotting and GPS capabilities. The nice thing about using a laptop is that the computer is not only a great planning tool, but when under way (depending on the hardware and software) can also be used to oversee any equipment that has been linked together—such as radar, autopilot, waypoint adjustments—overlaying charts with weather information and everything else that is typically needed. Laptop computers can even monitor SSB frequencies and store weather faxes.

Tablets, smartphones and laptop computers are not waterproof and are very susceptible to damage from moisture and shock. It is often highly recommended that they be kept safely down below. It is possible, however, to run a *remote* waterproof screen to the cockpit for use by the helmsman without endangering the computer.

With all of that said, I strongly prefer my marine chartplotter. There are no laptop risks, it can become soaked with water and its screen is clear and vivid even in bright sun.

Autopilots

Autopilots are amazing: Not only will they steer a boat on a heading far better than a person ever could—at least consistently over time—but so many features can be integrated into them that for many boats, they seem almost invaluable.

Autopilots can be set up to steer on headings or toward waypoints when connected to the boat's GPS, and relative to wind direction (helpful for sailboats). On long trips they allow the crew to do other things in addition to manning the helm...of course, while still paying attention to the surroundings. When I'm alone or with inexperienced crew, I can step away from the helm to take care of other essentials without fear that the boat will veer off course. And they are indispensable for night watches when the weather is cold and wet, for they allow the night watch to stay warmly wrapped in blankets and less exposed to weather.

Many autopilots can be controlled from below deck; these are particularly useful when there are chartplotter and radar screens down below so the navigator knows that the boat is on a safe course with no traffic or obstructions ahead.

There are many different kinds of autopilots, each rated for the size and weight of the craft. Some control a tiller, others a wheel; all control the direction. A sailboat may also use a wind vane autopilot, or an autopilot that uses no electricity and keeps a course relative to wind direction. A little research will tell you what's available and necessary for your specific type of boat. Systems can still be expensive and can become quite addictive, but don't forget that you still need to keep watch or else bad things might happen (there are some scary autopilot stories out there). Boats really don't just drive themselves.

Weather Reports

Every boat that leaves the dock should be able to receive weather reports and warnings. The most common system for inshore and coastal cruisers is the weather broadcasts and alerts aired and received by VHF radio. Once offshore and out of range of VHF signals, the SSB radio becomes the best source of weather reports. SSBs, when equipped with a weather fax receiver and printer, can provide weather faxes as well as audio weather reports issued by the weather service.

With the advent of e-mail, new options are available for transmitting weather reports and advisories, as e-mail permits the transmission of full color/full resolution graphic files.

Anchor Alarms

Anchoring out is one of my favorite activities, a sentiment shared by many. Many liveaboards, particularly the cruising variety on a budget, will rarely pay for a slip at a marina or even pick up a mooring ball. Over time, that gets expensive. Anchoring, in contrast, is free.

Anchors drag from time to time. It's important to ensure that this doesn't happen, but it's equally vital to know when it does. Add chain and weight and lay out the proper scope. Power in reverse and possibly add a second anchor. But eventually we have to sleep.

Many GPS units now come with an anchor alarm, a sound made when your boat changes position by more than a desired distance. There are dedicated anchor alarms, as well, such as systems based on the amount of load placed on the anchor chain (see www.anchorwatch. com). Note: While these systems are available, I have never used them and cannot speak to their effectiveness.

My favorite system is to drop from the boat a weight tied to a slack line connected to a cooking pot on my galley counter. When the pot falls, it is time to take an immediate survey of the circumstances. (Once, I was dragging anchor and this technique was a lifesaver. Although false alarms will routinely occur: On one such occasion my cat had gotten caught on the line. A decrease or shift in wind may produce the same result.)

If you want this added peace of mind and don't want to sleep with your handheld GPS, some system, either with a louder speaker, a speaker output, or a dedicated alarm system, might be in order.

Many liveaboards have a tendency to wake up throughout the night to check their position. I'm the same way. I'll be up one or two times a night to check the handheld GPS placed next to my berth, and will get up once to take a look to make sure that everything is fine. I don't sleep soundly at anchor.

Other Safety Systems and Equipment

The U.S. Coast Guard dictates much of a boat's required safety gear. You are required to have life jackets and throwable flotation devices, fire extinguishers and flares, horns and navigation lights. Common sense should dictate those requirements as well as many others. Moving forward on deck in heavy weather or at night should dictate that jack lines be installed. Harnesses are a good idea during evening watches and heavy weather. Man-Overboard (MOB) systems are vital enhancements to help ensure that a person overboard can be located and recovered. Strobes on life jackets and harnesses are helpful. Personal EPIRBs offer satellite tracking and assist in recovery. Foul-weather gear and survival suits and life rafts may be important, depending on cruising grounds and conditions. And always pack your ditch bag. If there is a potential danger at sea, there is probably a solution.

Other Cool Things

Other wonderful amenities (or in some cases necessities) follow, the goal being to introduce the systems so you can decide which features you want and which you don't. Remember, though, that these are for the most part niceties that hopefully will make life more comfortable or convenient. Typically there are many options to solve any one problem, and many solutions often can be achieved with no additional purchase of equipment.

Anchor Windlass

Anchor windlasses are designed to help raise the anchor, although many do an excellent job at helping to lower the anchor as well. They must be properly installed because of the huge amount of torque and weight they generate and the significant amount of amps they require. Particularly if you do much single-handing, or use a heavy anchor with lots of chain, a windlass might be for you. For my boat, a windlass is overkill.

Windlasses are fitted to particular chain sizes and rated for maximum pulling strength. They are either manual or electric. Electric windlasses require very significant electrical draw; great care must be taken in configuring the electrical system, particularly if the windlass battery is also the house battery and located aft.

Dinghy

A dinghy can be a necessity or merely a recreational toy. It can act as a tender under typical conditions or as a lifeboat under more trying circumstances. Of course, if you want to use the dinghy as your own personal water taxi, you'll need a dinghy dock where you can safely keep it.

There are dinghies that are simple rowboats, inflatable boats, sporty zippy boats, and combinations of all of the above. Inflatables can come with hard shell bottoms. Some have engines, others oars, and still others have both.

Dinghies tend to be expensive, and some require expensive engines as well, so care should be taken to ensure that you are spending your money for the right system. Many boaters spend more than $2–$4,000 on the dinghy, $1,000 on the davits and $1,000 on the engine—for a quick $4,000 added investment, and all these things have to be maintained. Add that to the cost spreadsheet table as "other equipment," if you want. And you may also need to register the dinghy as a separate craft.

You also need to know whether you plan on keeping the dinghy on deck, on davits, or towed. Towing is the most economical solution, although it increases drag, danger, and the risk of losing the dinghy.

Dinghy Davits

Davits are manual cranes, allowing heavy things to be raised and, in some cases, brought aboard. They are commonly used for bringing outboard engines aboard and raising a dinghy.

It is not uncommon to tow a dinghy, but towing creates additional drag on the boat and risks damage. Many boaters will either: lift and tie the bow of the dinghy up on the transom; place the dinghy on deck; or raise the dinghy up on davits, dropping the dinghy back in the water only when needed. Davits are expensive and require proper installation.

Laundry

Washing machines and dryers are additional luxuries. They use lots of fresh water, lots of electricity, and take up a large amount of space. There are units intended for marine conditions that are designed to function on less water and electricity than domestic units. As far as amenities go, onboard laundry machines are reserved for those with resources (both money and space) to spare.

Some laundry machines are designed to wash and dry the laundry in the same unit. I have heard mixed reviews of these units. There are also manual machines that allow for the effective washing of clothes, along with a manual spin cycle. They need very little water and no electricity.

Lights

Courtesy Lights. It is easy, economical, and aesthetically pleasing to run courtesy lights in white or amber (among other colors); these provide a nice romantic ambiance at night without undermining night vision. They draw low voltage and were my primary lights for entertaining.

Cabin Lights. Cabin lights come in all varieties, including the kind that switches between white light and amber for improved night vision. It is not always necessary to drill and run wires to install added lighting, because there are wonderful battery options that last quite long, as well as 12 and 110-volt solutions for those who reside primarily at dock.

Lights is another area that has changed dramatically through the past few years. The number and quality of LED lighting is a tremendous upgrade, utilizing less power and offering far more light than many former solutions.

Lanterns/Oil Systems. The greatest ambiance is provided by lantern/candlelight. Beautiful systems can be installed that are safe, efficient, and effective. Remember to overstock on the fuel and wicks so the system is available whenever you desire.

Flashlights. You can never have enough. Flashlights should be mounted either visibly or inside cabinets so they can be found instantly in an emergency. My recommendation is to purchase at least one battery-free light (powered by shaking the flashlight) and one good hands-free flashlight that can be worn on your head for engine repair problems or when you have to go to the foredeck to do something. Also, hands-free lights are wonderful to read by, often offering multiple power settings.

Marine Heads and Sewage Treatment

Marine heads are generally short and stubby, making the user almost have to do a partial squat. More expensive models might be more typically sized. Some have an up-and-down pump, and others pump back and forth, which is regarded by many as much easier but more space intensive. Electric heads are nice because they don't require any special training for use, while manual heads must be explained to guests and have been known to flood a boat or two by unsuspecting users not remembering to switch the toilet back to "dry" when finished (causing water to siphon into the toilet). Electric heads typically require more maintenance than manual heads, and can have significant power draws, albeit for very short periods of time.

There are some interesting options for sewage treatment, and it is important to know what is and is not permitted in your cruising area. Chemical treatments designed to kill coliform bacteria may be used without a holding tank in areas where pumping treated waste overboard is permitted. Incinerating heads turn sewage into ash; these systems also claim to be legal for overboard discharge. Non-holding tank solutions have the potential to allow for the removal of the smelly holding tank, also allowing for much more space. Do pay careful attention to the rules set forth in no-discharge zones, as an inspection finding a head without a holding tank might result in very significant fines if the type of waste treatment aboard is not permitted.

There is also a variety of holding tanks and odor treatments available economically. Everything helps a bit, but as long as there is sewage on board, nothing is likely to entirely solve the odor problem.

Security Systems

Boats have always been easy targets for theft, particularly when allowed to sit unattended for days at anchor or mooring. Gear is often placed aboard with only a couple of adjustable screws on either side, making for the easy removal of electronics. Stereo systems are often easily removed, as well. Many boaters work toward solving the problem by taking gear below deck and locking the boat before departing. Still, because typically only a padlock separates the thief from the interior, some boat owners opt for more protection, such as motion detectors and alarm systems just like those used for land-based residences.

The pessimist complains about the wind; the optimist expects it to change; the realist adjusts the sails.

- - *William Arthur Ward*

10

Cruising Considerations

When this book was first being conceived we conducted an informal (read: unscientific) survey among liveaboards and found that the average liveaboard is tied to just one or two locations. Marinas reported that liveaboards, like most boaters in general, rarely take their boats from their berths—many head out just a handful of times during the season. We also found that although the dream of cruising is a major draw to the lifestyle, few truly cruise, instead living aboard happily for a period of time, whether months or years, eventually moving back ashore a more satisfied and complete person.

The typical liveaboard is very much a dreamer, either striving to live the dream or one day hoping to unplug, untie, and head off. Internet forums (and my inbox) are filled with ideas of freedom, independence, and separation from society/civilization. Many first boats are chosen in anticipation of ultimately being retrofitted for cruising. As we have discussed previously, this is one dream that is often left unattained and, when attained, can end up being experienced in ways that are not found to be as pleasurable as anticipated.

Preparing for an extended time away is hard work. Often, quite expensive and major boating projects are abandoned prior to completion. As we discussed in the first chapters of the book, it is the dream that gets us to buy into the lifestyle and it is the hard work that tempers our goals. For better or worse, many (most) of us have found that sitting dockside or anchored off of some nearby shoal can be completely satisfying.

The cruising liveaboard has very little in common with the typical localized liveaboard. Some cruisers live for the adventure, being one with nature and/or seeking to experience different people, places, and things at their most natural. In other cases, cruising liveaboards are making a more complex decision based on their personal philosophies or a desire for individual freedom. Some share an overwhelming desire to live their lives free from society or the influence of others. Tom Neale's book *All in the Same Boat: Living Aboard and Cruising* addresses this issue right from its first page, describing a desire to be able to live life on your own terms, the personal desire to educate your children in your own way, and so forth.

Regardless of what brings you to sea, you will find yourself very much on your own. Your life and the lives of your crew, family, and guests depend on smart decision-making, intuition, and a savvy for mechanical maintenance and repairs. Mother Nature and her big blue will always win in a direct challenge, and thinking that you have the upper hand is one very easy way for you, your crew, or your guests to pay a dire price. I have personally experienced situations where, absent proper readiness and fast/coordinated decision-making, we would have found ourselves in serious trouble.

In fact, the non-cruiser and the cruiser are so different that I don't regard the cruiser as much of a liveaboard at all, but more aptly as a boater who happens to be living aboard. The skills are sufficiently different. However, by popular demand we will still take a few minutes to address some of the issues faced by the typical liveaboard cruiser.

If you want to learn more, I would strongly encourage you to join the crew of a vessel that is taking extensive time away and to head out for extended vacations and time offshore. When it comes to cruising, it really is the only way to learn.

Heading Off

Success in cruising is often determined by the preparation. Are you ready? Is your crew ready? Is your boat ready? Are you properly provisioned?

Training

The ocean is a tough place. Unskilled or negligent boaters endanger theirs and others' lives. Different ports and cultures can introduce challenges and dangers. Although no person can ever be completely prepared for everything, being prepared does not involve so much knowing the answers as being a problem solver and capable of learning and adapting quickly—sometimes in mere seconds—to situations that may arise.

Not only can Mother Nature play the role of antagonist, but so can other boaters, and your skills will need to be sharp enough to overcome the lack of training or attention by your colleagues. Many of the most dangerous circumstances are created by human error and the failure to pay attention; your welfare can be endangered either by being around inattentive, error-prone people or by ineptly getting involved and trying to help them out.

Just as you cannot learn to play golf by reading a book, you cannot really prepare to cruise by reading a book. If you are going to be prepared for heavy weather then you must have been in heavy weather—not just once, but over and over again. It never ceases to amaze me how many boaters first experience what might be otherwise routine heavy-weather conditions when they are alone and unprepared. We hear many stories of boaters' first attempts at using a storm chute or heaving-to only in times of absolute necessity, not in situations of drilling and practice, and there are a myriad of examples of situations resulting in serious injury to boaters who tried learning this way.

It's impossible to learn from a book how to overcome difficult situations; it's very difficult to learn how to be a master cruiser by yourself. Not every person with lots of hours under way is competent, and practicing bad technique over and over again assures you'll have a very sound bad technique. Just to watch an accomplished captain respond to different situations is a fantastic learning experience by itself.

In my two most harrowing situations (occurring years apart), I was on board with two very accomplished sailors. The first could seemingly sense problems with the way the boat acted even while the mechanical problems were still unknown to the rest of us aboard. He was able to position the boat in a way to try to ensure that we would not run aground nearby shoals in sub-freezing weather, all the while staying calm, troubleshooting the problem, and providing different orders to help manage the crisis. On another trans-ocean cruise I watched our captain navigate ten days of 20-foot-plus seas and erratic waves and breakers while managing a torn mainsail and a collection of malfunctions on a 50-foot sailing vessel. In many ways, I've learned more watching these real pros during these isolated incidents than during all my decades of sailing.

That is not to say that you shouldn't read up on cruising and off-shore incidents. I highly recommend books by Lin and Larry Pardey, Tom Neale, and so many others. And don't forget books such as *Force 10* (by John Rousmaniere) and *Fatal Storm* (by Rob Mundle) discussing actual life-and-death situations in extreme conditions.

When it comes to training, it is not enough for just you, the captain, to know how to handle the boat; it's important that your crew to be equally capable. Offshore, we all take turns on watch. Every person on board should understand how to use the communication and emergency systems, since we depend extraordinarily on each other.

Unanimous Consent and Role Assignment

While a bossy captain may be unpleasant, a single dissenting voice on board can introduce a dangerous dynamic. Everyone aboard should want to be aboard, and everyone aboard should willingly and skillfully perform their assigned tasks.

Different cruisers handle tasks in different ways. Some assign specific people to do certain things, meaning that some person will be assigned to tasks such as captain, navigation, cooking, cleaning, setting the anchor, communications, laundry, provisioning, and so on. Some crews rotate tasks. Others take instructions from the captain. Some crews rotate captains. There is just too much to do to have to constantly fight about who will do what.

This role assignment takes on greater significance when the cruise encounters an uncomfortable situation, whether it is heavy weather, mechanical issues, or anything else that can arise. Someone must be in charge, and everyone else must move quickly and without hesitation or second thought as orders are given. If ego or attitude can interfere, then the personalities are not properly suited for offshore.

Respecting each other is the first step. It is rarely enough to have members of your crew acquiesce to the challenges of the lifestyle.

The Right Boat and Gear

Many cruisers have backups for every piece of essential gear, and backups for backups. While the coastal liveaboard's primary requirement is comfort, the cruising liveaboard's primary goal is safety. A bilge pump failure at shore if caught fairly quickly usually means nothing more than having to head to your local marine store for a replacement. Offshore a bilge pump failure can become a major problem. The offshore cruiser, perhaps while under way in less than calm seas, will have to make the repair or prepare to pump and pump and pump.

Many offshore boats maintain complete tool kits, at least two spare bilge pumps, a fixed topside manual pump and a portable manual pump, extensive backup safety gear, ditch gear, and so forth. It could be said that only a fool would travel with less.

> *Engine, Rigging and Hull.* When choosing a cruising boat, start with a good hull, properly installed and sealed through-hulls, and well-built/properly installed seacocks (no gate valves) for every through-hull—and don't forget those seacocks for above but near the waterline through-hulls. Cruisers tend to like stable boats with heavy displacements. Draft varies. A deeper draft can help with stability but limits flexibility.
>
> The engine and rigging should be carefully inspected and prepared, and once again, backup gear should be brought onboard for all essential systems. I have been onboard with a torn mainsail and no backup, and had we not had sufficient fuel, we would have faced a significant and egregiously expensive problem. Carry extra sails, lines, and hardware—and don't forget to inspect the backups, as well, from time to time.

Many cruising boats, particularly cruising sailboats, have smaller galleys and heads because the confined space helps to prevent great injury, falls, and spills during rocky or unexpected conditions. This depends on personal taste but is another consideration.

Tools and Power. You never want to be without the tools to make necessary repairs. A complete heavy-duty marine tool kit is essential. Don't forget those special marine tools, including stuffing box wrenches, heat guns, and shrink tubing as well as marine grade wire, screws, and bolts. Screwdrivers should have long handles. One of my favorite all-around tools is the Dremel, capable of sanding, drilling, grinding, cutting, and so many other helpful tasks.

Cruisers are power-conscious, and cruising boats often have complex gear for monitoring power usage. This means amp draw as well as voltage, and some systems calculate remaining amp hours, and so forth. Power generation is often recommended to avoid having to use fuel to generate power. Many cruisers, particularly sailboaters, use solar or wind power systems to keep the batteries topped off. It is strongly advisable to isolate the starting battery from the general use "house" batteries as well, allowing batteries to be entirely drained without jeopardizing the ability to get back under way. Inverters and generators are also common.

Safety. Safety harnesses, jacklines and handles should exist everywhere in a cruising boat, including in the galley, head, salon, and so on. I am a fanatic for fire extinguishers being reachable throughout a boat since a fire anywhere onboard is often devastating. Offshore vessels require other safety gear as well, including easily deployable lifeboats, Electronic Position Indicating Radio Beacon (EPIRB), or a Global Maritime Distress & Safety System (GMDSS) for detection when in distress. The list of possible safety gear can go on and on.

The list of preparatory items can go on and on, as well. For instance, anchor safety requires a heavy anchor and lots of chain. This can be so heavy that a windlass is helpful. Sea anchors, drogues, and storm sails are important. Never forget your foul weather gear. One potential problem for some sailors is that in the event that the main needs to be dropped quickly the sail would fall all over the place. For those sailors, lazy jacks would be extremely helpful to keep the sail contained so that the crew can work on other items. Other common requirements are boarding ladders, stern anchors, and so forth.

Storage and Stowage. If you want to fish, you need room for your fishing gear. If you want to surf, you need room for your board. Some like to drink wine, play guitar, get dressed up for nice dinners, watch TV, surf the Internet, etc., and whatever you bring must be kept in a very safe condition when under way. But don't forget that your most important items are food, water, fuel, power, tools, and gear. You need to be prepared for any contingencies (such as extra time at sea), so anything that prevents you from bringing necessities on board is another thing that should be left behind.

Stowage means having the gear placed securely away so that nothing gets in your way or falls on your head or floor. Commonly, storage areas are so limited that every spare space is taken and essential items, such as seacocks, can become blocked. Now, rarely does an emergency require that the seacocks be closed (some sailors can go a life-time without having an emergency requiring that they be closed); in addition, seacocks tend to be placed in remote areas, so blocking access to them is exceedingly easy. Consequently, boaters either may not know where the sea-cocks are, or they may unthinkingly block access to them. When an emergency (such as a broken hose) requires that a seacock be closed or a bung inserted, the vessel is flooding and will sink unless things happen quickly. Any delay is too long.

Communication and Navigation. Communication and navigation gear should be duplicated. Many cruisers use a permanently installed radio and a handheld (useful when on shore), and also use SSB, satellite, and other forms of communication. Duplication is key.

Dinghy and Ditching. For all those moments when you might want to access land or another boat while anchored or moored, a dinghy is essential cruising gear. Since dragging a dinghy offshore can result in all kinds of problems (most notably, a lost dinghy or fouled prop), a means for bringing the dinghy onboard is quite helpful as well. Can you just feel the cash register ching-ching away as the money flows?

Some cruisers use their dinghy as a life raft. Most, however, do not. Conditions that might result in an abandoned boat are exactly the same kind of conditions that can result in an abandoned, flipped, or filled dinghy. A life raft not only keeps its occupants sheltered, dryer, and higher out of the water (helping to stay warm), but also helps secure the other most essential piece of physical gear: the ditch bag.

Speaking of the ditch bag, never head off shore or into difficult conditions without one. The bag should be buoyant, waterproof, easily accessible, portable—and ready to go at all times. The bag, at a minimum, should contain flares, signal gear, flashlights, EPIRB, GPS, handheld radio, a handheld water maker, a folding jug, high calorie bars, sun protection, medical supplies, thermal blankets, passports as well as money/credit cards, and so forth. Some bags include many other items, including gear for fishing, personal hygiene, sea anchors, and the like.

Don't forget your creature comforts. Microwaves, coffeepots, wine, refrigeration, water makers, hot water heaters, televisions, stereos, etc. are all nice to have as well. There are ways of minimizing space usage (*e.g.*, instant hot water heaters) but this stuff all takes up space. Perhaps the greatest invention for the cruiser is digital media.

Provisioning

Provisioning, for most cruisers, is about keeping things complete, simple, and light. Too many ingredients or cooking phases require more pots and utensils and therefore more cooking time, cleaning time, and water. There are some great resources for recipes with fewer provisions. Start with a provision list and acquire your goods accordingly. Re-provision liberally whenever you can and you can use the ship's provision list to shop with after taking an inventory. But don't forget the towels and toilet paper.

Although canned goods will last a long time if unopened, the cans are heavy and they themselves do not last forever, particularly if they start to rust. Also, dampness will cause the labels to fall off. Cruisers who bring cans aboard often remove the label and write the contents directly onto the can with a Sharpie or other permanent pen—or even a Dremel. Some cruisers will actually rust-proof or varnish the cans, a detail that many would not take the time to do.

Dry goods (that do not require refrigeration) are a real favorite for time at sea. These include flour, pastas, sugar (try to use cubed or lump sugar to avoid sticky spills), oats, and rice. Dried eggs, powdered milk, cereal, dried fruit, and coffee are common onboard as well. Be careful of insects and mice: it is quite common to transfer the dry goods to airtight buckets, or zip lock or vacuum pack bags. Properly stored, these goods can be maintained in bulk for a very long time.

There are lots of tidbits and pieces of advice when it comes to provisioning. Wash your fruits and vegetables with a splash of bleach to help kill any bugs. Buy pre-ripened tomatoes and store at cool room temperature. Ripen tomatoes in newspaper. Do not wash your apples before storing, and quickly remove rotten/spoiled apples or they will contaminate the rest.

Do not use your valuable refrigeration space for things that do not need to be refrigerated (yes, that means drinking warm drinks from time to time). Many drink mixes are now so tasty that all you need is a bit of water and you can enjoy a wide variety of different beverages. (For us big people, the great taste even comes with no calories at all.)

It may surprise you (it surprised me) to hear you don't need to refrigerate eggs. Preserving eggs requires that the pores in the shell be sealed. Some cruisers use Vaseline (a bit slimy) but a more proven technique is to dip the egg in a combination of waterglass and boiled/cooled water. This kills the bacteria that cause eggs to spoil while sealing the pores, keeping water and moisture in and bad things out. Unrefrigerated eggs have been known to last upwards of nine months using this technique. [NOTE: consider poking each egg with a pin before cracking to let any accumulated gasses escape, since the egg has been air-proofed for this period of time; AND, without failure, crack each egg into a separate glass before mixing with the other eggs, because one egg in the bunch still always seems to spoil]. Visit motherearthnews.com to read about their detailed study on egg preservation.

Keep pans with locking lids (pressure cookers work as well); don't forget to store knives safely and put plates on non-sliding surfaces. In any kind of rolling condition, get that galley strap on to protect you from falling. Try to keep a temperature-resistant apron in case hot liquids spill. Definitely consider rubber hot-temp cooking mitts that will not absorb moisture and will survive any kitchen temperature (wearing these you can dip your hands directly into boiling water).

If you haven't cruised before, this might seem like tough stuff. Just start slow and keep the recipes simple and you'll do just fine. And be sure to pick up a couple of cruising cookbooks (such as *Care and Feeding of Sailing Crew* by Lin and Larry Pardey and *Cruising Cuisine: Fresh Food from the Galley* by Kay Pastorius) for some amazingly helpful information.

Heading Off

When it comes to heading off, the cruiser wraps up his/her/their personal business. All possessions that will not come aboard must be sold, stored, or given away. With the advent of online sales and auction sites such as *Ebay* and *Craigslist*, selling possessions is far easier than ever, and there are storage facilities all over (but don't forget to pay your bill).

The kinds of predeparture errands that you should be sure to take care of include mail holding/forwarding services, transfer or termination of accounts, prepayment of bills (if necessary), and so on. Upon deciding that you might cruise one day, or even liveaboard one day, open up a full service bank account and a mail forwarding box. Since global anti-money laundering rules prohibit or obstruct the opening of accounts for people lacking a physical address, it is much preferred to open the accounts before you give up your physical spot on land.

Traditional mail forwarding is exceedingly archaic, although digital mail services have been slow to evolve. Over the next few years, major evolution seems certain to occur.

Even though it costs more money up front, even in this world of online bill payment consider paying for certain important things in advance. For instance, my life as I know it is suspended if my e-mail goes down. I use both a paid service and a free service and I need them both working, so I prepay for the service for two or more years in advance. Don't be thrifty in this regard. For me, I can only have so much space in my e-mail accounts, enough so that one e-mail sender can fill my entire inbox with a couple of large photos, so I buy extra storage space for my free account and I pay for that well in advance as well. Other big prepayment things for me include my cell phone, online photo album, personal web sites, and so forth. They are all paid in advance for the next five years.

If you maintain a storage facility, consider prepaying for that as well. If there is ever a mistake in the bill payment, you run the risk of having your most prized possessions auctioned off from right under your nose. If this happens, whether by oversight or accident, you will lose your stuff and you will never get it back. So prepay to avoid any chance of this occurring.

If your contact information will change, allow sufficient time to circulate that information. Folks are lazy about updating their contact lists and often need to be told more than once. Nevertheless, web-based e-mail addresses such as a Gmail address never need to change, so if you don't have a free account, this might be a good time to secure one.

Prepare for any direct deposits as required. Salary checks, social security checks, and the like all can be directly deposited. Online bill payment and check writing is unbelievably convenient (I could not imagine any cruiser doing without it), so be sure to investigate your financial institution to be certain they can perform all of these essential services.

Finances and Making Money

It is not possible to tell how much money a cruise will cost; in fact, I've never heard a number that felt reasonable to me. Each cruiser is different—it's possible to cruise for nearly nothing or spend millions of dollars annually. Some sailors use their engines more than others; some strive to make their journeys without ever turning on the engine (preferring to sit dead calm rather than keep on the move), comfortably tolerating stagnancy. Some would rather pick up transient slips; others will just drop the anchor and dinghy where they need to. Some like eating dinner in fancy restaurants; others cook up beans, rice, and grain aboard.

International cruisers do not tend to carry too much cash for two reasons: the first is that many international ports have limits on the amount of cash that can be carried (often limiting the total amount to $10,000); the second is that cash can so easily be damaged or stolen. If a local bank or brokerage is used, money can be deposited into the account and accessed via ATM, check (if permitted), or wire. Also, if your financial institution provides a bill payment service (and you should make sure it does), bills can be paid and checks cut to anyone whenever the institution's site can be accessed. This convenience was unheard of just a few years ago.

Making money on board is quite specific to the cruiser's own unique situation. Some cruisers have more than enough money and don't need to worry about additional sources of income. Some have a pension/retirement check routinely deposited into their account. Others earn money by working remotely, using satellite or other means of communication to work with their clients or their home company (this is what many writers do, as well as photographers, graphic designers, and the like). Writing is a popular endeavor, with cruisers blogging and travel writing to their hearts' content. Still others seek employment wherever they might happen to be. I've known my share of liveaboards who seek to make money laboring or maintaining other people's boats along the way, some who try to get hired for construction/handyman tasks, and another close friend makes a good living as a street musician.

Pay attention to local laws, regulations and customs. Some locations will tolerate just about anything, while others require permits or visas to perform work of any kind. Different marinas have different policies for on-site contractors, so be sure to do your homework to avoid a surprising heap of trouble.

Firearms and Protection

One of the most hotly debated online subjects relates to firearms. Though cruisers debate this issue at length, the use of lethal or non-lethal force onboard is another of those very personal decisions that only you and your crew can make. This book will not offer a recommendation and, to be honest, offers no real preference. That's not an attempt to play it safe, but an honest respect for the complexity of the debate. Responsibility and a perfect understanding of local laws are important, since mess-ups can cause you to end up in a foreign jail in a foreign land lacking any of the rights that you might have otherwise thought you'd be entitled to.

The debate rarely centers on a cruiser's political views, particularly since most independent cruisers are all for the freedom to bear arms, and many of those who cruise without firearms still have some stored back at the home port. The most relevant portion of the debate centers more specifically on whether guns aboard will offer more benefits than risk. Protection typically regarded as non-lethal (such as tasers, mace, pepper spray, stunt wands, and the like) are equally debated.

If you decide to carry protection on board, be certain that you know how to secure and handle the weapon. There have been heavily reported situations in which a gun onboard was very helpful, such as the Pirate's Alley incident involving the two sailing yachts *Mahdi* and *Gandalf,* in which pirates approached firing submachine guns with an intent to kill and the attack was miraculously thwarted by a shotgun on one of the boats.

Brandishing a gun without knowing how to use it is one way to get you or someone you love killed. The gun, after all, exists for only one reason, and bad people at sea tend to be very good at being very bad. Secondly, carrying weapons subjects you to a world of new rules. In all waters you should expect to be boarded at some point, whereupon the weapon adds an entirely new dynamic.

Whether or not you choose to be armed, your primary protection is your understanding of your cruising grounds. Do not forget to visit Noonsite (http://www.noonsite.com/) for updated information, and confirm with information supplied from various governments.

Getting Along

Life at sea is a combination of wildly different experiences. Depending on the cruising schedule and other conditions, the crew may work in assigned shifts throughout a 24-hour watch. When a watch is around the clock, members of the crew will be napping at practically all hours of the day. Other days may involve no work at all. Days in port can range from very intense (such as provisioning, cleaning, and repair days) to very relaxing.

Non-heavy weather cruising time tends to be routine and predictable. Many cruisers have certain daily and weekly traditions that provide great meaning aboard. We'd have a glass of wine every sunset and toast to the ocean and Mother Nature. Shifts are planned.

Some meals are always taken as a full group. Children are typically held to greater structure, with home schooling and study built into a fairly rigid framework. Our clock tends to be based on the daylight the sun gives us.

Usually, board games, cards, and other games can be found onboard. Musical instruments are common. Books, computers, movies, and so forth are often readily available as well. The nice thing about instruments, computers, and board games is that they can continue to be entertaining for unlimited periods of time. Many cruisers have interesting exercise routines, as well. Personally, my favorite activity on board is learning, whether it is how to play music or how to navigate celestially. Many people are surprised to hear that many cruisers do not drink alcohol very much when under way. Down time and in port, however, all can be a different story.

Contacts with friends and relatives are also best accomplished by routine. Set certain times and dates for phone calls, e-mailing, blogging, and posting photos. Not only does it help keep focus, but your landlubbing loved ones will appreciate and look forward to the contact.

So go learn, sign up for crewing opportunities, and get out there. Spend time in heavy weather and learn everything there is to know about your engine and how to repair every single thing aboard. Stock up on great tools and supplies, and one day you'll find yourself exactly where you'd dreamed you'd be.

Also, be sure to learn in advance about your cruising destinations and activities ashore so that you don't run into complications (such as having your pet, provisions, or other possessions quarantined or confiscated). Hop on forums and ask about those special little secret locations that only cruisers know about. And radio in when you get there. You might find new friends, old friends, and tour guides.

Safe seas!

Tarps provide protection from the sun, wind, and rain.

11

Climate

Liveaboards in temperate or tropical climates will have a much different experience than liveaboards in a cold-climate area or in an area in which the temperatures are extreme, both hot in the summer and cold in the winter. Pretty obvious.

There are many other climate issues in addition to temperature that impact the liveaboard, the boat and boater safety. The prevalence of rainy conditions, humidity, exposure to hurricanes and other tropical storms, wind, snow, and blizzard conditions will all certainly have a significant effect on your experience. Competent marinas employ measures to protect boaters from climatic conditions that could damage boats or injure boaters. I believe that beyond providing a slip to the boaters, every marina should protect the boats and provide safe conditions for boaters; the best marinas perform this task with a stunningly effective and efficient process.

My marina, for instance, runs safety lines across the docks and boats when heavy weather is forecast, to aid in withstanding storm conditions. These lines are tied and maintained through the entire winter as a critical safety procedure. While ice buildup in the water is not as big a problem (because of a more than nine-foot tidal range in Boston), ice can still develop in extremely cold weather. The marina regulates this and ensures that ice buildup does not occur in the areas surrounding the boats. The marina removes snow from the docks and will salt the docks to remove ice. Finger piers, however, are the responsibility of the individual boat owners.

Know what to expect, and know how to prepare yourself and your boat for weather and temperature fluctuations and the change of seasons. Many books have been written on handling various weather conditions at sea. Our focus is limited to the things that need to be understood to aid in comfort and safety while living aboard in more typical circumstances.

Dampness/Humidity

Boats are designed to be waterproof, and clearly no boat should have water coming through the hull or the deck, regardless of weather conditions. Boats, however, are not air proof, and air contains moisture in a range from virtually none, to up to 100 percent.

The higher the temperature, the more of this humidity you will feel. In hot and humid conditions, moisture such as sweat will not evaporate; you will feel damp, sticky, and in need of a shower. Remember, waterproof means water inside the boat stays inside as well.

The interior of a boat constrains warm, humid air; the boat will act like a steam room and be increasingly uncomfortable. This can even lead to heat exhaustion or heat stroke, so drink plenty of water and remove yourself from these overheating conditions before things get too dangerous. If this is occurring in your boat, in addition to decreasing the boat's temperature, it is important to address this problem in two ways: by ventilating and by reducing humidity.

Ventilation

It is not enough simply to open a port or hatch, because good ventilation requires that stale air be removed and clean air be brought in. Manufacturers of ventilation systems often recommend that at least two fans be installed, one that adds fresh air and one that exhausts stale air. Often, the best system brings in fresh air from the bow and exhales toward the stern.

A variety of products and methods can accomplish this purpose: Cowls can be installed and aimed in the direction of the nearest breeze; you can also use solar vents/fans, 12-volt vents/fans, or wind chutes (like parachutes that capture fresh air and force it through a hatch into the boat), as well as many other systems.

Good ventilation is not only an invaluable enhancement for comfort, but also an essential safety requirement, because oxygen can be depleted and replaced with carbon dioxide as people breathe. Also, ventilation is critical for protecting against carbon monoxide accumulation if internal systems break down or if neighboring boaters have their engines running. Good ventilation also protects against fumes generated from epoxy, fiberglass, varnish, paint, and fuel as the result of boat improvements or spills. More discussion on carbon monoxide will follow in the chapter *Safety and Sanitation*.

Moisture and Humidity

Reducing humidity is one of the more challenging and frustrating aspects of living aboard.

Moisture is by definition wet (yes, I'm also a rocket scientist), and we don't like the inside of our homes, or our clothes, skin, cereal boxes, papers, computers/iPads and so forth to be wet. We are surrounded by water, which already has a tendency to end up inside our boats, being brought in on our shoes and clothes (and cat) after rains and wet cruises, or entering through ports and hatches inadvertently left open or unsealed. Non-liveaboards get to leave to allow their boat time to dry. Liveaboards are relegated to sleeping on wet berths and sitting on wet cushions.

Moisture also brings odors and mold, which can make life aboard less appealing, and can ultimately damage possessions and even cause illness.

Condensation

Moisture that occurs inside a boat by virtue of spills, drips, or leaks is manageable because you either know how it got there or can work to clean it up. When you see something wet, you can take care of it immediately, taking measures to dry any wet cushions and possessions so you can avoid unwanted by-products of the moisture. [While tracking down the source of a leak can be a difficult challenge, a good trick is to use water-soluble markers. After drying the wet areas, use the marker to write or line across an area where the water might be coming from. You'll see the marked areas become impacted by the water and will be able to follow the path back toward the water's source.]

Condensation, however, is a different matter. As seen on the outside of the drinking glasses of our cool beverages and the dew/ wetness on the grass (and our decks) in the morning, it is moisture that has left the air and appears on surfaces as water droplets. Condensation will appear over the entire exterior deck of a boat; in the interior, it might appear on the ceiling, walls, floor, and surfaces under cushions.

You know that you're the victim of condensation if your ceiling starts to drip on you (i.e., it starts to rain inside your boat), or you lift up a cushion or mattress and find that the underside is soaking wet and possibly moldy and stinky. Also, you know that you've been the victim of condensation when all of your clothes in drawers and lockers are damp.

As a liveaboard, it is helpful if you understand how condensation occurs, and more particularly, what can be done about it.

Water stays in the air only so long as the air temperature stays warmer than a certain point, and when the temperature drops below that point, the air can no longer hold its moisture. That temperature point fluctuates and is called the dew point. The factors that cause the dew point to fluctuate aren't our concern, but the result is.

Let's say that the dew point is 60 degrees Fahrenheit and the temperature outside the boat drops to 55 degrees. Water will form on the deck and other surfaces on the exterior of the boat, since the temperature is below the dew point and the air can no longer hold the water. The moisture is "falling" out of the air. Inside, as long as the temperature is maintained above 60 degrees, there will not be moisture forming on the interior surfaces (with the problem exception we will talk about shortly). If the interior temperature of the boat drops below 60 degrees, moisture will form.

Accordingly, avoiding condensation is a primary reason to heat your boat if there is any chance the interior temperature will drop below the dew point, even during periods when the boat is left unoccupied. Otherwise, you might return to a boat in which everything is soaking wet.

Got it? Unfortunately, there's more.

There must be some explanation for how water can form on the outside of a cold glass on an 80-degree day when the dew point is 60 degrees. The condensation occurs because the temperature *on the glass* is below the dew point, even though the surrounding air is above the dew point. The surface of the glass is itself colder than the dew point.

And this is the liveaboard's problem. You live on the surface of the glass.

What if the water or outside air temperature is 50 degrees and the dew point is 60 degrees? Even when you heat the interior of the boat to 70 degrees, the inside of the hull making contact with the cold water or air might easily be colder than the dew point, even if the air itself is warmer - exactly like the glass. When that occurs, water will form on those surfaces, tending to be areas of the boat much harder

Condensation: The Bane of a Liveaboard's Existence
"Raining Inside the Boat"
Photo by Chris Birch

to heat or even monitor; places like closets, drawers or lazarettes where clothing or other personal possessions might be placed. The only solution is to warm the interior surfaces themselves (in addition to the interior air temperature).

The problem is, unlike a home, or even a car/RV, there is no insulation helping to keep the cold out separated from our interior surfaces. Even worse, many areas of the interior of the boat are extremely difficult to warm because they are not exposed to and even protected from the interior air, particularly the areas under cushions/mattresses, lockers, and drawers. Ironically, these areas are difficult to warm not only because they are either behind closed doors where the warm air does not circulate, but because they *are* in fact insulated— by our clothes and cushions—ironically keeping the warm air away. Water forms on the surfaces and then infiltrates everything in our lockers and drawers as well as the underside of our cushions and mattresses. You already have limited locker and drawer space, and now what space you do have is acting as a magnet for moisture, ultimately damaging what you are trying to store and protect.

Reducing Humidity and Condensation

Your ongoing challenge is the avoidance and removal of the moisture. This moisture can damage *everything* and cause odors and health-impacting/property-damaging mold.

Step 1. Keep the interior temperature above the dew point. If you do this, you will be on the right track. Some heaters produce very dry heat, which will also act to dehumidify the air.

Step 2. Reduce the moisture from the air. Dehumidifiers can be used, but may be expensive and incompatible with your electrical system or space limitations. Marine retailers sell products that are designed to act as sponges for the moisture, such as small cup-like moisture-absorbing containers that can be placed in the lockers and other storage areas.

Step 3. Use a system designed to heat your lockers and storage areas. There are some interesting methods for this, including a system of metal bars that, when run from a 110-volt source, will put out just enough heat to safely increase the ambient temperature of the small area in which the bar is used.

Step 4. Keep your clothes and non-water-resistant possessions away from the exterior surfaces of the boat, since you know that moisture will form on those surfaces. There are creative ways to ensure that your fabrics do not make contact with these surfaces, such as foam or bubble wrap reflective insulation sold in home improvement stores, wooden separators, and other solutions.

Step 5. Marine stores sell a paper-type product that works quite well when placed under cushions and mattresses to absorb wetness and keep it away from the cushions. Not only will this paper become wet, but it will also get quite moldy over time, so it is important to change it as needed.

Step 6. Lift the cushions and mattresses when you leave the boat, to allow air to circulate around them and to allow residual moisture to dry and surfaces to warm.

Step 7. Periodically open all lockers and storage areas to allow warm air to circulate and to dry moisture that might be accumulating.

Step 8. Avoid showering or boiling water on board, particularly in damp weather or when there is limited ventilation.

Step 9. Consider a central heating system. The venting of a central system will act as a near-hull space heater.

The sooner you become aware of the nuances of your boat, the sooner you will be able to develop a system to reduce moisture and keep odors and mold away. Knowing that moisture and condensation will permeate your living space, I suggest buying moisture-proof containers and desiccants for storage. Your marine retailer will have a collection of options as well. Be sure to put all of your paper documents and special possessions in moisture-proof containers, perhaps also adding a desiccant.

Another suggestion is to keep your tools and equipment cleaned and well-oiled. This will help protect them for use when needed.

Moisture and condensation pose significant problems when running a home office or personal electronic gear from your boat. While this is something that I and most liveaboards do, your challenges are not only to allow for the space for a computer, printer, and supplies (such as reams of paper)—but also to figure out how to heat the electronic gear when not in use so that condensation doesn't form. For instance, moisture (and salt, in certain conditions) can appear on the motherboard of your computer, which can easily destroy the entire computer. While taking measures such as covering computer ports and connectors will prevent liquid moisture from penetrating (some recommend using duct tape, which concerns me since the glue residue can damage the equipment), liquid moisture isn't really your problem. It is condensation that can wipe out your gear and destroy your supplies. The best recommendation, an unfortunate one at that, is to leave your equipment out in the open so that it is surrounded by warmer air. If you put the equipment in a cabinet away from circulating air, you might be inviting the problem.

Also, never buy the kind of envelopes or stamps that require moisture to seal, since you already have plenty of moisture and they will seal themselves into a giant mess. And keep all of your paper supplies and files either in warm air or in moisture-sealed containers.

Temperature

A nice temperature is quite helpful for comfort. If you are not comfortable, you won't live aboard long-term.

My marina charges for electricity during the winter. I would have been more comfortable and would have saved a substantial amount of money if I had avoided using electric heaters as my primary heaters and instead installed a forced-air diesel central heating unit. I'd seal up the v-berth (effectively cutting my small amount of living space in half) and run two space heaters: an oil-filled heater, which was kept on every day all day, and an electric space heater I only used while aboard, for safety reasons. My electric bill got pretty high.

One of the leading causes of boat fires is electric heaters. The leading causes of death among occupants of boats are boat fires and poor ventilation; both risks substantially increase in cold climates during the winter season.

Heating

In cold climates, your boat can feel quite confining, and anything that detracts from the comfort will diminish your quality of life. There are specifically two ways to heat the interior of a boat: radiant heat and forced air (central) heat.

Radiant Heat

Radiant heat is heat that *radiates* or spreads out from a source. Space heaters are classic methods of heating a boat; the portable ones are predominantly electric. Quality units can be found in RV and marine stores. There are other variations as well, such as portable units that use small propane canisters or mini diesel tanks, and bulkhead-mounted heaters that operate on propane or diesel fuel.

The principle advantage to a space heater is that it allows you to target the specific location you want to heat. The disadvantage is that the heat is limited to the area surrounding the heater, and the heat diminishes significantly as you move away from it. Also, space heaters don't heat well through bulkheads, walls, locker doors, or under cushions.

Electric space heaters can be placed anywhere and produce a hot/dry heat. The disadvantages to electric space heaters are: (1) They cost a lot to operate, since they draw significant amounts of electricity; (2) the house wires, outlet, and cord can heat up if the wires are not of an acceptable grade, causing a risk of fire in *non-visible* areas of the boat; (3) the space heater becomes very hot and can burn anything that makes contact with it; and (4) in the event that the space heater falls over, which is common in a boat, the space heater can self-ignite or ignite the surface or object proximate to the fall. Every year, boat fires are caused by the use of electric heaters.

Bulkhead space heaters use predominantly propane or diesel fuels, and avoid many of the otherwise potentially dangerous conditions discussed above, provided that the use of propane is handled in a safe and responsible way.

Propane bulkhead space heaters preclude the risk of *electrical* fires, since they can be operated with no electricity at all, although it is advisable to use a low-draw fan to help circulate the warm air. Small, one-pound propane tanks are quite economical and can last a long time. Fire is still a risk, since the heating element or flame can become very hot and propane is a highly explosive fuel. We'll talk about the safety issues with the use of propane later, but propane gas, when released, can be very dangerous, particularly on a boat.

Diesel bulkhead space heaters have the same benefits as propane heaters, some generate even more heat than propane. Their fuel, however, is not explosive.

Be aware of ventilation requirements of your propane and diesel heaters (as well as other combustion heaters such as solid fuel heaters). It is extremely important that you vent out any fumes produced by the heater, as burning fuel produces carbon monoxide. Also, propane and diesel heaters heat by burning their fuels, and therefore require oxygen to work. The oxygen is drawn from the air surrounding the unit; while this helps to reduce moisture in the air, it can deplete the oxygen to dangerous levels, particularly during the winter when boats are sealed.

Bulkhead propane and diesel heaters do not have heavy electrical draws, although some have added fans, often running on 12 volts at very low amperage to help to circulate the heat. Consequently, there is very little risk of an electrical fire. Bulkhead heaters generally require venting, and some are designed to both bring in fresh air for combustion and exhaust the fumes. While this does not help as much to pull the moisture from the air (at least, not to the extent of a heater that combusts surrounding air), the result is a clean heat that does not deplete oxygen levels inside the boat.

Diesel bulkhead heaters can be fueled by separate tanks, such as gravity tanks, or can even pump diesel fuel from a tank in another part of the boat (including your diesel tank if your boat uses diesel fuel). This is typically done with a low amperage 12-volt fuel pump.

Be watchful of the temperature of the chimney and follow the recommended guidelines. If the unit is mounted too close to the deck, or the chimney property insulated, the deck can become extremely hot, which will damage the boat as well as introduce risk of fire or fumes.

I installed a bulkhead diesel heater that pumped fuel via a 12-volt pump from a portable plastic gas tank, which I fitted with a system that would allow the fuel hose to be snapped on and off. I bought a separate tank, and when one tank was almost depleted, I could go to any gas station, fill up a second tank—also fitted with the snapping system—and swap the tanks instantly, with never a moment of downtime or risk of a spill. Even in very cold weather, this tank switch could be done quickly and safely.

I supplemented this diesel system with an oil-filled electric space heater, which I liked because there is no exposed heating element, and there is a more manageable electrical draw. The unit works safely to warm the ambient air, bringing my living quarters to comfortable temperatures more quickly than diesel would alone—the downside to diesel heaters is that it takes about twenty minutes to get them going, and the process takes some supervision.

Central Heat

If I had it to do all over again, I would install a central heating system immediately upon moving aboard.

There are many advantages to central heating systems. The system uses a fuel, whether propane or diesel, that is far more efficient than electricity, therefore saving you money over more common electric space heaters. Another major advantage is that the heat is distributed throughout the boat, and a multi-zone thermostatically-controlled system can be installed. This means that you are only heating the boat (or select sections of the boat) when the ambient temperature drops below a designated level—as compared to other systems that must be manually controlled. Vents can be installed and adjusted to better target the quarters you want to heat. Another major advantage is that the heat is forced air, which is distributed by ducts hidden underneath the cabinets, berths, and benches. This means that the heater is not taking up valuable floor or bulkhead space in the boat, and that the ducts themselves give off radiant heat that is now capable of warming previously unheated areas of the boat, reducing condensation in hard-to-reach nooks and crannies.

Another advantage of many central heating systems is that they are often 12-volt systems allowing the boat to be heated effectively while underway.

The disadvantage to central heating is the initial cost and periodic maintenance costs of the unit. Compared to a $100 electric space heater, a central heating system can run in the thousands of dollars, not to mention the labor necessary to run the duct work and electrical lines. Much or all of this added cost can be recovered over time through decreased electric utility bills. Another disadvantage of the unit is that if the boat is not operational for the winter, fuel will need to be brought aboard regularly in containers and poured into the main tank (absent a workaround), a task that might have to be done in extremely cold temperatures—and fuel can be easily spilled, resulting in diesel odors and slick conditions (diesel fuel is very slippery).

Shrinkwrapping and Canvas Covers

Liveaboards in cold winter climates face a significant challenge not only in heating their boat, but also in keeping snow and ice off her. Snow and ice can cause dangerous conditions for standing and maneuvering on deck, trap occupants aboard or prevent access to the hatches, cut airflow and oxygen from getting to and escaping from the boat, and can damage the boat by causing pooled water around fittings. Moreover, if water pools in or under any fittings, or gets into the deck and freezes, the consequential expansion will pry any gaps apart, creating increased openings for water to leak and pool and cause increasing structural damage to the boat.

The only acceptable way to deal with freezing water on the deck is to prevent the snow and ice from accumulating on deck in the first place. Shrinkwrapping is a common method that boaters in cold climates use to prevent this from happening. It also adds a significant amount of protection from wind and weather.

Shrinkwrapping—Critical Protection!

Shrinkwrapping means building a frame over the structure of a boat with a door built into the frame, and putting plastic over the frame anchored to a line run around the deck or hull. The plastic is then heated, causing it to shrink into a taut shell.

The frame is typically made of disposable wood, but can be built out of metal conduit for boaters who expect to be shrinkwrapping year after year, as the conduit can be stored and reused.

The downside to shrinkwrapping is that it carries an expense, both in parts and labor, and the boat is not operational during the time the boat is wrapped (although this isn't typically a problem, since the engine may have been winterized and the boat is unusable anyway). One upside is that the shrinkwrap traps heat like a greenhouse on sunny days, and protects the deck from wind and weather. There were many subfreezing sunny days when the greenhouse effect allowed me to sit or work on deck in shorts and a T-shirt, and from time to time I would even have to open up the door to cool off both me and the boat a bit with a blast of arctic air.

There are several options for creating a door through the shrinkwrapping shell. These include zipper cutouts, plywood doors, and even some thermally insulating doors. Zippers, while the cheapest solution, are fragile and small, making for difficult entry and the possibility that the door might not even survive through a winter season. Plywood doors are the most common, and are typically disposable. Thermal doors are effective although rarely utilized—and unless you want to incur substantial expenses every year for a new door, often need to be stored. Thermal doors work well with conduit (reusable) systems.

A great alternative to shrinkwrapping is the use of a canvas cover. There are companies that create custom covers with transparent windows and easy-install/reusable frames. The advantage to these systems is that the canvas lasts a long time (although the windows do need to be replaced every few years), breathes well (obviously far better than plastic), and is environmentally responsible—all while doing an excellent job of retaining heat. The disadvantage is that canvas covers are expensive, much darker than translucent plastic shrinkwrapping, and require storage when not in use. Still, if you are planning to keep your boat for many years, this could be another possible solution.

In the Boston area, I know only a handful of liveaboards who do not shrinkwrap or cover their boats. While some of these liveaboards justify their decision by their desire to continue using their boats during the winter, this choice requires not only that the engine compartments be heated (since freezing temperatures could destroy the engine or even sink the boat), but that the boat be positioned on the far outside of some marinas so she will be able to leave a place highly susceptible to winter storms. (Cool-weather marinas may tie the docks together in the winter to better withstand heavy weather. This magnifies the exposure of the boat to weather conditions and storm damage.)

Cooling

In hot weather, ventilation continues to be one of the most important solutions for cooling a boat. Two other solutions for controlling hot temperatures and cooling a boat are (i) maintaining shade over as much of the boat and its ports as possible, and (ii) air conditioning. All of these solutions are commonly employed by liveaboards.

Shade

Shading your boat is easy and can be extremely effective in providing relief from the summer sun. A good shade system can even protect from the rain and can provide a wonderful opportunity to sit on deck and read, eat, drink, talk, or just watch the rain (one of my favorite activities) during less-than-favorable days.

There are many systems for shading a boat. Some boaters buy tarps and drape them over sailboat booms or hang them from high points on decks. Other boaters build or install frames made out of wood or metal, or even just rope. Other boaters have enclosures or *biminis* custom-built, creating actual sitting areas or rooms.

"A Very Hot Day"
Photo by Captain
Rob Jackson

C. Robb Worthington
S/V *Tara Rose*
Catalina 30
Living Aboard, Bermuda

The best solution is any one that gets the sun off the deck, hatches, and ports. Canvas makers can often very economically make wonderful creations that are durable and UV resistant and that will last for years. Any department or painting store that sells cheap tarps will do just fine, as well. A little creativity can dramatically increase your comfort.

Air Conditioning

There are three methods for air conditioning a boat: central air, hatch air, and portable air conditioning.

Central air conditioning units require a central unit as well as duct work to distribute the cool air. Some air conditioning units cool the air from the water (requiring one or more through-hulls) and work well in cool-water climates (poorly in warmer-water climates), while other units use coolants to do the same thing. Central units are highly effective and often work well with centralized heating systems, and like these, can be expensive to purchase and install. The upside to this type of system is that units are typically 12-volt systems and therefore can be used while cruising.

While houses can use window-sized air conditioning units, typical boats don't have that luxury. The second option is to purchase a unit that simply fits over a deck hatch. Some of these units can generate cool air as well as warm air (called reverse cycle) and can be very effective at helping to create a wonderfully comfortable environment without requiring structural modifications to the boat.

Be aware that you may or may not be able to use these systems while cruising, and depending on the boat and installation, you may need to remove them and seal the hatches before you leave the dock. The units tend to be bulky and take up deck space, as well.

One final option for air conditioning is the portable unit. These can be carried aboard, though they often require a port for venting. The advantage to these units is that they can be used anywhere, they will help to reduce moisture from the air, and they can be implemented with only a moderate cost and without labor or modifications to the boat. These units tend to be AC units and as such, are not designed for use while cruising.

Storms and Blizzards

Storms can cause problems for boaters, and while many boats are designed to handle heavy weather at sea, conditions encountered at dock can impose danger as well as significant discomfort.

Hurricane Francis Takes Her Toll
on Sam Densler's *Stories She Could Tell*

Throughout this book we've talked about ensuring that your marina is well-protected. Under normal conditions, this is simply a comfort issue. But when storms hit—particularly in marinas exposed to long fetches, such as coastal marinas—they can bring waves, tides, and extreme wind. You will most assuredly appreciate a well-protected marina under these extreme conditions.

It is incumbent upon all liveaboards, just as it is upon all boaters, to follow the weather closely. When difficult conditions are expected, it makes sense to add fenders and dock lines to keep the boat from contacting the dock or any other boats. In extreme conditions, it makes sense to remove electrical and water lines that can be ripped from the boat and/or dock, causing electrical damage or otherwise damaging or flooding your home.

From Paradise to Hell

Also be certain that anything that could fly off the boat has been secured or removed from deck.

Since there is no place to hide when a storm is inbound, preparation and a well-protected marina are the keys to managing safely and responsibly.

Snow and Ice

I want to expound further on the subject of snow and ice, for they can introduce several potentially serious dangers for the cold-weather liveaboard.

Snow and Ice on the Dock

I once walked down the metal ramp onto the dock at low tide (in Boston, it is a very steep walk down at low tide) and as I stepped onto the slick dock, I slipped and fell down toward the water. I stopped before I hit the water, but learned that hitting the dock even under the best of circumstances can be painful. Care should always be taken when the docks are wet or slick. Snow and ice require even more care.

If there is snow on the docks, it is a safe assumption that the water is "friggin cold," a temperature just a bit colder than "cold." As we all should know, swimming for even moderate lengths of time in "cold" water can result in diminished capacity, and ultimately hypothermia. Any time spent in "friggin cold" water can cause diminished capacity and hypothermia (and ultimately death) in an extremely short period of time. Cheap advice is that when the water is friggin' cold, don't go in. And if you enter accidentally off a dock, it might be quite difficult or impossible to extract yourself, even under the best of circumstances. If you're alone, you have big problems.

Remove snow and ice as quickly as possible. My marina is responsible for the docks, while the individual boaters are responsible for their finger piers. Have a snow shovel and bag of salt to help remove any residual ice, and if there is ice, do everything necessary to ensure that you don't slip and fall in. In the event that you *do* fall in, it would be nice to have a ladder around. Consider installing a swim ladder on your finger pier or otherwise near your boat, and hope you never need it. For those of you who reside in marinas that house liveaboards in the winter, it is your responsibility to make sure that the marina performs its obligations when it comes to maintaining safe conditions. For what it's worth, there may be laws requiring that common areas be maintained in a safe condition.

Snow and Ice on Deck

The first problem with snow and ice on deck is the danger inherent in any slick deck surface: You can be seriously injured with any slip or fall on deck, since fittings, lines, and obstructions abound. Falls off the boat can be equally dangerous, since a fall might involve hitting the fittings on the boat as well as the dock on the way to the water. It is hard enough to get back aboard when you are healthy, but getting back aboard once injured, particularly in cold conditions, could be impossible. I couldn't imagine myself being able to get back aboard if I fell off, but my cat has managed to climb back onto the dock on two occasions.

Obvious slipping and falling issues aside, freezing water is not supposed to be on your deck. Water has an amazing tendency to work its way into every available crevice—one perpetual challenge of boating is to find the newest leak and seal it. Aging fittings and sealant will ensure that water will always have some interesting and unexpected place to seep. Ice introduces major problems, since water expands when frozen and will pry the fittings off the deck, open up holes in the sealant, and cause deck delamination by prying the fiberglass off the deck core.

Once, after I had removed my shrinkwrapping, a late-season winter storm produced so much snow that I could not easily get out, and opening the companionway hatch caused a substantial amount of snow to enter the living quarters. I told the story over some drinks to some other liveaboards and it turned out that many others had similar stories, including one person who spoke of being entirely unable to get out of her boat, a rather dangerous proposition.

This leads me to one last point regarding snow and ice. Snow is heavy and ice is heavier. Put some of it on deck and you have a boat that will sit a bit lower in the water. Push the boat down far enough, and water could start siphoning into the boat through through-hulls that were previously above the water line , such as sink drains and vents.

This isn't a theoretical problem. This situation occurred on a large scale in the Pacific Northwest of the United States in a region that does not often experience extremely heavy winter weather conditions. A series of late winter storms caused boats to become so heavy that many sank because of water siphoning in through their above-the-waterline through-hulls, openings that the boat manufacturers never expected would be below the waterline.

The only solution to this is to make sure that every through-hull that could ever be below the waterline has a seacock installed, and that these seacocks are closed when necessary or not in use. This would have saved many boats that day.

Other Safety Issues

Every year, liveaboards in cold climates die as a result of their efforts to heat their homes. There are several initiating events, but typically two causes:

fire and improper ventilation. Fires occur when hot space heaters make contact with flammable items contained within the boat. Space heaters can ignite when tipped over or when run for lengths of time. The wires can overheat over time and can ignite. Propane, a highly flammable gas, can explode. Improperly vented heating systems can release carbon monoxide into the living quarters.

Boat fires are devastating. Boats provide very limited means of escape, and are often constructed entirely of materials that are flammable and/or release highly poisonous gases when burned. Boat fires often result in the loss of life; they have been known to travel quickly from boat to boat.

Freezing docks and decks, as well as snow and ice, have already been discussed. A conscientious liveaboard can help to mitigate these significant problems with proper care and planning. Other issues to be aware of are:

Hoses bursting. An internal hose that freezes can lose its integrity. In that event, when the ice thaws, water passing through a damaged hose will leak and depending on the water source may partially or totally flood the boat. Common burst hoses include those in the fresh-water system (the flood is limited to the amount of water in the water tank), city water system (the flood will occur under high pressure and will sink the boat), raw water intake or outtake (including engine, air conditioning and refrigeration through-hulls), and sewage through-hull (this may be prohibited by law, or the seacock may be required to be kept closed under coastal conditions). In general, it is recommended that responsible boaters close these seacocks when not in use, and when in use, owners should be aware and careful under all conditions, particularly cold weather.

Many liveaboards in freezing conditions will shut down their internal water systems in order to prevent this type of damage. It is not sufficient merely to cease using these systems; it is critical that water be drained. It is not uncommon to add antifreeze to these systems and circulate the mixture until the fresh-water system is filled *entirely* with antifreeze.

Another solution, for those liveaboards who wish to continue using their systems, is to heat all the areas where water resides (which may be difficult or impossible because of the proximity of water and holding tanks to the external walls of the hull), and to also wrap the water lines with insulation and heating tape, which can be plugged in and used to keep hoses warm.

Surrounding areas freezing. Some environments freeze regularly, other environments don't. All cold environments, even seawater, can and will freeze at some point. The freezing temperature for salt water is a little bit colder than fresh water, which freezes at 32F degrees, and moving water is not as prone to freezing as stagnant water. (As a fun tidbit, the freezing temperature of salt water is based on the amount of salinity of the water, typically about 28.5F degrees, although a physics guy on the Internet says that technically, salt water can't freeze, for the salt and water separate at the water's lower freezing point—explaining the salt mountains that form on glaciers. I haven't verified this.)

When water freezes around a boat, additional problems are introduced. Since water expands when frozen, surrounding ice can stress or even crush the hull. Even if that doesn't happen, the ice is rigid and the boat could be damaged by colliding with it.

There are a variety of methods to prevent ice from forming, including regularly breaking up any forming ice and placing bubblers around the boat to help keep the water moving and therefore liquid. Because of the damage freezing water can cause, this matter should be obsessively overseen.

Protecting key systems and the engine. Water enters boats in a variety of locations; this is very normal. Many stuffing boxes (points where the rudder and propeller shaft enter the boat) are designed to allow water to move through in order to provide some lubrication so the shaft can spin. Over time, this water will accumulate in and around the engine and engine block as well as in the bilge, fresh water system (obviously), and holding tank. If this water freezes, your engine or other key systems may be damaged.

Part of your winterizing function is to get this water out of the engine and the boat and "winterize" the engine and other systems to protect them. Often the best solution for this is to pump antifreeze throughout the engine and pour antifreeze in all locations where water might accumulate, namely under the engine, grey-water containers, fresh-water system, holding tank, and bilge. After the cold weather passes, this process is reversed.

Ventilation. Another unfortunate cause of injury and death is poor ventilation. While this topic has already been discussed a bit and will be discussed at more length in the Safety and Sanitation section, we should at least here state that ventilation not only helps create a comfortable living space by reducing heat, but also ensures safety by adding fresh, clean air to the living space and getting rid of bad air. Heating systems might deplete oxygen. Heating systems that incinerate propane or diesel fuels, or other solid fuel, will produce noxious/toxic gases such as carbon monoxide, which could result in death. A leak in the exhaust system of a boat could do the same. A simple installation of a smoke detector with a carbon monoxide detector that operates on a 9-volt battery can be a very economical protection against this danger.

Make sure that your home is properly vented so you can keep on living safely and comfortably.

12

Safety and Sanitation

Most of the liveaboards I know care very deeply about their surrounding environment. No one wants to sit on deck with the water surrounding his boat filled with floating sewage. Most of us like the smell of clean air and the look of clean water. We like to use clean bathrooms and keep our garbage contained in garbage cans and dumpsters with as few insects, rodents, and odors as possible. And we like to be safe and healthy.

Unsafe or unsanitary activities have an immediate and direct impact on ourselves, our neighbors, and our environment. Not all liveaboards cherish the protection of the environment and overall boat safety to the same extent as the rest of us. I've been to marinas that have resembled dumps, where sunken boats remain in their slips and where there is evidence of oil and fuel leaks, as well as garbage on the docks, and dirty and smelly bins and bathrooms, all creating dreadful conditions. Liveaboards clearly come in all types.

Safety is another concern that deserves our attention. Boats contain many things that can be extremely hazardous, both in terms of our health and in regard to the structural safety of our boats. Our safety problems may not be as noticeable as sanitation concerns, but they have a direct impact on our neighbors. Fire and storm damage are seldom limited to one boat, and it is often the heroic measures undertaken by fellow boaters—such as cutting boats loose from the dock—that save the marina and other boats.

Safety Precautions

Maintaining our boats in a safe condition is our most important job as liveaboards; this requires some work. It is our duty to be aware of potential dangers to ourselves, our crew, our passengers, and our boats.

I have had the privilege of sailing with a terrific captain during one blue-water cruise and another highly skilled trans-ocean sailor during another ocean voyage. There were problems during both trips, and each captain reacted with lightning speed, thinking clearly and coming up with a plan of action before I had even grasped the problem. I have also sailed with captains who couldn't tie their shoes during an emergency.

On one trip in particular (the maiden voyage of the *Fog*), the captain and I were sailing around Cape Cod in subfreezing weather and I had just brought lunch up from below. With the captain at the helm, we had only just taken our first bites of lunch when all of a sudden the captain tossed the meal aside. Before I even asked him why he had done that, the captain was already reacting to the fact that we had lost our steering. We later learned that the rudder had jammed against the hull after a rudder stop had fallen off. Because of neighboring shoals, this had very quickly become a life-threatening situation, and the captain's reaction may have saved the vessel and perhaps our lives.

Solving problems quickly, as a captain of any vessel must be able to do, not only requires a helmsman's knowledge and engaged awareness, but also a thorough knowledge of the mechanics of the boat and the proper way to use safety gear. At that stage in my sailing experience, I don't think I could have figured out the source of the problem. I wish that more boaters could have the opportunity to watch a top-notch captain react during an emergency. There is a calming nature to the decisions, to the thoughtful process and the brilliant reaction. Ultimately the trick is to identify the problem early and know how everything works so you can quickly troubleshoot the problems that are sure to arise.

As liveaboards, we are most typically our own captains, and yet it is surprising how many of us ignore the simplest safety precautions or, even worse, accept safety risks in order to save a small amount of money.

In addition to having the proper safety gear aboard, be certain that you have the tools to handle most types of repair situations, including screwdrivers, pliers, wrenches, an electrical repair kit, plumbing repair kit, a knife, extra wire, hoses, wooden bungs, and hose fittings. In addition, filters, belts, impellers and other replacement parts should also remain aboard.

Be sure your boat is properly secured to the dock with high-grade dock lines and high-quality fenders. Always have extra dock lines, of extra length, on board; these should be easily accessible to deal with other needs and emergencies that may arise…not just for your vessel, but also for others. Everyone will surely appreciate it when you have the basic equipment to react to the various situations that occur away from the slip.

Potential problems such as falling overboard are situations that can apply to all boaters, and those risks, as well as prevention and rescue procedures, will be discussed in virtually every other boating book and course offered. I'll leave those subjects to the boating experts, except to mention that great care should be taken to learn to use the safety gear you have on board. It was surprising to me how many captains in one particular transocean race had sea anchors on board that they had never deployed; they didn't know exactly how they worked. The faulty use of safety equipment can be as dangerous as, if not more dangerous than not having it. I've heard of a situation in which a sailboat *heaved to* with its sails configured so that the boat was kept with its beam *to* the rough seas.

This misapplication of one of the safest defensive sailing tactics ended up severely damaging the boat and seriously injuring one crew member.

These problems are not theoretical. I, and many others who have spent time on boats and on the water, have many stories about difficult times. When I tell you that these things *can* happen, I mean to say that these things *do* happen.

Fire and Fire Suppression

Fire is extremely dangerous to people aboard boats, as well as to other boats and neighbors. Boats incinerate very quickly, generating poisonous gases, and are fueled by the many flammable items kept aboard, such as propane gas, cooking alcohol, and alcohol-based cleaners and thinners (acetone, methanol, paint thinner, and so forth).

In addition, a boat, unlike a house, is not subject to zoning codes requiring multiple exits. Houses have windows of sufficient size for escape. Most boats generally have only one way out, and otherwise require exit through narrow hatches. To compound the problem, many boaters and liveaboards use space on deck for securing life rafts or other gear, particularly when under way, which may cover and prevent the hatches from being used. It is easy to get trapped in a boat.

Boat owners react differently when they see a boat on fire at a dock; some will cut the flaming boat loose from the dock, and others will cut the non-flaming boats away. The logic to keeping the flaming boat at the dock is so the fire can be treated. If the flaming boat is cut, no one really knows what the boat will float into, which risks additional unknown damage. I don't often read about fires being put out, but do usually hear of ignited boats burning to the waterline. I don't know the right answer, except to say that many of these fires were preventable.

The key to fire safety is not only preparation, but also detection and proper use of fire suppression equipment. Fire detection usually means smoke detectors. Be sure to install smoke detectors throughout, and test them periodically to ensure that they are in proper working order. Economical smoke detectors are fine; battery-operated units are easily installed and can work for extended periods of time with only a 9-volt battery. Combination detectors are better, combining smoke detection with carbon monoxide detection, a critical issue that will be discussed shortly. I understand that smoke/CO detectors can sniff out propane as well (although the problem with this is that since propane is heavier than air and sinks, by the time the propane rises to the level of the smoke detector, typically placed high up in a boat since smoke rises, the boat will be nothing short of a huge bomb).

With respect to fire suppression, the Coast Guard has requirements for fire extinguishers. Personally, I don't care what those minimal requirements are, since the best suggestion is to have more than the required number on board, in every berth and living space, with easy access. The fire extinguishers must be monitored and maintained to make certain that, if needed, they will function properly.

There are fire suppression systems that may be used in the engine compartment as well. There is very little risk of a fire with a diesel engine, but because of the explosive nature of gasoline, a fire suppression system is often suggested for gas engines. These systems are typically halon and, if fire is detected, the system sounds an alarm and triggers the fire suppression system immediately.

Propane

Propane, often used aboard boats for cooking and heating, is an economical and efficient gas, but is extremely flammable and explosive. As an added problem, propane is heavier than air. A hull, which is by definition air proof and waterproof below the waterline, is the perfect basin to store the escaped gas. Leaked propane gas will sink and fill the bilge where, unable to escape, the gas will just wait to be ignited. And it doesn't require a 30-pound tank to provide enough propane to explode; a leaking one-pounder can do the trick.

There are many places in a propane system from which gas can leak: at the tank, the fittings, the hoses, or, in the event that a pilot flame goes out, right out of a burner.

There are some highly recommended procedures that will significantly reduce the risk of a propane explosion on board. First, be sure that the propane tank is a "vented locker." A vented locker is a location where any gas spilled or leaked out of the tank will be unable to escape to any point except through a vent placed at the bottom of the storage container, directing the propane off of the boat.

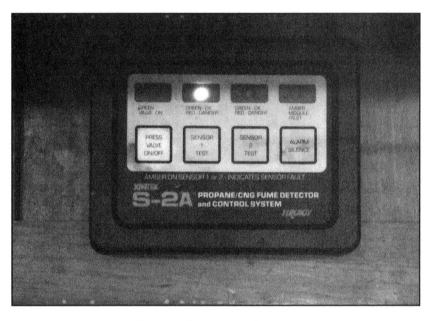

Propane Detection System

On my boat, I do not have room for a dedicated locker, so I store my one-pound containers in a forward locker used for spare dock lines, which has a water drain that drains overboard. When I used a propane bulkhead heater (before upgrading to diesel) I would place the tank either on the dock or the very front of the bow so that leaking gas would spill away from the boat.

Since the fittings and hoses may also leak, it is critical to test the connections (often done with soapy water) and install a propane detection system with sensors in the lowest parts of the boat, as well as an alarm and emergency shutoff, so that if propane is detected, the passengers can be notified and the gas flow terminated.

It is surprising how many boaters do not follow these simple safety rules, or are even aware of the consequences, and it is agonizing whenever there is a story of an explosion caused by a propane leak. On the water, even great care cannot prevent all circumstances in which something might go wrong, whether it be a malfunction, a storm, or, as is often the case, a mistake. Adequate safety precautions and systems might be the difference between a safe outcome and a less desirable one.

This type of disaster could have happened to me one night when some friends and I were having a barbecue at anchor off of one of the Boston Harbor Islands. After we finished cooking, a passenger who was taking the barbecue off of the rail unscrewed the one-pound propane tank, went below, and placed it on the galley counter. I was down below and heard the tank still releasing gas. The safety mechanism on the tank had jammed open and propane had leaked for an unknown length of time. Knowing the risk, I had that tank off the boat in one or two seconds as if it were a grenade. I was very worried, since I did not know how much propane had already accumulated in the bilge. The boat never did explode, but had there been a propane bubble, it could have ignited at that time or sometime later. I consider myself lucky to have escaped this problem.

Alcohol Stoves

There are two kinds of alcohol stoves: pressurized and non-pressurized. Non-pressurized stoves are quite safe, but pressurized stoves can be quite dangerous. Pressurized alcohol stoves are known as "curtain burners." My boat, like many other older boats that do not utilize propane or electricity for cooking, has such a stove.

Many boat owners do not like to use alcohol for various reasons: the added time spent to get the burners lit, the high initial flame, the low temperature cooking heat, and the fact that food can be tainted with the taste of alcohol fumes.

The reason for the nickname "curtain burner" is that pressurized alcohol, when being ignited, is pooled in the burner and lit. While it is heating the burner to allow for a traditional stove burn, it burns erratically and high. This flame can rise more than a foot above the stove. Lighting my stove on one occasion actually scorched the bottom of my curtains, and I ended up discharging a fire extinguisher—what a mess.

If you do use alcohol, store it properly and safely, and follow the lighting procedures. Move flammable items away from the flame and carefully supervise the initial lighting.

Space Heaters

Every winter, fires are started by space heaters. Electric space heaters can start fires in many different ways: by being plugged into outlets that are wired with insufficient wiring (causing resistance and heat), by the heaters being placed too close to flammable items, and by being tipped over.

To ensure that the wiring is safe, inspect the system to see that the wires are marine grade and of a sufficient gauge, properly connected to a circuit breaker or fuse, and that all connections are made with marine connectors and protected with heat-shrink tubing. Anything less will corrode and can significantly increase the risk of an electrical problem.

I purchased my boat from a lifelong boater who, as it turned out, had taken some shortcuts with the electrical wiring, and had wired the bilge pump with household wiring and wire nuts. Sure enough, all of the connections failed and the interior of the boat flooded. Don't take anything for granted when it comes to a safe electrical system.

Some space heaters have safety mechanisms that are supposed to shut down the heater in the event that the heater is tipped over. I can tell you from experience that these safety mechanisms do not always work. The only safe way to use a portable space heater is to supervise it when operating.

My closest call with an electric space heater occurred when I was reading in my v-berth and the heater was down on the floor outside the cabin. A blanket had fallen off the berth and landed on the heater. I soon smelled the smoke, and the smoke detector went off immediately after that. Though a serious fire was prevented, some bad odors lingered for a while and that blanket had a bit of a burn mark.

There are viable alternatives to space heaters with ceramic or exposed heating elements. Oil-filled heaters are regarded as much safer, having no exposed heating element; they become quite warm, but not so hot as to risk igniting anything around them.

Be very aware of the risks associated with these heaters and take careful precautions. Smart people die every year from circumstances that could have been identified and rectified with a little effort.

Gasoline Fumes

Gasoline vapors are flammable. When gasoline inboard engines are used, the engine compartments often collect fumes that need to be flushed out prior to starting the engine. That's why boats that use inboard gasoline engines have a bilge fan, which must be turned on for a designated length of time before the engine is started. Failing to do this creates a fire hazard.

Water, Floods, and Sinking

Despite the existence of millions of boaters, scuba divers, water sports participants, swimmers, and beachgoers (and I fall into all of the above categories), humans do not mix well with water. We require a breathing apparatus when under it, and can be swept away by an unexpected current. The water and the various creatures in it can hurt us in many ways. The sea is not our element.

Boats, when working as intended, do a wonderful job of protecting us by keeping us up and out of the water. Boats do this particularly well when the water is kept on the outside of the hull.

Yet water does come into the boat naturally. Many stuffing boxes are designed to leak a drop or two a minute (which will add up significantly over time). Water will gradually accumulate in the bilge from this and other sources and, when the water level rises to a certain point, the bilge pump turns on and takes that water overboard.

Boaters don't like to see water accumulate inside their homes and are fanatical about locating its source when they see it. While some boats can actually float when flooded, most cannot. Even the boats that can float will sink much lower in the water, becoming inoperable and more susceptible to other dangerous marine conditions. The idea is to take steps to ensure that the boat is safe and dry and, in the event of a problem, have provisions on board to deal with it.

Bilge Pumps

The bilge pump sits in your bilge and switches on when the water rises to a certain level, draining the water overboard.

Keep this pump in working condition. It is not sufficient to know that the bilge pump works—you must periodically inspect the wiring and bilge for anything that could indicate an impending failure or otherwise block the water flow or drainage. Bilge pumps do fail and burn out over time. When the pump fails, you do not want to be in a situation where the water level can rise above the floorboards or to any unsafe level. Have a replacement on board.

An examination of the bilge typically turns up visible water, which should be well within safe limits. Be sure that your bilge pump float switch is set to a level that does not keep the bilge pump running, but does not allow the water level to get too high. It is recommended that you consider adding a second or even a third bilge pump, each slightly higher than the last for redundancy and added capacity. Also consider installing a high-water alarm in connection with the second pump level, so you know when both pumps are engaged, or to indicate the failure of the first pump.

Be certain that the bilge pump(s) is/are wired in such a method as to ensure that the pump(s) will work even when all of the electronic circuits have been shut off, as many boaters shut all of the power down when they leave the boat.

There might be occasions when either the float switch fails or you need to operate the pump manually. I highly recommend a bilge pump switch that has three settings: on, off, and auto. "Auto" allows the pump to operate when the float switch is triggered, "off" disables the bilge pump, and "on" will override the float switch. This system has come in handy for me on many occasions and only failed me once, when I inadvertently hit the switch to the off position. Don't do that.

A boat can flood for two reasons: the bilge pumps fail, or the water enters the boat too quickly for the bilge pump to keep up. A reliable backup (capable of operating under all conditions including power loss) is the incorporation of a manual bilge pump with a handle placed topside so that, in the unfortunate instance that there is too much water below or some other failure, the bilge can be cleared of water without your having to get wet. Also, if the bilge pump below cannot keep up with the influx of water, another crew member can operate the manual bilge pump in addition to the pump below to drain the boat more readily. Many new boats are now shipped with this as a standard safety accessory. I would have much appreciated this when, in the middle of winter, my boat flooded with frigid water.

Lastly, before talking about the various ways water can enter a boat, it is important to mention the final, and critical, safety precaution. *Listen.* If the bilge pump turns on often, water is entering too quickly. Find out where the water is coming from!

There are many areas for water to enter. Assuming that a boat's hull is structurally sound, water can enter anywhere there is a through-hull, any hose or system connected to the through-hull, anywhere that a shaft passes through the hull (such as a propeller shaft and rudder shaft), or any leak in the fresh-water system. Water can also enter from the deck, ports, hatches, and companionway during wet and cruising conditions, but those are not the types of concerns we are talking about.

Through-hulls and Seacocks

Through-hulls are holes through the hull. Any through-hull below the waterline will flood a boat if water is allowed to enter in an unconstrained manner. Therefore, a leak in any system connected to a below-the-waterline through-hull will flood and sink the boat if unattended.

Through-hulls are necessary. Engines that use outside (raw) water to stay cool use a through-hull to bring in water from outside the boat, and they exhaust that water through a second through-hull just barely above the waterline. Most heads use raw water to flush, and those boats that are equipped with a macerator to remove waste, or even a direct-to-overboard toilet, will have another through-hull where the waste exits the boat. Air conditioning and refrigeration systems often use raw water, as well. Offshore vessels may have a salt-water faucet in the galley so dishes can be washed with raw water before being rinsed with fresh water, in order to preserve fresh-water supplies.

Any through-hull below the boat's waterline *must* have a seacock, a valve that can be opened and closed with a simple 90-degree turn of the lever. Older boats were equipped with "gate" valves (valves that look like those on a gardening hose), which have a dial that must be turned many times around to open and close the valve. Not only do gate valves fail, but in an emergency you do not want to spend your time turning the dial around and around.

Your primary defense against flooding is the seacock. It is incumbent upon you that you know exactly where all of the seacocks are, so you can quickly access them in the event of a leak in any system. Liveaboards have a tendency to expand their possessions into every crevice, and seacocks tend to become more inaccessible. Be careful of this. Moreover, it is recommended that seacocks be closed for any system when not in use, as well as when there is no one aboard. This suggestion is often disregarded.

It is also recommended that seacocks be installed on through-hulls above the waterline, as well. The boats in the Pacific Northwest sank when above-waterline through-hulls without seacocks sank below the waterline as a result of the added weight of snow and ice. There was no way to stop the water from entering these boats.

When I was sailing, my boat commonly heeled over to the point that the through-hulls for the drain for either my galley sink (when heeled to port) or head sink (when heeled to starboard) would drop below the waterline. On a gentle heel, the sink would fill with sea water. On a hard heel, I have watched my sink overflow. Holding this position would have flooded the boat. I resolved this by adding seacocks to those through-hulls and closing them when under way.

If water is coming in, you must find it. If you don't know where it is, shut every seacock first and test the systems one by one. When you find the system that is leaking, figure out where and why. If the leak is from a faulty hose, cut the hose and add a hose connector and clamps. If you don't have the proper equipment, you may use a wooden bung to temporarily block the problem hose.

Water Hookups

"Water hookups" refer to what is often called "city water," or a water connection that allows an external hose to be connected directly to the fresh-water system, bypassing the water tank. This has the benefit of allowing water to be used without filling a water tank.

There are two problems: One, the water is coming aboard at a very high pressure, more than most on-board fresh-water systems ever typically endure; and two, in freezing climates, both the external and internal hoses can freeze. We'll deal with the issue of freezing hoses in a bit. The problem with the high-pressure flow of water, however, is a very real safety concern.

When a boat is connected to a water hookup and any part of the fresh-water system develops a leak, an unlimited quantity of water will flow unimpeded at high pressure into the boat, flooding her. Safety procedures should require that the city water be turned off when not in use and certainly when away from the boat. This can often be achieved with a simple 90-degree valve, like a seacock. Like closing other seacocks, boaters often neglect this task as they become more convinced that their systems are functional and reliable.

Another safety mechanism is a flow gate that opens when triggered by an internal system or closes when the water flows aboard too quickly. These are helpful systems, but can be very expensive and are typically not part of a standard installation.

The only safe protection against flooding from city water is not to use city water. Inevitably, one day you will forget to turn off the water when you leave the boat. While many liveaboards enjoy the benefits of city water, it is easy to read about the boats that have gone under from what would have otherwise been a small problem.

Stuffing Boxes

Different systems are employed to permit equipment that passes through the hull, such as propeller and rudder shafts, to function properly without leaking. Many boats use a stuffing box, or a system in which the shaft enters the boat through two nuts that tighten onto a mechanism through which the shaft is passed. This mechanism contains a "stuffing" to both allow the shaft to spin and prevent water from entering. Some stuffing boxes are designed to leak water at a drop or two per minute to maintain lubrication, and others are designed not to leak at all.

If your boat has a stuffing box that is designed to leak (some aren't), be sure that the flow is at the recommended rate (*e.g.*, perhaps one drop per 60 seconds). If your stuffing box is not designed to leak, make sure that it doesn't.

For stuffing boxes that leak, as the stuffing gradually compresses, the water will flow more quickly and the stuffing box either needs to be tightened or the stuffing replaced. It doesn't take long for a faster flow to have a material impact on how often the bilge pump will need to cycle on. If you can't find any other location for the water accumulation, be sure to check these locations. Many young boaters do not even think to examine the stuffing boxes, or even know what they are, but it is important to be aware of every source of water.

Engine (Raw Water) System

Some engines require that raw (sea) water flow through the engine to cool it. This water runs into the boat past a seacock—typically into a strainer to filter out grass and things that can cause engine problems— runs into the engine, exits the engine, and passes out through a through-hull that is typically above the waterline.

It is important that you not only understand the flow of your engine but also know which hoses are carrying this water. If one of them breaks, you will sink unless you get that seacock closed. If the strainer lid is too loose, the water will continue to flow into the boat as well.

I once tried to clean my raw-water strainer without closing the seacock. The water flowed in so fast that it was extremely difficult for me to close the strainer to stop it. I closed the seacock and tightened the strainer lid. I learned a lot about water pressure that day.

Freezing Water

For those liveaboards in cold-weather climates, freezing temperatures can be not only uncomfortable, but also dangerous and highly destructive in the event that water freezes inside a hose or the engine, or the water outside the boat freezes. This danger is substantially increased if a burst hose is connected to an unlimited supply of water, such as external seawater through a through-hull or a city water hookup. In that case, if the seacock is not closed and the leak repaired, the boat will flood.

Damage can also be caused when internal hoses freeze and burst. The freshwater tank in my boat has a capacity of approximately 70 gallons and the water heater another 6 gallons. Pump that into the cabin floor and that's one hell of a flood, even if it is not enough to endanger the boat.

Also, as mentioned previously, water in and around the engine can freeze, severely damaging the engine, engine block, and other key equipment.

Liveaboards in cold climates have to make some decisions about their engines and water systems during cold seasons. Hoses that run through areas of the boat that are not constantly heated are highly susceptible to freezing. Unless the engine needs to be used during freezing conditions, it is strongly suggested that the engine intake seacock be closed and water in and around the engine and hoses be evacuated and replaced with antifreeze.

Regarding city water, cold-weather marinas typically run their water lines deep enough underwater so that they are not exposed to freezing temperatures. But near the waterline and above, the water hoses could burst and, if used during the winter season, should be protected, even though their bursting is an inconvenience that will not affect the condition of your boat.

If city water is to be used, the hose bringing the water to the boat will have to be insulated and heated, probably with (electric) heat tape, which will heat the hose to keep the water above freezing. The water lines inside the boat will also need to be insulated and heated, and electric heat tape is a common solution for that as well. Bear in mind that if the electricity fails for any reason, the heat will turn off and the hoses again will be susceptible to freezing.

Many liveaboards want to continue to use their toilets during the winters (I don't blame them!). I, however, am not willing to leave any seacocks open for fear of having to wake up wet one morning. In lieu of using raw water to flush, I use a mixture of water and antifreeze kept in a five-gallon bucket. That is also critical to ensure that the contents of the waste holding tank do not freeze, as well.

Also, I elect to winterize my entire fresh-water system, as my primary water tank is in the very bow of the boat and impossible to properly heat. Accordingly, I drain the water and run antifreeze throughout the fresh-water system to ensure that no water line can freeze. Unfortunately, that means that during the winter, I have no running water in the galley and head, and am relegated to using the marina's showers, sometimes having to wait in line. It is an inconvenience that cold-climate liveaboards are subjected to in order to ensure that their homes are safe and their health is preserved.

Slick Docks

Another safety issue that should be discussed is slick docks and dock safety. I have seen people fall and hurt themselves without making any mistake at all other than a false step. I've seen very competent boaters misstep getting onto their boats, and in one case watched a lifelong liveaboard walk right off the end of a pier (he had had a few drinks and was walking with a pretty woman while engaged in conversation—perhaps one of the funniest things that I've ever seen).

Some of the stories told on the docks are even scarier, and involve drunken or otherwise stupid behavior causing falls and slips. Just as this book is being written, a newspaper reported a story of a woman who fell into the water while trying to fend off another boat and was killed when crushed by the two boats, even though many people tried to keep the boats apart.

Docks are dangerous by their very nature, as they are bordered by water and have sharp edges, inflexible piers, metal faucets, very sharp cleats and dock boxes, and other obstructions that can cause serious injury and/or send the victim into the drink. Also, many docks can be very slick in wet weather and downright dangerous with snow or ice.

A person who falls in the water might not be able to get out, and if the person falls in during the winter, he might be exposed to temperatures that can first disorient and then incapacitate, making escape from the water impossible. I will repeat a previous recommendation that you or your marina install a swim ladder at some point near your boat so you have a way to get out in the event that you fall in.

Carbon Monoxide

Every year there are stories told about disasters caused by carbon monoxide, a gas that is colorless and odorless. Exposure starts with a headache, then kills by gently putting the unfortunate victim to sleep.

Carbon monoxide is released by the exhausts of engines as well as through the use of certain heating systems (such as my bulkhead heating systems) and generators; it can invade a boat's living space and areas surrounding the boat in any number of ways, including a leak in the venting or exhaust systems. Carbon monoxide can also invade through ports or hatches if being generated by neighboring boats running their engines.

In well-publicized cases, there were deaths caused by carbon monoxide generated by the exhausts of some houseboats. In several cases, exhaust was released and pooled under the boat's swim platforms, and children playing in the water spent enough time around and under the platforms to end up being poisoned by the fumes, knocked out, and killed.

Contrary to popular belief, a person does not need to be in a confined area in order to become poisoned. In no-breeze conditions, studies have shown carbon monoxide levels to increase quickly to very high levels on the deck near the boat exhaust, often more than ten times the safe limit throughout the aft (outdoor) portion of a boat. Activities such as playing or getting towed closely behind a boat, setting fishing lines, or even sitting on the back rail near the exhaust have been known to endanger boaters.

The symptoms of poisoning might include a severe headache, dizziness, confusion, nausea, fainting, and ultimately death, while low or accumulating levels of poisoning might involve shortness of breath, mild nausea and a headache, and symptoms similar to the flu or seasickness. Low levels can also lead to drowning if the person faints.

It's important to mention that even a low level of carbon monoxide, if exposure is continuous, will gradually aggregate in the victim's bloodstream, eventually becoming dangerous or fatal. This is called *cumulative poisoning*.

The best defense against carbon monoxide poisoning is a combination of awareness and one or more carbon monoxide detectors. This should be an absolute requirement. Venting systems should be carefully checked and maintained and the engine and exhaust systems examined periodically. Nonetheless, since carbon monoxide is odorless, it is a very economical and important investment to install detectors that will warn if carbon monoxide is starting to accumulate. Many of these detectors double as smoke detectors as well. If carbon monoxide is detected or suspected, get the victim to fresh air and immediately seek medical care.

There are pamphlets warning boaters of the risks of carbon monoxide, including pamphlets developed by the U.S. Coast Guard and many states; any search of the Internet should identify several sources.

General Health

While ours is a world surrounded by carcinogens and pollutants and things that can inflame allergies and cause discomfort, there are three general health issues that liveaboards need to be aware of: safe food, safe water, and mold/mildew.

Safe Food

Safe food is a product of good refrigeration and proper cooking temperature (for most food, excluding staples such as chips and pop tarts). Great care should be maintained to ensure that food is adequately maintained and prepared.

Moreover, it is sometimes difficult to clean dishes, utensils, and cooking essentials to the extent we would like, particularly if we are trying to conserve water while cruising. Additionally, due to the excess moisture in the environment, even clean dishes can show mold after a very short time.

Safe Water

Water hoses and holding tanks are prolific areas for the growth of bacteria that can result in off-putting odors, bad tastes, and illness. Water that is kept aboard for extended periods will be more likely to become stale and contain bacteria.

Many liveaboards will not drink water that flows from the water tank, and always have gallons of fresh water for drinking.

Many other liveaboards use only one tap in the boat for drinking water and install filtering systems to try to improve the taste and cut down on bacteria (often a designated drinking water faucet so as to preserve the life of the filter). More aggressive filtering requires that water be filtered while being brought aboard as well, and some liveaboards have set up very impressive systems designed to make drinking water safe.

Tablets should also be purchased for the water tank; adding small amounts of bleach can help to improve the situation. Be sure to run the water sufficiently, if necessary clearing one or two tanks of water in order to help clean the tank and move any antibacterial chemicals through.

Mold and Mildew

Mold and mildew can often be handled with a good cleaning program, ventilation, and a dry boat. Mold that permeates fabrics and other similar materials may be hard to clean. There are also air filters that help to clean the air of contaminants and particles; these can often help as well with the interior atmosphere of the boat.

Sanitation

Common sense and decency should dictate behavior with regard to general cleanliness. In the event that common decency is not a sufficient incentive to be responsible, there are laws and health codes that make certain actions illegal.

One of the traits of liveaboards is that we pay attention to the details that surround us, and can quickly identify unsafe or unsanitary conditions as a community. With regard to sanitation issues, we are often the first to complain in order to make our lives more comfortable.

We're talking, of course, about things like leaving garbage on board boats or on the docks or pumping out our boats in the marina. Unfortunately, there is clearly not enough common sense or decency in this world, and the behavior undertaken by many members of our community and the world is not only indecent, but deplorable. On more than one occasion I have awoken to a marina whose water left the hull of my and many other boats coated with a layer of human excrement. On occasion I'd hear the macerator in a boat and know which boat was emptying its holding tank. Ironically, my marina provides a free pump-out service, and the boat owner does not even need to be available, for the marina staff will just swing by and do it. Was it so difficult that the guilty boat owner did not even want to call the marina to schedule a pump-out?

I appeal to common decency, but absent that, think we should take a moment to talk about the laws regarding sewage and sanitation issues. While I personally don't like laws telling me what I can and can't do, I believe the law telling people that it is illegal to cover the environment and neighbors' homes with sewage is a pretty good one.

Sewage (Also Known as Black Water)

It is illegal to discharge your holding tank or otherwise release sewage within a certain number of miles of the coast of the United States (currently three miles). There are similar laws in much of the world. Confined waterways have their own rules and regulations, but most are "zero-discharge" zones, meaning that regardless of where you are in that body of water, it is illegal to discharge any sewage at all. Many confined waterways even prohibit treated sewage. Penalties for failure to comply with this requirement can be very severe.

Many boats, mine included, are equipped with a variety of options for dealing with sewage. Your boat may be configured to flush not only to a holding tank, but also directly overboard. In addition, many holding tanks can be connected to a macerator that processes and then pumps waste from the holding tank overboard.

The Coast Guard and other authorities that police boats for sewage discharge are familiar with these systems. Marinas may police this, as well. If you are in regulated waters at a marina or cruising, you are subject to inspection for sewage discharge. The authorities expect that the direct discharge valve is off; indeed, they might require that the valve be *taped* in the off position with a specific kind of tape that cannot be removed without being torn. The authorities might drop dye tablets into your head and flush out the system, and should the outside water change colors will cite the boat owner for violation of this law.

Also, for boats with macerators and the capability of discharging holding tanks overboard, the authorities will often require that the discharge seacock be closed at all times while the vessel is within their jurisdiction. Sometimes the authorities will even require that boats in particular jurisdictions disable overboard systems entirely. Failure to follow these laws will result in a citation or more significant penalty.

Gray Water

Gray water refers to waste water that is not sewage. Examples of gray water include shower water and water that has run through either the galley or head sinks (used for washing dishes, brushing teeth, and the like).

Gray water regulation is fairly new, but appears to be gaining momentum. Boats were typically fitted with through-hulls for direct discharge of sink water, while shower water was often discharged with a separate bilge pump and pumped directly overboard.

Gray water regulation raises many complications for liveaboards should boats be prohibited from discharging gray water directly. What do we do with the water? Should boats add an extra holding tank, like RVs? Boats lack excess space, and the amount of gray water created from a shower or resulting from washing dishes can be significant, and can quickly fill up the sewage holding tank. Some boat owners in no-discharge zones mount buckets below the sinks and handle the discharge manually. Obviously, there are very real dilemmas in this regard, and as the rules develop, there will be more to come on this.

Pollution Generated from Cleaning and Washing Solutions

Boaters wash their boats with boat soap and waxes. They clean their bilges with bilge cleaner. They wash their dishes with detergents. All this gray water is often permitted to be released directly overboard.

These soaps, or the things we are washing, might contain pollutants. It is important, therefore, for the environmentally conscious liveaboard to pay attention to the soaps and detergents that are used on board. Marine stores often offer a wide variety of choices. (Choose non phosphate, biodegradable products.)

Garbage

Mice and rats and cockroaches and other insects like food and garbage. Garbage smells.

Many marinas have rules regarding the handling of garbage, requiring that garbage be placed in containers or a dumpster provided by the marina. Health codes probably require this as well, and if there is an increasing sanitation problem, there is typically some recourse.

Personal responsibility suggests that liveaboards should remove garbage from their boats regularly so as not to attract unwelcome animal guests, and not store garbage on the docks for the same reason. There's not much else to say on this issue.

13

Government Oversight

It seems unfortunate that we have to take time to speak about government oversight and regulation, but while some of the applicable laws are important for *all* boaters, some are exceedingly relevant to liveaboards - since our boats are our homes and we open up our homes to the inspection of our government. This section is intended to provide a brief overview of the types of laws and rules that impact liveaboards.

The discussion of law is offered with great respect for the safety concerns as well as the risk of tremendous misconduct and harm to society. The water not only causes countless injuries and death, but also provides traffickers of illegal items (including sex, drugs and weapons) a significant path in and out of the country, direct access to areas of national security and historic monuments, and so forth, each justifying increased oversight over our coasts and waterways. Moreover, in today's climate of violence and terrorism, we all recognize that ports and ships—including cruise ships, LPG and natural gas tankers, cargo ships, and many other types of ships and property—provide high-profile targets for terrorism and importation methods for contraband. The U.S. Coast Guard, as well as law enforcement and U.S. Customs Service, are working very hard to ensure that illegal activity, including terrorism, does not strike U.S. ports or enter through U.S. waters. While this oversight has always been an imposition on boaters, its current increase is a symptom of the times.

As you get to know more members of the liveaboard community, you will probably find that many of us enjoy the idea of departing from civilization. We like to be left alone and want to be able to head out to the wild blue whenever we seek freedom from interference. And while many of us excel at the legal requirements for safety and care more deeply about sanitation issues and environmental concerns than does the general public, the additional governmental scrutiny is contrary to our lifestyle. It pains me to know that by virtue of our life on the water we have largely waived our rights of privacy and freedom from unreasonable search and seizures within our homes. Essentially, as a matter of law there is little "expectation of privacy" in boats (the laws did not expect them to be used as homes) and the greater mobility have together justified diminished protections from state intrusion.

Governments and states generally create their laws assuming that people live on land. This is quite a problem for liveaboards. Perhaps in a water-bound society the laws might be more considerate of the liveaboard lifestyle, but in the United States they are not. As an example, many liveaboards use post office boxes as their only means to receive mail, and find that they cannot register their driver's licenses or register to vote because in some jurisdictions a P. O. Box is not legally sufficient. Problems such as registering a car make simple tasks far more complicated. Also, in the modern climate of the world's battle against terrorism, under the U.S.A. Patriot Act's money laundering provisions, all financial institutions (banks, stock brokers, etc.) are required to receive a physical address as well as other forms of verifiable identification from their clients. Will your bank be willing to take a P.O. Box as an address anymore? No. What about a marina address? Maybe.

One solution to this has been is to use a service provider that provides a legal address for cruising liveaboards. They provide an address for mail delivery and vehicle registration and are supposedly experts at mail forwarding. I don't know how these providers will fare in the evolving climate but more and more of these service provider addresses are included in the PO Box databases resulting in declined accounts. While these rules largely make sense in the grand scheme, this is a real problem for us liveaboards, and it is getting worse.

As we delve into the subject of law and rule, we should start with the general principal. In the United States, laws are created by the federal government, as well as state and local governments. Sometimes these governments delegate rule-making authority to agencies that, after following certain procedural requirements, establish rules that also have the power of law. Laws can be criminal—meaning that a person convicted of the law can be charged a monetary penalty as well as sentenced to serve time in jail—or civil, in which the sole penalty is monetary (except as you will read below in the subject of forfeiture). Criminal offenses must be proved beyond any reasonable doubt, while civil judgments can be rendered whenever it is "more likely than not" that a civil offense was committed.

General Requirements

When we take our homes for a cruise, we are no different than pleasure boaters and are subject to all of the same rules as the rest of the boating community. Many laws and regulations are based on important safety concerns, and responsible boaters are often great advocates for their and others' compliance with these rules. We all recognize that failing to keep a good watch, overindulgence in alcohol or drugs, lack of extra safety precautions for children, and failure to use proper lights can all easily endanger our lives as well as the lives of our passengers and fellow boaters. Almost daily we hear of a boater who has become endangered because of something that he could have easily prevented. And we hear of drowning and boat accidents every day.

While it is your responsibility to learn and know the laws that apply to you, you should be quite certain that there are laws related to the following offenses:

- Reckless operation of a boat
- Operating while intoxicated
- Operating or giving permission to operate an unregistered boat or boat with an expired registration (or an undocumented boat)
- Failing to properly display any required registration/ identification insignia
- Failing to maintain proper registration identification or present it to boarding officers
- Operating a boat more than a designated number of days without notifying and possibly registering in a jurisdiction
- Failing to report a change of address of a registered boat (not always obvious for transient liveaboards)
- Failing to exhibit lights as required between sunset and sunrise
- Failing to stop, assist, and give name and address at the scene of a boating accident or incident
- Failing to obey water markers
- Operating in an area designated for swimmers or too close to a scuba diver flag
- Depositing, throwing, or discharging any refuse matter of any kind into certain water (rule varies based on type of refuse and location)

- Cruising or anchoring in an area prohibited for such activity
- Failing to maintain required safety gear on board or not utilizing safety gear as required by law
- Maintaining or transporting illegal contraband

Although laws and regulations may be issued by different authorities, including the U.S. Congress, the Coast Guard, the Environmental Protection Agency, the Commonwealth of Massachusetts, etc., they may be enforced by multiple agencies including, for instance, the Coast Guard and state and local police, as well as a harbor master.

It is rare to find a boater who, having spent any time on the water, has not been boarded and inspected by some enforcement entity at one point or another. Engaging in activities that draw notice or are of higher risk will attract more attention and draw greater scrutiny. I, in my sailboat, have never been boarded but have had the state police pull up alongside and ask me to provide documentation as well as show them various safety gear, including life jackets, flares, and a fire extinguisher. I did and they left. It is unlikely that the authorities would have believed that my boat, with a hull speed of just under seven knots, would ever be used to smuggle anything. Nonetheless, take a tour of the postings in the liveaboard email groups and you will read countless reports of stories told by various liveaboards that reflect more difficult experiences, situations in which the authorities conducted armed boardings randomly searching for more than just required safety gear or properly instituted sanitation systems.

Limitations on Liveaboards

Marinas have differing views on liveaboards, and impose various policies and restrictions. A marina's ability to establish its own rules should be championed. Some governments and agencies around the world have taken it upon themselves to come up with their own requirements or limitations for liveaboards, passing rules instructing marinas on what they can and cannot do.

There are obvious albeit sometimes misguided politics in the passage of many of these rules. For instance, a government that is trying to demonstrate to its constituency a policy that is tough on pollution may target liveaboards, a small, unorganized, and politically weak group. The allegation that liveaboards are major polluters is often rebutted but seldom successfully defended against.

As an example, the San Francisco Bay is a body of water overseen by the Bay Conservation Development Commission, a state agency. BCDC has passed a rule prohibiting a marina from allocating any more than 10 percent of its total slips to liveaboards. To make matters worse, while BCDC has stated (to me) that the definition of a liveaboard is a person who has no other residence, many marinas have developed more stringent policies in order to ensure compliance, such as defining a liveaboard as someone who spends, on average, more than two nights per week aboard. If a boater violates this rule, the boater will be asked to depart the marina, whether or not he is in fact truly living aboard.

Liveaboards who attempt to skirt the liveaboard rules have been dubbed "sneak-a boards" and live under the constant risk that they will be without a home port with little or no notice. Some marinas are, to the contrary, extremely lax in their enforcement of these rules. As long as the system remains one of self-enforcement, we will see this wide range of marina compliance, but any change in the enforcement of these limitations will have a dramatic effect on the lives of a large number of liveaboards.

On the bright side, one example of similar legislation that was successfully rebuked was in the Seattle/Puget Sound region, in which various agencies attempted to pass legislation prohibiting liveaboards from living on certain waters. My friend Don Stonehill organized the Liveaboard Association of Puget Sound and successfully lobbied, sued, and succeeded in preventing the ban. The group now enjoys a good and informative relationship with governmental bodies, and continues to work for the general benefit of boaters nationwide.

Safety

Federal as well as state and local laws and rules require that certain safety gear be maintained on board in an accessible and operational condition, and that boats be operated safely in accordance with local requirements as well as responsible behavior. It is incumbent upon you, as a boater and captain of your vessel, to know, understand, and comply with these rules.

Alcohol and Drugs

Laws relating to the use of drugs or alcohol, or possession of illegal substances, are generally pretty uniform across many jurisdictions. Those of us who are sharing the water want fellow boaters to conduct themselves in a manner that does not endanger us, our passengers, or our boats.

Use

The law related to the use of alcohol aboard a boat was formerly one that required reckless boating as a prerequisite, and the penalties often were quite light. There were many very serious injuries and deaths caused by intoxicated boaters doing some fairly egregious things, and the laws became stricter.

These days, boating under the influence (BUI) laws exist; they read similarly to driving under the influence (DUI) laws. Just as a sample, the Commonwealth of Virginia prohibits a boat from being operated while under the influence of drugs or alcohol, and presumes that blood alcohol concentrations of 0.08 percent or more constitute being under the influence.

The penalties for violating the Virginia law include fines of up to $2,500, imprisonment for up to 12 months, revocation of the privilege to operate a boat for up to 3 years, and enrollment in an alcohol safety program. Other states have set more stringent requirements, including tiered penalties for multiple offenses and revocation of vehicle driving privileges for boating violations.

In addition to these BUI penalties, reckless behavior that risks injury or death to another may also justify a criminal complaint if the actions of the person, intoxicated or not, rise to the level of a criminally negligent activity. Speedboating in a no-wake zone or swimming/diving area is an example of criminal negligence, and can justify a criminal charge, including a manslaughter charge (an unintentional murder caused by a grossly reckless act) or significant civil award if the behavior is "reckless" or performed under the influence.

Possession

The mere possession of illegal drugs is illegal (again, I'm a rocket scientist) and can have particularly bad penalties as a liveaboard. Pay close attention to the gun laws, as well. If you get caught, it doesn't matter whether the boat is under way or not, since it is the possession that matters. Depending on the item and the amount, as well as the waters and your boating operation, the possession is either a misdemeanor (punishable by a period in jail of less than one year) or a felony (punishable by a period in jail of potentially one year or more); the charge could even rise to the level of drug trafficking or smuggling. With little or no protection from search and seizure, violations are more likely to be identified.

Search and Seizure

With all of the above as prelude, let's turn our attention to search and seizure. The Fourth Amendment to the U.S. Constitution provides that people shall be free from unreasonable searches and seizures, and the Supreme Court has defined this protection as one of many granting a right of privacy to the people. The Fourth Amendment does not prohibit all searches and seizures, but merely the unreasonable ones, and a system has been put in place whereby under most circumstances, probable cause is needed before a search, and a judge is asked to approve the search in advance, issuing what is called a "search warrant."

Exceptions to this rule that have been permitted by the Supreme Court include circumstances in which there was a belief of an immediate threat of harm or other life-threatening situation, or where the evidence sought is of a nature allowing it to be easily hidden or removed. These searches are considered "reasonable." Consequently, motor vehicles are permitted to be searched without a warrant since any evidence that is sought can so easily be driven off and hidden or destroyed. Motor vehicle searches do, however, require probable cause that a crime has been committed. For these cases there is a *reduced standard of privacy.*

The Supreme Court, however, has held that law enforcement authorities do not need to have probable cause as a prerequisite for searching boats (and property on boats), regardless of how unreasonable. The Court considered random boardings of boats to be a "limited" intrusion supported by the need to "deter or apprehend smugglers…" One of the Justices who did not agree with the decision was concerned that the Court, for the first time, was approving a "completely random seizure and detention of persons and an entry onto private noncommercial premises by police officers, without any limitations whatever on the officers' discretion or any safeguards against abuse." The case is called U.S. v. Villamonte-Marquez (1974).

The Coast Guard statute recognizes this right of law enforcement. No boat owner has any right of privacy or freedom from interference aboard his boat, and therefore no right to be free from searches and seizures, unreasonable or otherwise. The U.S. law permitting the Coast Guard to search a boat is U.S.C. Title 14, Part 1, Chapter 5, Section 89, which reads in part:

Sec. 89.—Law enforcement

(a) The Coast Guard may make inquiries, examinations, inspections, searches, seizures and arrests upon the high seas and waters over which the United States has jurisdiction, for the prevention, detection, and suppression of violations of laws for the United States. For such purposes, commissioned, warrant, and petty officers may at any time go on board of *any* vessel subject to the jurisdiction, or to the operation of any law, of the United States, address inquiries to those on board, examine the ship's documents and papers, and examine, inspect and search the vessel and *use all necessary force* to compel compliance. When from such inquiries, examination, inspection or search it appears that a breach of the laws of the United States rendering a person liable to arrest is being, or has been committed, by any person, such person shall be arrested…if it shall appear that a breach of the laws of the United States has been committed so as to render such vessel, or the merchandise…on board of…such vessel, liable to forfeiture or so as to render such vessel liable to a fine or penalty and if necessary to secure such fine or penalty, such vessel or such merchandise, or both, *shall be seized* [italics mine].

This law, by its own words, deprives boat owners of any right to resist any inquiry, inspection, examination, or search, provides no safeguards, requires no cause, and, as we shall discuss in the next section, allows the Coast Guard to confiscate the boat for nothing more than a suspicion that a crime *might* have been committed (i.e., *any* crime at all might have been committed). The Coast Guard's written boarding policy also reminds boaters that the boarding team is permitted to be armed.

The problem is compounded for liveaboards, who are now required to open up their *homes* to inspection, for any reason or no reason at all, and without any need for a showing of cause or restraint.

It is worth mentioning that boat searches are not a function of current events with the world's new battle against terrorism, for searches and seizures have been going on for quite a while. The only evident difference between searches prior to the attack on the World Trade Center and those conducted later is that meaningful public support for the proposition that boaters should have some right to privacy has eroded, and searches are now often conducted at gunpoint just like any other military operation.

Civil Forfeiture

As if unreasonable and unwarranted searches weren't enough, all citizens of the United States should be aware that the federal government (as well as state government) is permitted to take away their property, even if no crime is ever shown to have been committed, and even if the person who has lost his or her property is entirely innocent. The laws authorizing the government to take away people's property are called forfeiture laws. The general public has not only tolerated these laws, probably thinking that the government would never take away *their* property, but has continued to allow their representatives to pass so much legislation in this area that I understand there now to be hundreds of forfeiture laws in the books of federal and state governments. These laws are designed not only to be punitive, but also to raise significant amounts of capital.

The government can take away your property, whether it be your cash, home, boat, land, business, or any other assets, if it believes that the property was, in any way, used in a crime. These laws were originally intended to dispossess criminals of their ill-gotten gains, such as confiscating property acquired by a drug dealer, but have escalated into many governments taking highly expensive property away from property owners as the result of petty crimes—or even worse, from people never charged with crimes as the result of conduct of third parties. The government doesn't even have to ultimately bring a criminal action, but if it does, even if the person is found not guilty, the property can be kept and either destroyed or sold at auction.

How about this: What if you catch a fish that is one inch below the legal minimum? It's a crime, and many states have statutes authorizing the taking of the boat since the boat was used in the commission of a crime. What if a marijuana joint is found on board? What if your Y-valve for sewage discharge is inadvertently left in the wrong position? No charges ever need to be brought. These are not merely exaggerations. The law is clear on this point and if the triggering circumstance occurs, the forfeiture laws do permit the property to be taken.

There are horrible stories of real-life forfeitures, including authorities taking a 133-foot, $2.5 million yacht when a trace amount of marijuana was found in a dresser drawer, and a lady who lost her house and property when her son, who was renting her in-law apartment (not even connected to the house) was found to have some marijuana in his possession (no charges were ever filed and she did not even know that her son had ever smoked or possessed marijuana).

The federal government finally made some amendments to its seizure laws, requiring that the government now has to show that *it is more likely than not* that a crime was committed (a civil standard, not a criminal one, although here the judge and jury is the government itself), and it is now easier for an innocent person to recover property. Innocence, however, requires that when a person finds out that illegal conduct has occurred, he or she must contact the authorities immediately. Therefore, every mother who finds out that her child has experimented with drugs in the house is under an obligation to call the authorities right away. If the son is later arrested for drugs, even if the family thought that the child had ceased his activities, the family can have their house taken away.

Also, even though the federal government now has to show that it is more likely than not that a crime was committed, many states have not reformed their forfeiture laws, and are permitted to take the property for any belief whatsoever. Luckily, there is more awareness to this issue and we have seen a pickup in some state civil forfeiture protections. Not enough, but some.

Ohio law, for instance, provides that any personal property used or intended for use in the attempt, conspiracy, or commission of any offense can be seized and forfeited to the seizing agency for its use or sale. A boat is subject to forfeiture if the possession of the boat is illegal, or if any "contraband" is found on board. In Ohio, the underlying offense needs to be a felony.

Since possession is attributed to the owner, if you are an innocent owner with no actual knowledge of any crime, you will be required to show not only that you did not know, but that you should not have known after a reasonable inquiry that your property was used or could have likely been used in a crime.

This is a complicated area and a source of great misuse. Awareness is the first step. Know your rights and the law.

Sanitation

Many legal issues related to sanitation were discussed in "Safety and Sanitation." Be aware of the rules in your marina as well as in your cruising waters and know what activities are permitted and prohibited. Some jurisdictions have some pretty significant penalties for illegally dumping sewage or other refuse; many jurisdictions and no-discharge zones ban gray-water discharge as well.

International Law

Cruising liveaboards who depart their home waters to explore other parts of the world need to be aware of the laws in the jurisdiction where they are headed. First and foremost, be sure to have passports for every single one of your passengers and crew, as well as any other registration and documentation information that might be required both by your home port as well as your destinations. In addition, you and all of your passengers and crew might need a health certification and proof of specific vaccinations.

Also, different jurisdictions have differing rules on drug/alcohol use and possession of firearms, as well as food products, particularly fruits, vegetables, plants, and other agricultural products. There may be specific limitations or rules related to your pets as well, and some countries have strict quarantining procedures.

Depending on your port of call, you may be required to acquire a visa in advance of your arrival, or participate in some other procedure prior to or during arrival. Become familiar with the entry procedures and follow them carefully, for the laws in your arriving jurisdiction may be quite different than you expect and penalties for violations quite severe.

14

Final Words

Thank you for allowing me the opportunity to share with you some of my experience and thoughts—and warnings as well. There are many other liveaboards and boaters alike who would love to tell you about their aspirations, shortcomings, and plans. They'd love to tell you how they came out of the landlubber closet to undertake this lifestyle, and how they decided on their boat. They'd love to show you their marinas and boats and tell you about their wonderful improvements and upgrades. We'll all talk as long as you let us—and I thank you for letting me have the opportunity for this short while.

Final Advice

Hopefully, you are now better prepared to overcome the challenges, and therefore have a better chance to enjoy all of the wonderful benefits that this lifestyle can offer. It's not easy—whether we are talking about the costs, maintenance obligations, space limitations, or perils of living on the water. But it's not necessarily all that hard either, and you will be joining the many thousands of us "normal" people who enjoy this lifestyle already.

Here are some final thoughts:

- Remember that the challenges of the lifestyle go with the territory and are the price to pay for the wonderful benefits.
- Talk to everybody who is willing to talk to you—and don't forget to listen.
- Don't sweat the small stuff.
- Read, learn, and experience everything you can.
- Invite yourself aboard a boat for a trial if at all possible.
- Be patient and thorough when choosing a boat—and remember that boats, good and bad, grow on trees.
- Be sure to make *smart* decisions, and don't let your emotions dictate rash or unwarranted behavior.
- Remember that your home must be a boat first and foremost (structurally, and, if desired, operationally).
- Remember that you are buying a home, and comfort is far more important than if you were just buying a pleasure boat.
- Be realistic in your needs.

- Be realistic in your budget, and prepare your cost spreadsheet.
- Be sure that your spouse/partner/companions want to do this at least as much as you do.
- Put your possessions into storage initially, if possible, to make sure that you will stick with the lifestyle. Some people keep the storage facility for life and factor the space into their life's working budget.
- Be patient and thorough when performing upgrades and improvements.
- Don't spend to the maximum of your budget; be prepared for unexpected costs.
- Centuries of boaters have gone without the state-of-the-art cruising equipment such as radar or chart-plotters, and unless you are cruising in difficult conditions, you don't *need*

this equipment either.
- Try to enjoy *all* of your neighbors.
- Stand up for the things that need standing up for, enjoying as much of the rest of the stuff as possible.
- Enjoy! And remember that you are living millions of peoples' dreams.

Some Opinions

Jessica's Favorite Things About Life Aboard:

1. The zen of water
2. The lack of traffic noise
3. The view at night
4. The community of helpful, knowledgeable, nice neighbors
5. The ease of changing neighbors!
6. Encourages organization and getting rid of junk
7. Never a lack of problems to attack
8. No lawn to mow
9. Nobody rings your doorbell and tries to sell you anything
10. Freedom from earthquakes!

Jessica Levant, Liveaboard
Ferrocement Motor Sailor
San Francisco Bay, CA

Robb's Favorite Things About Living in Bermuda:

1. Watching sea turtles surface nearby
2. Watching the glowworms on the second day after a full moon exactly 56 minutes after sunset
3. Watching 6-foot tarpon work the shallows feasting on fry
4. Enjoying the arrival of the long tail tropical birds every spring and the cormorants every winter
5. The morning commute involves kayaking
6. Bermuda
7. Not paying on $2,500/year in utility/cable/phone bills
8. Not paying on average $25,000/year rent
9. Collecting 10 gallons of water in one half-hour downpour
10. Staying with friends when hurricanes come to visit

C. Robb Worthington, Liveaboard
S/V *Tara Rose*
St. Georges, Bermuda

Jim's Favorite Things About Living Aboard:

1. I live somewhere I couldn't afford,
2. There are only two other part-time liveaboards at my dock—so life is very isolated
3. I "know" my neighbors. They know me.
4. We look out for each other
5. Sunrises and sunsets
6. Going sailing is a 10 foot commute

7. Being able to putter on boat projects without having to go anywhere
8. Women like to visit.

Jim Sims, Liveaboard

Chris' Reasons Why Liveaboards Succeed:

1. Keeping [stuff] on shore
2. Having mail delivered to work
3. Small, simple boat
4. Compulsive attention to gear stowage efficiency and neatness
5. Military-like attention to maintenance
6. All-around neatness
7. Abide by the Golden Rule: All personal gear must fit in one dock cart
8. Realization of the fact that boats need lots of attention
9. Enjoy providing that attention
10. "A clean boat is a happy boat"

Chris Birch, Marine Technician

Chris' Top Ten List of Reasons People Stop Living Aboard:

1. The smell
2. The motion
3. The clutter
4. The expense
5. The work
6. The sewerage
7. Deck leaks
8. No room for the snow skis and piano

9. Boat sunk
10. The significant other

Chris Birch, Marine Technician

Jim's Two Worst Things about Living Aboard:

1. The motion in bad weather—even at the dock
2. Morons who don't understand what "NO" means—as in NO Wake

Jim Sims, Liveaboard

Dave's Top 8 Things Missed By Being Aboard:

1. A good shower
2. My own washer and dryer
3. Hot tub
4. Ridiculous rents
5. Obnoxious neighbors
6. Long commutes
7. Mowing the yard
8. High property taxes

Dave R., Liveaboard

Resources

There are some terrific resources available to liveaboards, including some fine magazines, websites, and books. Take the time to read everything you can and learn as much as possible before making too many decisions. When we talk about learning everything, don't just focus on boats and boating systems, but also take the time to learn about your local marinas, climate issues, and safety rules and regulations. You are not just a liveaboard; you are a boater and you have the ability to lead by example. Be outstanding at what you do.

Magazines

I would recommend that you take the time to read the different magazines which are available. Unfortunately, *Liveaboard Magazine*, the only periodical geared toward the liveaboard population has gone defunct.

In addition, there are magazines dedicated to specific lifestyles and magazines dedicated to your specific type of boat (*Sail, Practical Sailor, Passagemaker, Trawlerworld*), magazines focusing on different usages (*Bluewater Cruiser*), magazines that focus on different geographical regions, magazines that provide insight into equipment and repairs, and many others that provide valuable information—and others that don't say very much at all.

One advantage to magazines is that those of you who like to read the advertisements can learn about all of the new technology and ideas. Aside from the cutting-edge technologies, advertisements and articles also contain practical ideas and tons of stories about people's experiences and difficulties. Magazines are often the best venues to learn about the hottest topics and biggest news stories.

Another advantage of these magazine rags is that they are cheap education and you can carry them and read them anywhere. Pick up a few and get familiar with your choices.

Forums

The best resource is to talk to people. While you can do this by going to different marinas, I would also highly encourage you to join an Internet community, also known as an e-mail group or forum. If you are not familiar with one of these, they are basically just groups of people that send e-mails to each other. One person with a question or something to say sends an e-mail to an address; the e-mail is then distributed to all members of the group. Anyone who wants to may respond to the group, or e-mail the sender directly. It is an open discussion.

There are literally thousands of e-mail groups to select from. The most applicable one for us is called "liveaboards." Also try,

http://www.life-aboard.com/forum/

There are numerous downsides to these groups, in that you tend to find yourself witness to discussions that would make an elementary school teacher squirm. Focus on the issues and solutions, particularly the *range* of solutions, and you will find much of the advice incredibly insightful or, at a minimum, highly educational. Also, you will find that there is no question that has not been asked, or is not a common concern among many of your peers. Also, you will see that there is not necessarily only one solution to any given problem.

You will learn that some people love the United States Coast Guard and others hate them, that some people love having guns on board and others take great offense at guns aboard, that some people are in favor of Jimmy Buffett and others against him, and that some people don't like other people and some people don't like anyone, and other people will come to the defense of the people who are not liked and other people will come to the defense of people who don't like anyone. You can join the community and in doing so, you will have the chance to participate or not. Regardless of your level of participation, you will be able to listen to this broad cross-section of liveaboards.

Since many of these lists have been around for a very long time, there are huge archives covering just about every topic imaginable. There are people asking about what kind of boats are the best, what marinas are great and not-so-great, and the virtues of different equipment and amenities. You will find opinions on thousands of topics and are likely to find that your question has been asked before.

Websites/Blogs

There are some very fine websites out there. The world has changed, and whether you are looking to research and purchase boats, learn about the craft of boating, determine weather conditions, locate marina, or find equipment or manufacturers, the Web offers a virtually unlimited collection of resources.

If you are researching living aboard, definitely check out www. livingaboard.net (the site for this book), which provides the cost spreadsheet discussed earlier in the book, as well as other valuable links. Other good links include:

http://www.houseboatmagazine.com/
http://www.sailnet.com/
http://www.yachtworld.com/

A quick search will identify many other wonderful resources.

Books

The first book I would recommend is the book you're reading, but you already know that! (Well, we've both made it this far, so I figured self-serving humor was in order.)

A wonderful book on living aboard is entitled *Gently With The Tides*, published by International Marine/McGraw-Hill. It was one of the books that got it going for me.

The other book that I think is a must-own for any economy-minded boater is *This Old Boat*, also published by International Marine/McGraw-Hill. This book teaches the various systems and provides economical solutions and repairs, as well as wonderful how-tos.

Acknowledgments

The advice and thoughts in this book are based on not only my own experiences, but also on the input of the many characters I have had the chance to meet through the years, as well as the delightful people I have had the privilege to interview in preparation for this book and the companion video. I am grateful, and this project is far more thorough and wonderful because of their contributions.

I want to take a moment to thank the following people who have been essential in providing wonderful assistance and advice in my liveaboard career, boat buying endeavors, boat repairing endeavors, and preparation for this book. All of the following people have taken an active role in their lives and careers to make sure that boaters and liveaboards are offered a safe boat, a safe marina, and knowledgeable neighbors to look out for them. They are all natural teachers and have given me their time in order to make sure that liveaboards and boaters get the best advice possible.

Chris Birch	Capt. Chris Birch, owner of Birch Marine, Inc., has been maintaining pleasure boats in Boston Harbor for over 20 years. Chris has lived aboard and sailed the East Coast and Bahamas on his 1971 Tartan 30 *Carina*. With the addition of a wife, two kids, and a dog, Chris now lives on land but still spends a good amount of time cruising New England with his family aboard *Fearless*, his "ne'" 1969 Tartan 34. Birch Marine is currently maintaining boats in Boston & Miami, building pedal-powered/prop-driven dories, and finishing ultra quiet lobster yachts.
Tom Cox	Tom has managed 8 marinas from Florida to Cape Cod over the past 30 years. He and his partner presently own and operate Constitution Marina in Boston's Inner Harbor, where he lives aboard his 59-foot sailboat, *Rosinante*, with his wife, Lynne. Tom is the President of the Massachusetts Marine Trades Association and sits on the national board of the Marina Operators of America. He holds a Certified Marina Manager's certificate from the International Marina Institute and is very active in local environmental organizations in addition to sitting on the board of directors of Save the Harbor/Save the Bay as its immediate past president. Tom runs a first-class and "liveaboard friendly" facility in Boston Harbor, from which he also offers the non-boater the opportunity to partake in the liveaboard lifestyle, albeit for only

a night or two, on various vessels in his marina that participate in the marina's Bed and Breakfast Afloat program.

Robert Doty Originally from Virginia and Hawaii, Robert has spent the majority of his time in Jacksonville, Florida and has lived aboard *Candide,* a 38-foot Hans Christian Traditional sailboat, since August, 1999. He is the creator and webmaster of a website (www.sleepingwithoars.com) dedicated toward providing liveaboards with valuable information. His site has received more than 100,000 visitors and has provided terrific advice to thousands of new and aspiring liveaboards.

Greg Emerson Greg grew up in Tampa, Florida, where he went to school and worked several years in Tampa's famous shipyards. Greg downsized from ships when he moved to Alachua, Florida in 1979 and began working at Hunter Marine, which at the time was a relatively new sailboat manufacturer. Greg worked through the ranks, becoming the production manager over the entire hull and deck construction for Hunter, where he spent a decade before moving to the customer service department, where he worked with customers and Hunter Marine's large worldwide dealer distribution network. After 26 years, Greg is still currently with Hunter Marine, now the largest sailboat manufacturer in North America and second in the world. He is the market development manager for the Northeast region of North America.

Norm Johnson

Norm has served in the Air Force, fixing electronic navigational aids on Phantom jets, and spent time in the aerospace industry until he found himself realizing (in a rum-induced state with boating friends) that he wanted to be the skipper of a chartered sailing vessel. After finding nothing on the market, Norm decided in 1973 to build himself a boat—a 74-foot LOA, 18-foot beam, 8-foot draft, 120,000-pound ferrocement boat. Norm and his partner Jan, a jeweler, are retired and cruising aboard *Bandersnatch*, and have tens of thousands of miles under keel. Norm and Jan want me to report that he and Jan can't imagine living any other lifestyle.

John Procter

John learned to sail at the age of 12 on the Charles River in Boston and fell deeply in love with sailing from that point on. He served in the Army during Vietnam, taught instrumental music in the Boston Public School system, earned a Masters degree in music education and an MBA, and has been a yacht broker and member of the YBAA for more than twenty years, serving on its board of directors for six years and as its president for two years. John is currently the chairperson of the organization's forms committee. When not working as a yacht broker, he is either playing his euphonium with the Metropolitan Wind Symphony or the New England Brass Band, or sailing the waters off Cape Cod aboard his 32-foot Pearson Vanguard sloop, *Hornblower,* with his wife Heidi and their two-year-old son Will. John, Heidi, and fellow broker Sam Lawson have worked together at Lawson

Yachts, Inc. in Hingham, Massachusetts since 1985.

Don Stonehill   A lifelong outdoorsman, "Stoney" began his love for boating with his high school freshman year shop project...building a boat. Don graduated from college with a degree in broadcast journalism and electronics technology and has completed a 36-year career in broadcast radio and television. For 14 years, he and his wife Joanne owned a boat shop, which they sold in 1986. Don and Joanne have lived aboard a Hunter 42-foot sailboat for more than 10 years on Lake Union in Seattle. Don and others organized the Liveaboard Association of Puget Sound when the government said they could no longer reside on protected waters. As chairman, Don and others were successful in achieving their goal of ensuring that liveaboards are still permitted to reside in waters of the Pacific Northwest. The group now enjoys a good and informative relationship with governmental bodies, and works for the benefit of boaters nationwide. Don & Joanne's sons, Gary and Mike, and their families live in Sacramento, California.

Afterwords

Thank you for taking the time to read *The Essentials of Living Aboard a Boat.* It has been our pleasure to bring it to you.

Please take some time to visit www.paracay.com for tons of additional resources on boating and the marine lifestyle.

Also, please visit www.livingaboard.net for copies of the cost spreadsheet contained within Chapter 6. And don't hesitate to e-mail me at mark@livingaboard.net with your comments, questions, and greetings. I'd love to hear from you.

Live smart and safe, and may your seas be fair.

Mark Nicholas
and all the great folks at
Paradise Cay Publications, Inc.

About the Author

Mark Nicholas has lived a bit of the Renaissance life, traveling the world, practicing law, playing music, and now the founder/CEO of a company created to help families prepare for crisis (Family Archival Solutions, Inc.). He continues to write books, take photos and wander the world.

Originally from the small coastal town of Bayville, New Jersey, Mark grew up in and around the water, sailing small boats for years. With only a rudimentary knowledge of the inner workings of larger boats and boat mechanics, Mark moved aboard his 33-foot Hunter Marine sailboat *The Morning Fog,*in Boston Harbor.

The *Fog* turned out not to be a competent liveaboard boat, requiring major sacrifices in every aspect of her design. Expenses skyrocketed and whole systems needed to be rebuilt. Through this experience Mark learned an unbelievable amount—things that someone should have told him, and lots that no one might have ever thought to tell him. He wanted to write a book that, had he read it, might have helped him make better decisions and save thousands of dollars.

Mark is a graduate of Syracuse University College of Law. He currently lives in Southern California with his beautiful wife and daughter. He is also a voting member of the Recording Academy; has been a musical recording artist; and has engineered, produced, and provided technical and consulting services to many other artists, musicians, and filmmakers.

The Essentials of Living Aboard a Boat is Mark Nicholas' first book, originally released in 2004, updated 2005, 2013 and 2018, now a mainstay of the aspiring liveaboard.

A home is meant to be lived in.